CW01160976

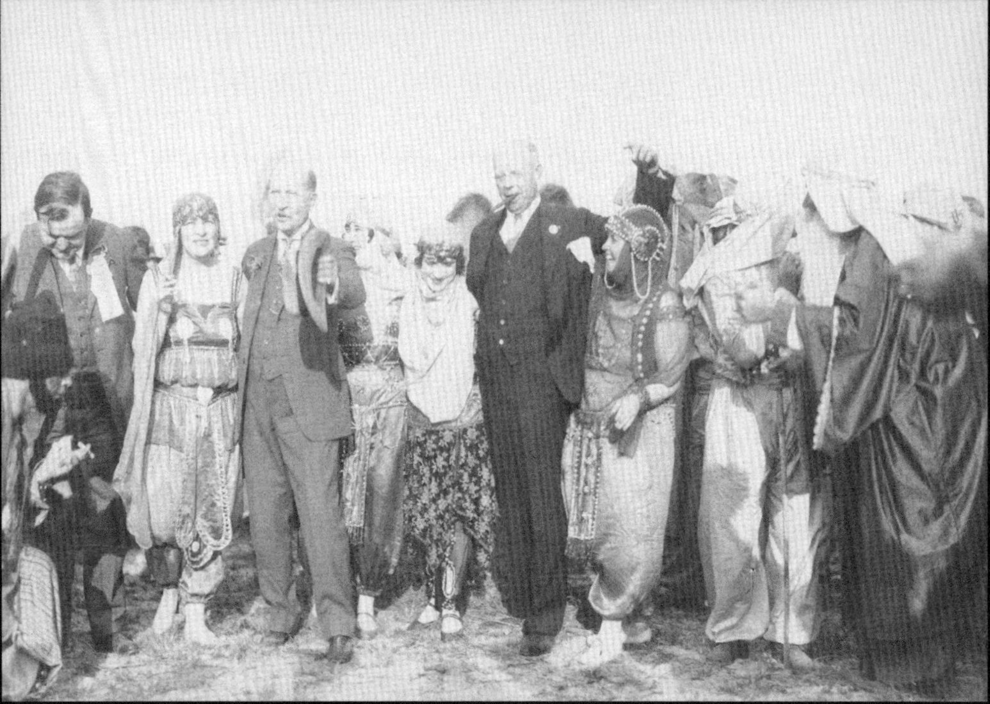

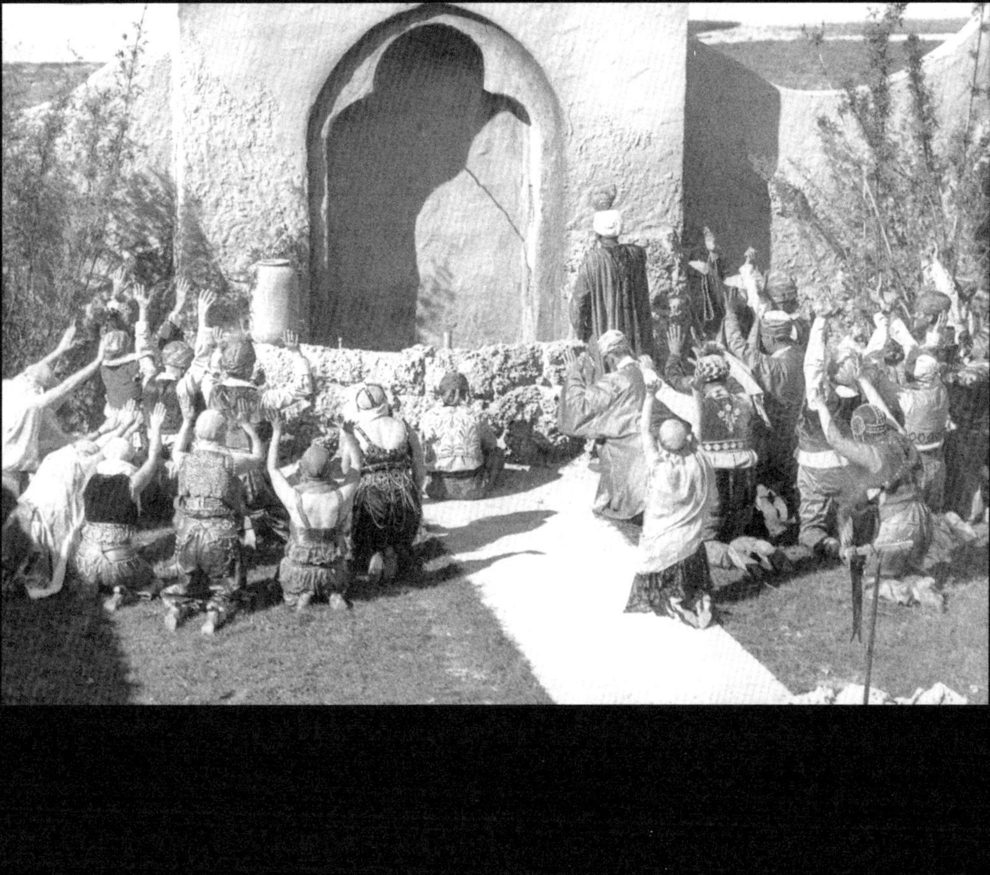

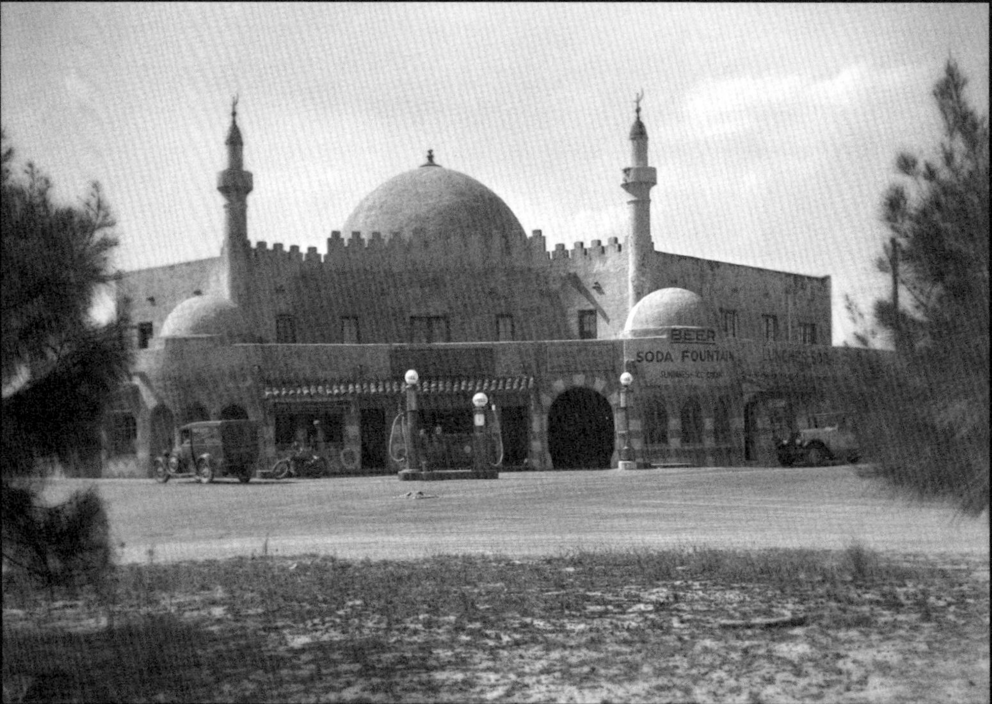
BEER
SODA FOUNTAIN

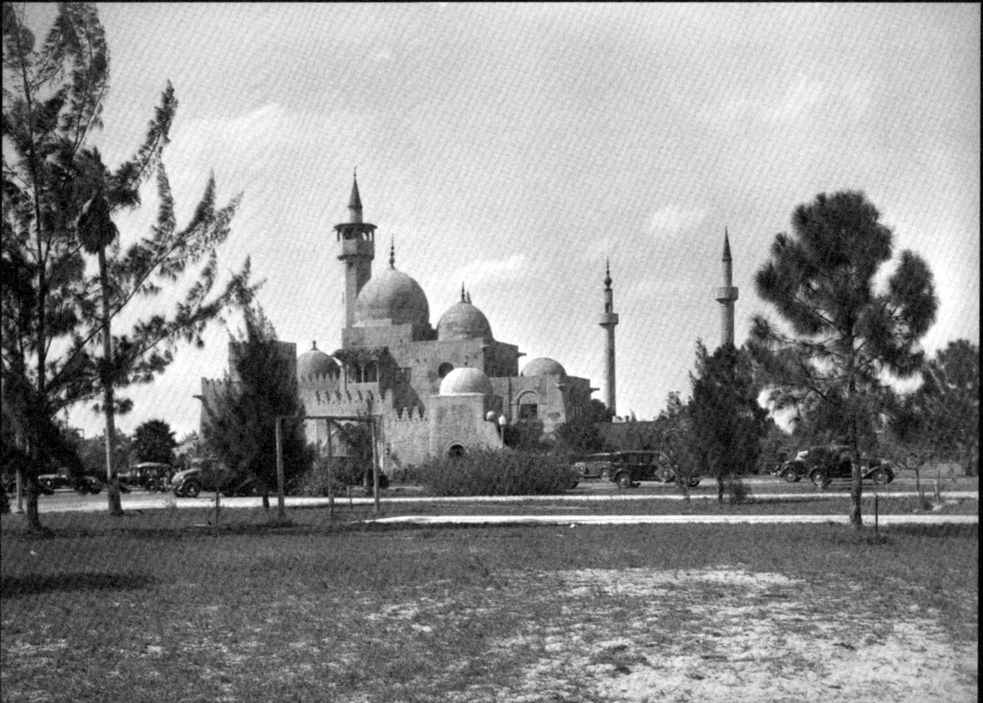

THIS SKETCH DOES NOT ADEQUATELY INDICATE
THE ACTUAL COLORS OF BATCHELDER TILES BUT
IS INTENDED TO SHOW THE DISTRIBUTION AND
GENERAL COLOR VALUE OF THE DIFFERENT UNITS.

4X4 BLACK PAVERS

1X4 RED & BROWN
PAVER STRIPS

2X2 & 2X4
PAVERS - RED RANGE

FIELD - REGULAR BODY
5 + 3 MEDLEY OF COLOR
SIZES 2X2, 2X4,
4X4, 4X6.
SOME 3/8 x 7/8 MOSAIC
IN BLUE & GREEN S.G.
& YELLOW & ORANGE E.G.

MAYA FIGURES

MOSAIC

GATE PANELS
SUGGESTED TREATMENT
IN
BATCHELDER TILES
SCALE 3/4" = 1'-0"

THE BATCHELDER TILES
Batchelder-Wilson Co.
101 Park Ave. New York

PRELIMINARY
NY DWG # 224-2
JULY 10/26 AR

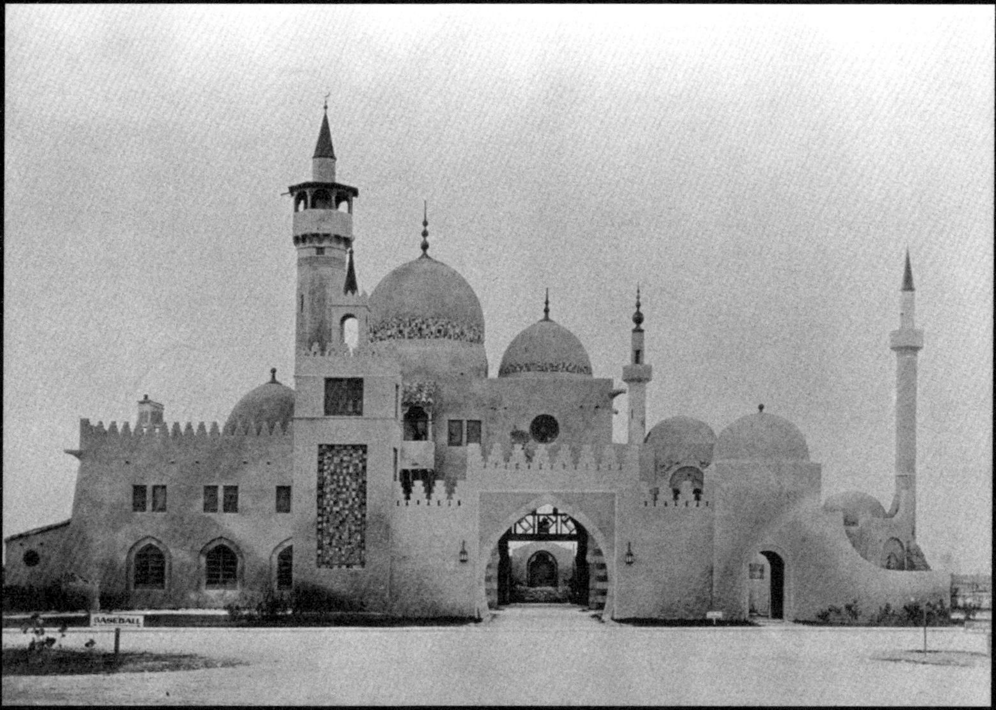
BASEBALL

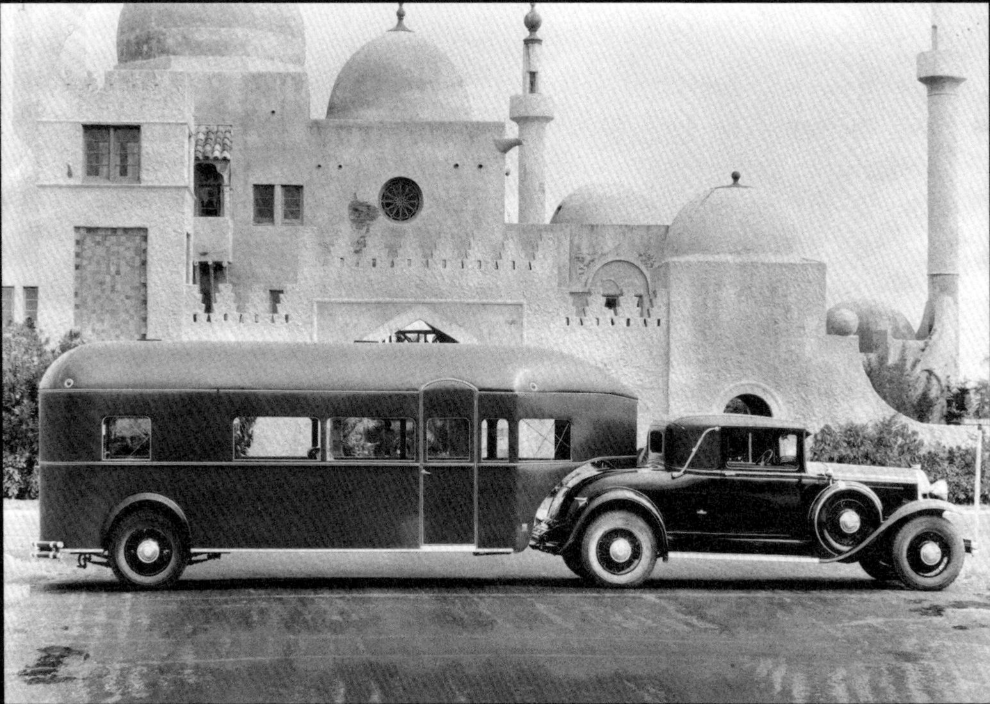

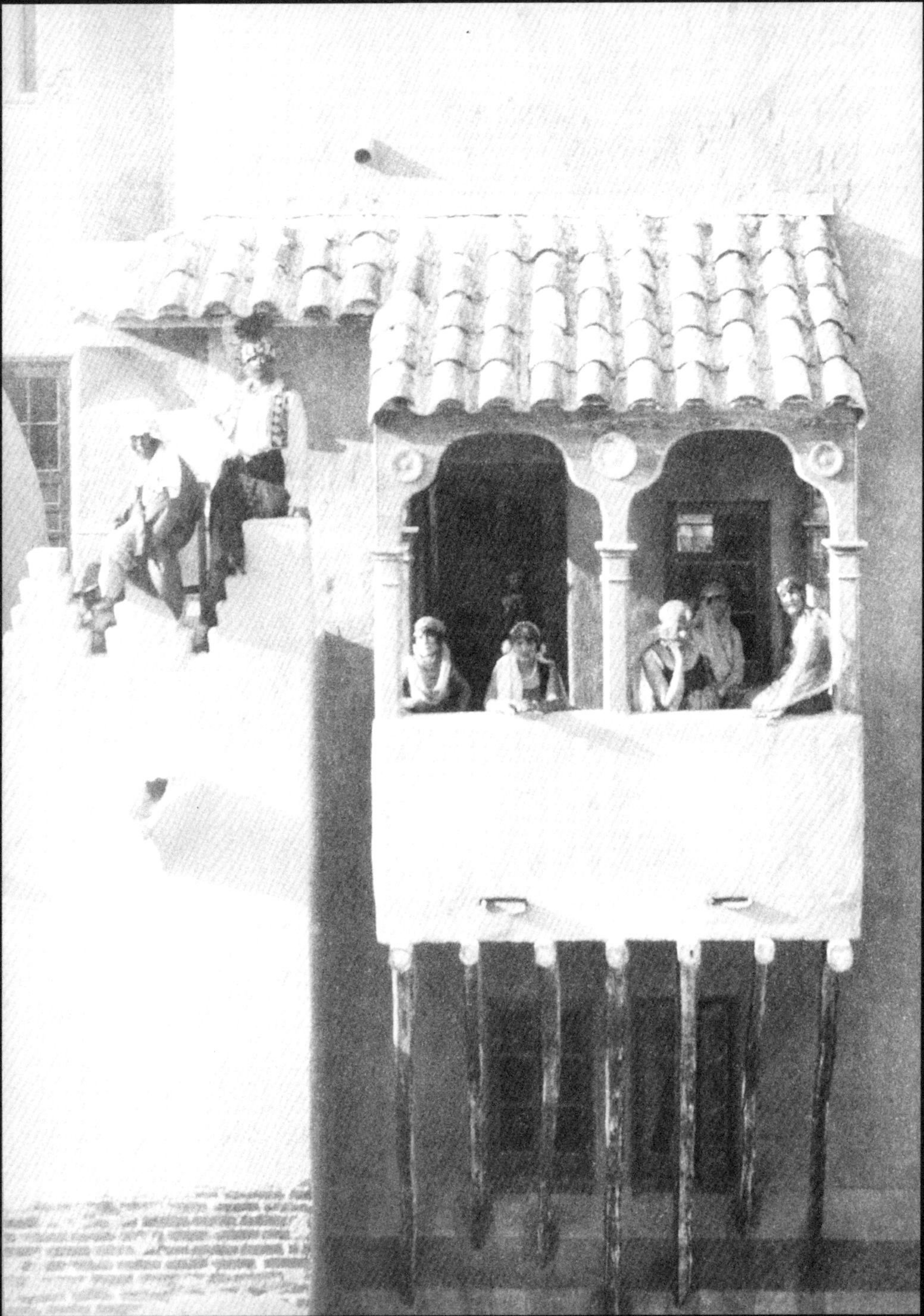

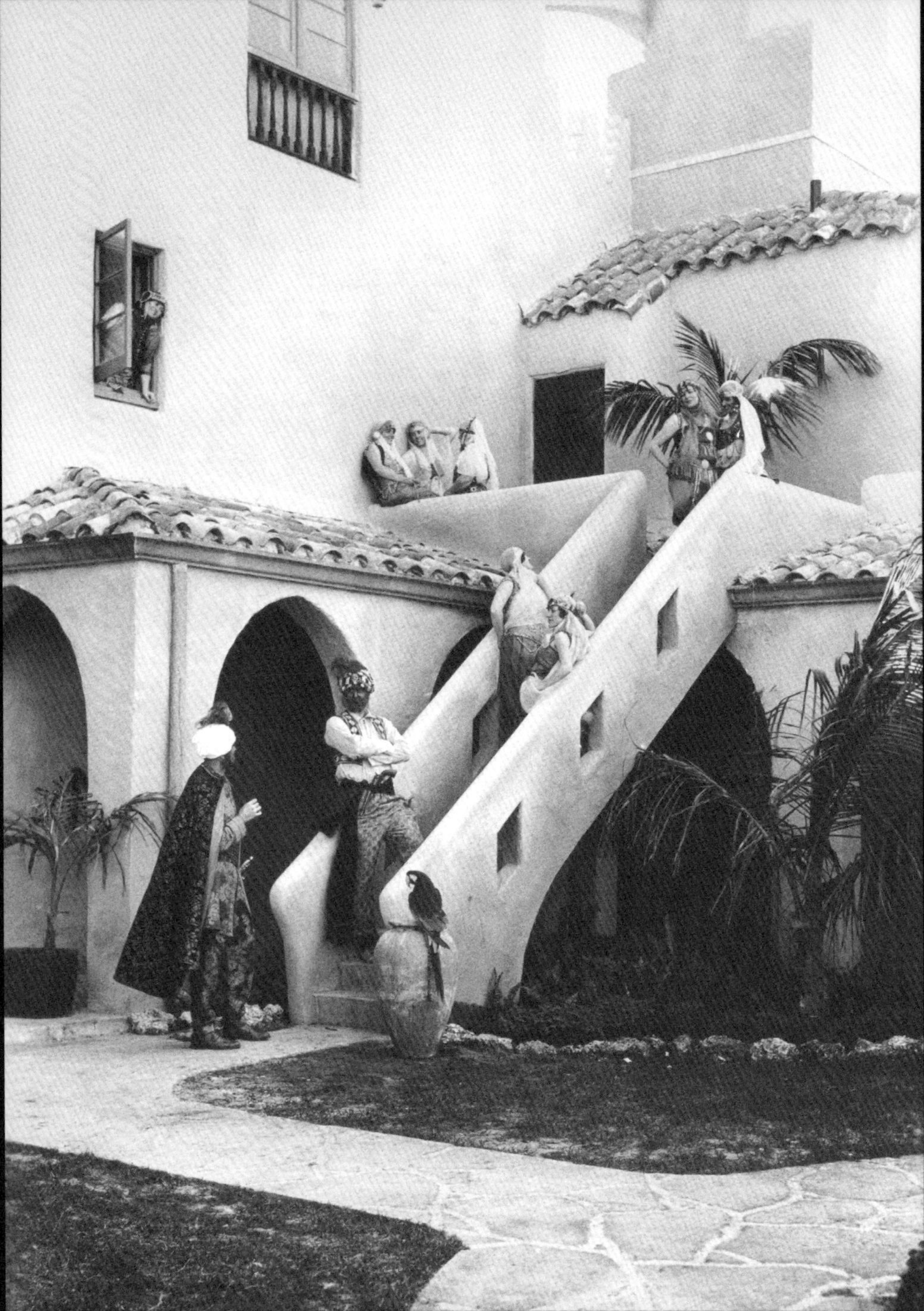

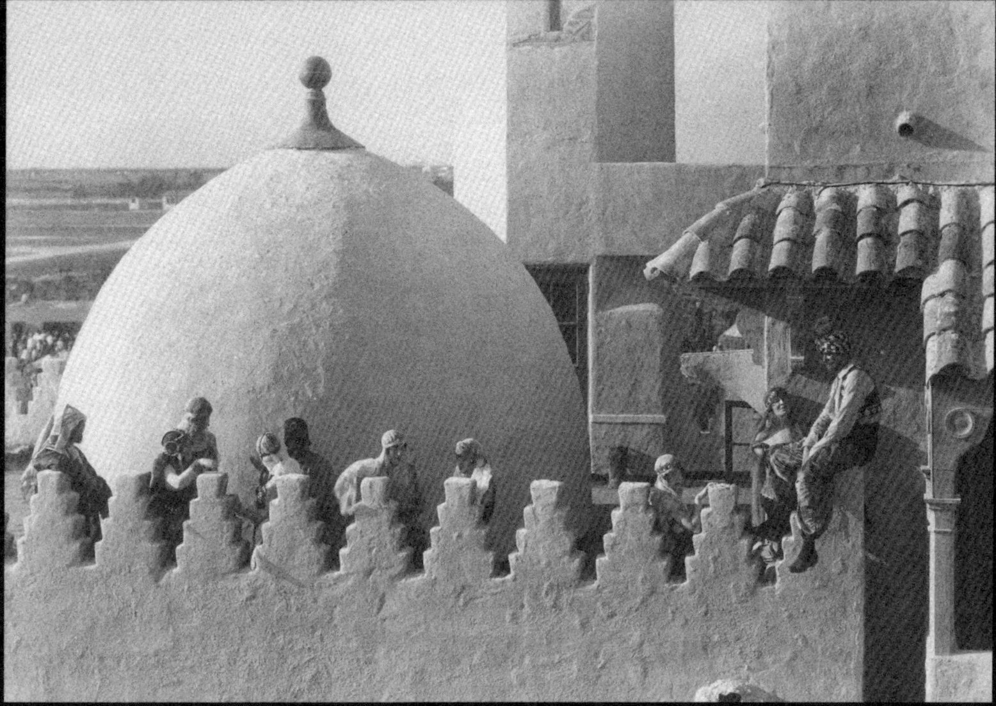

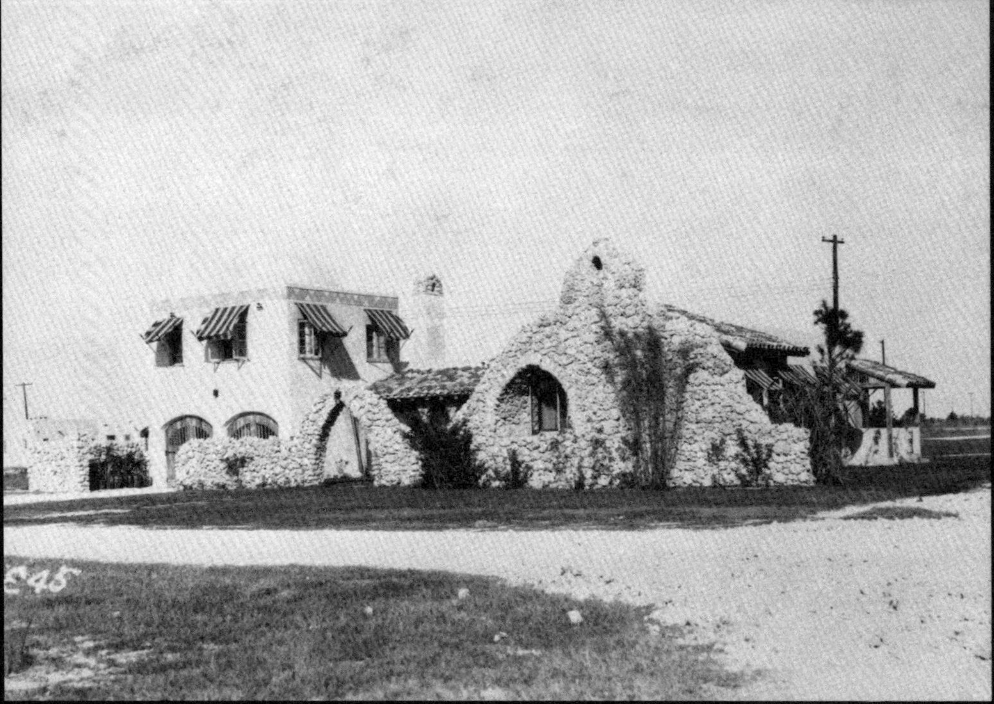

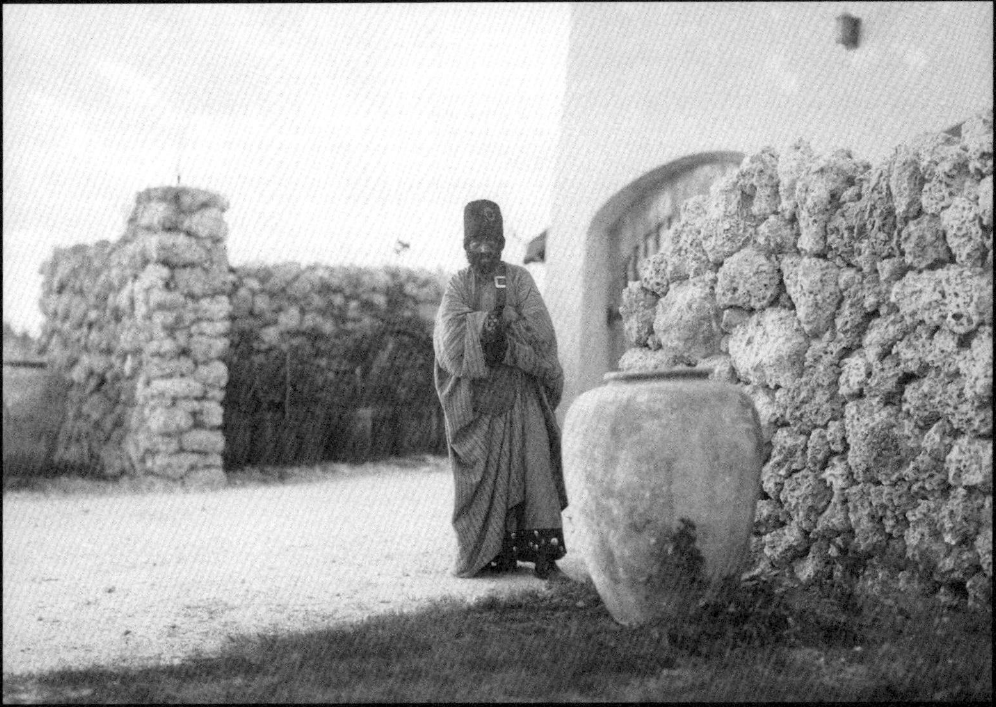

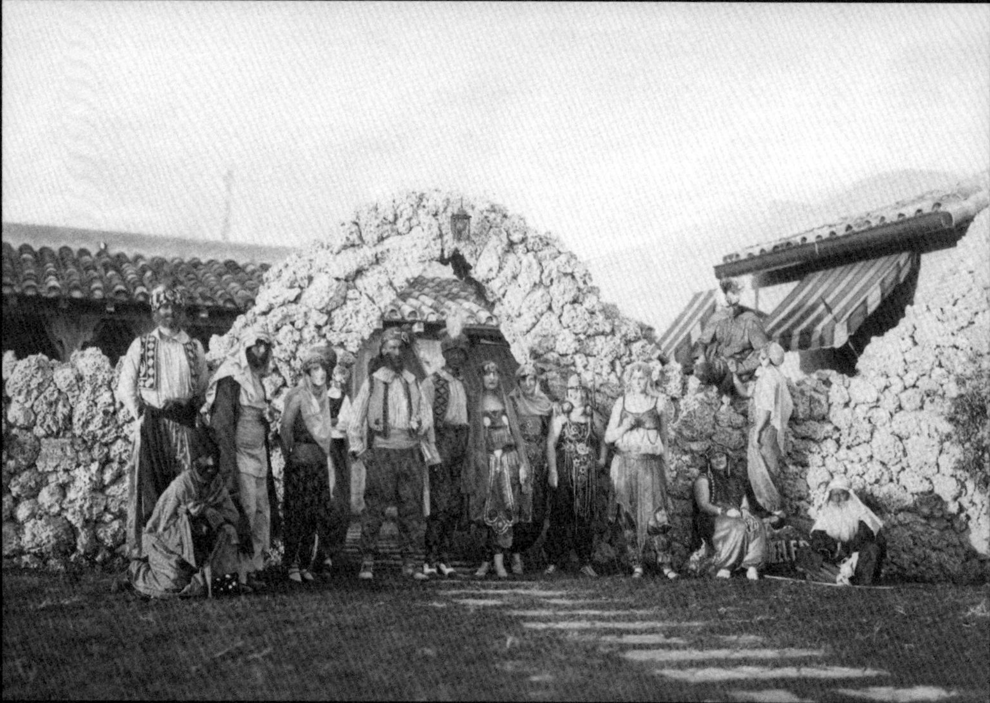

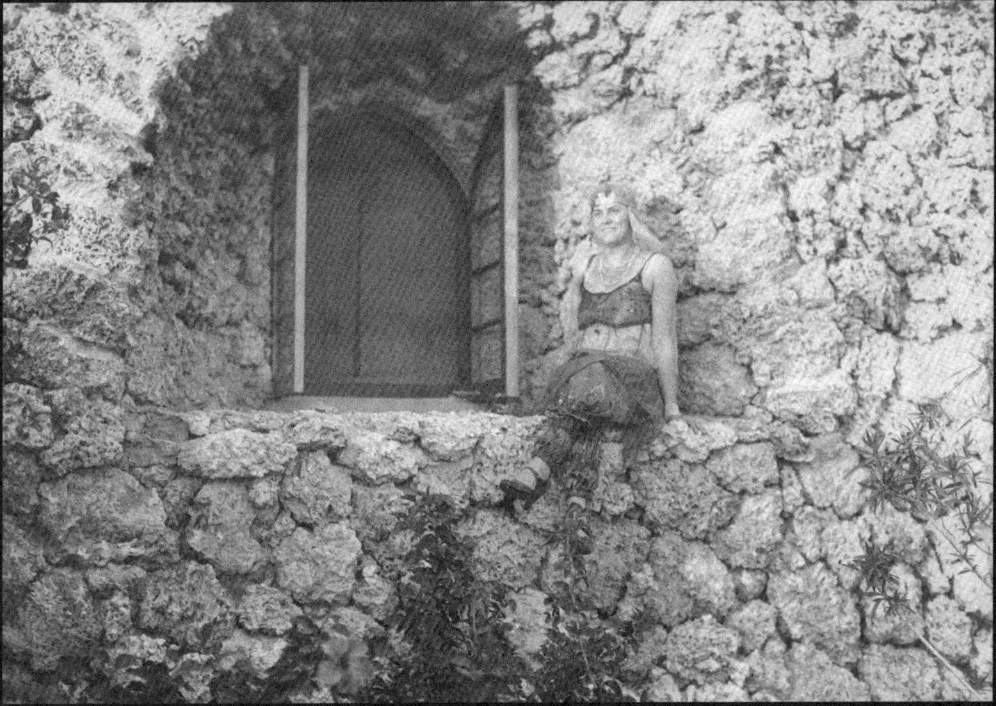

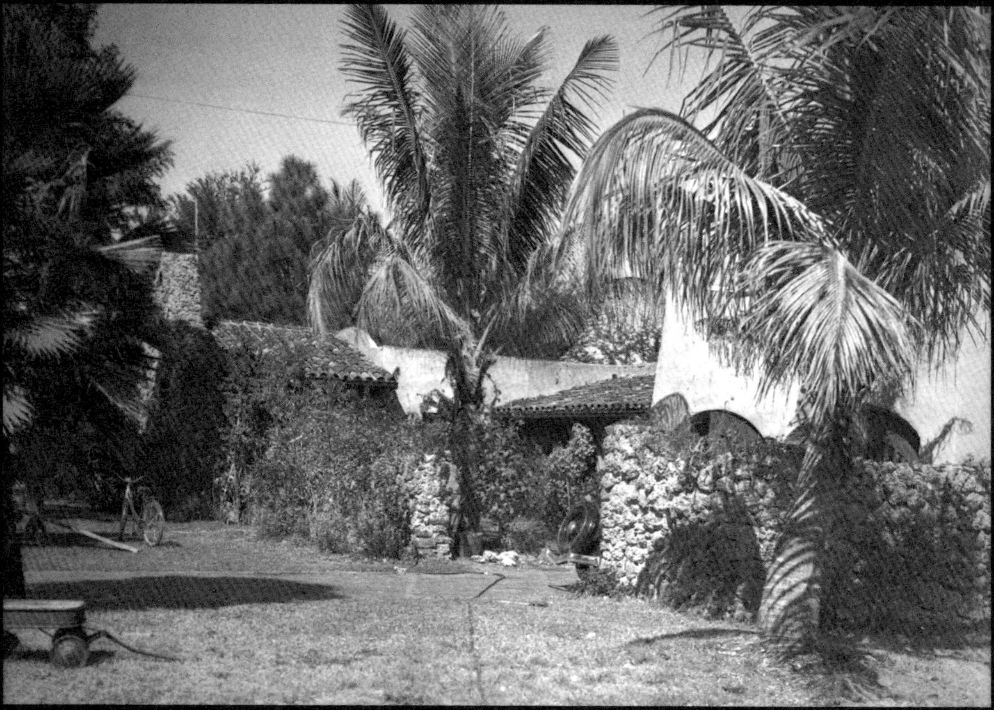

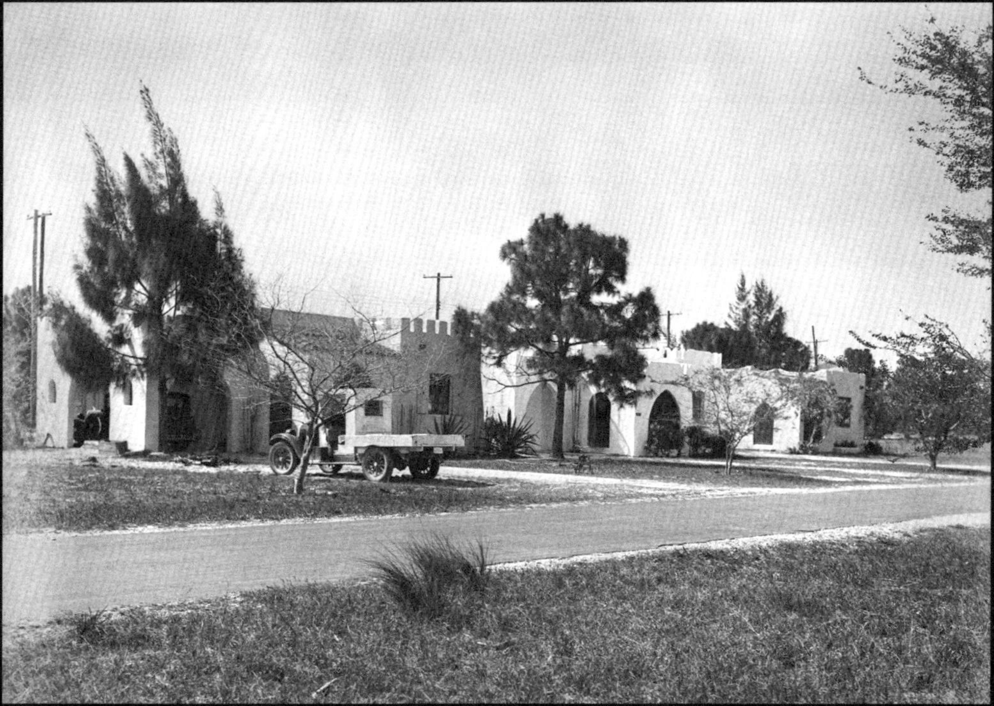

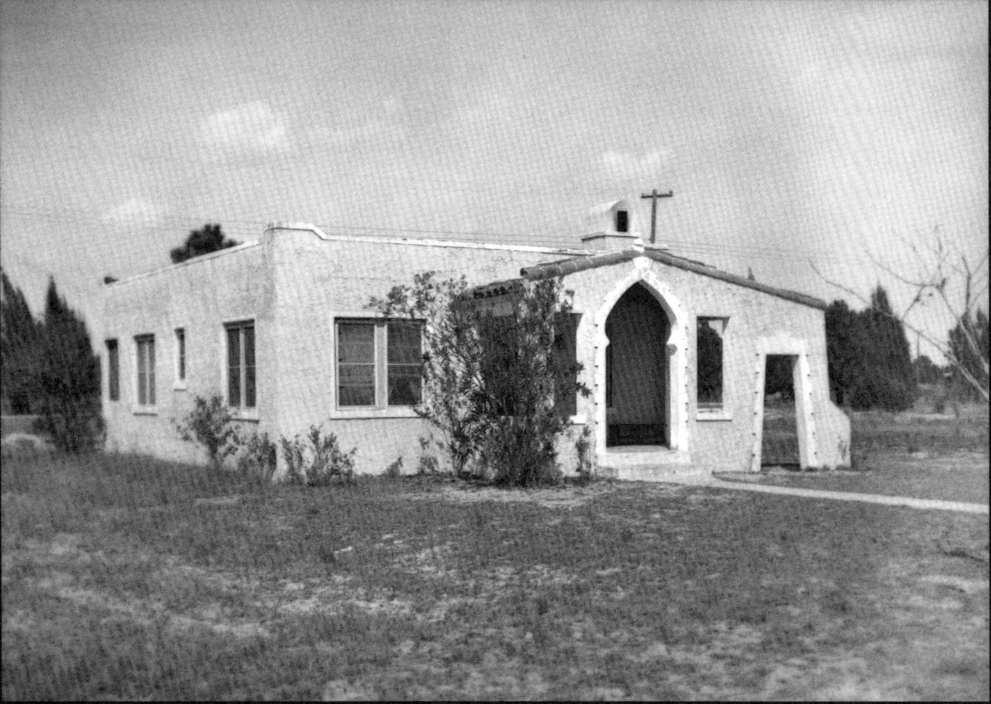

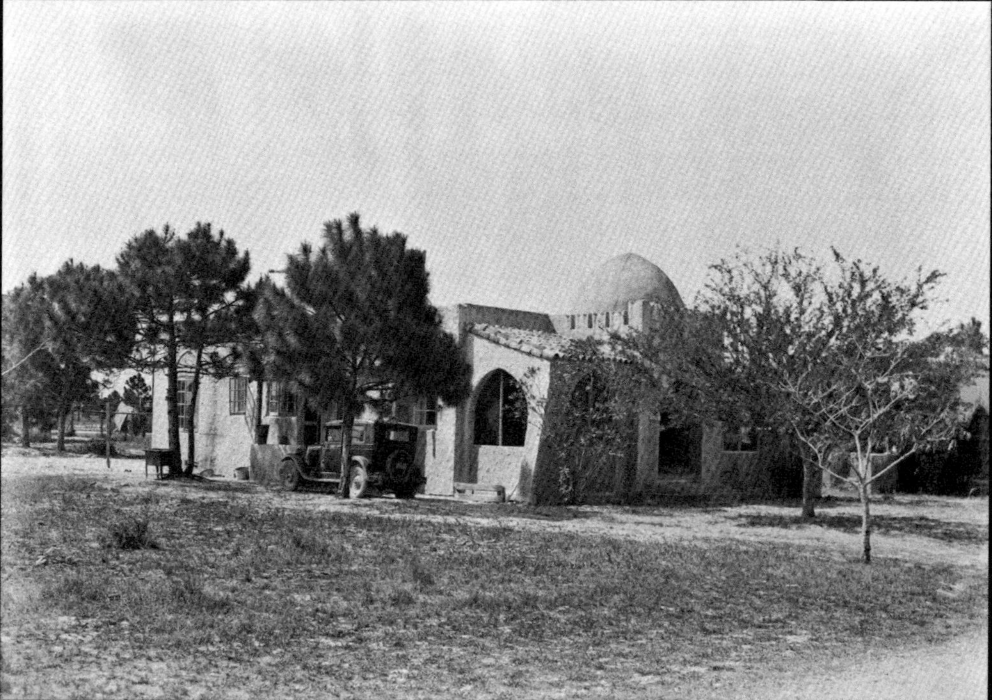

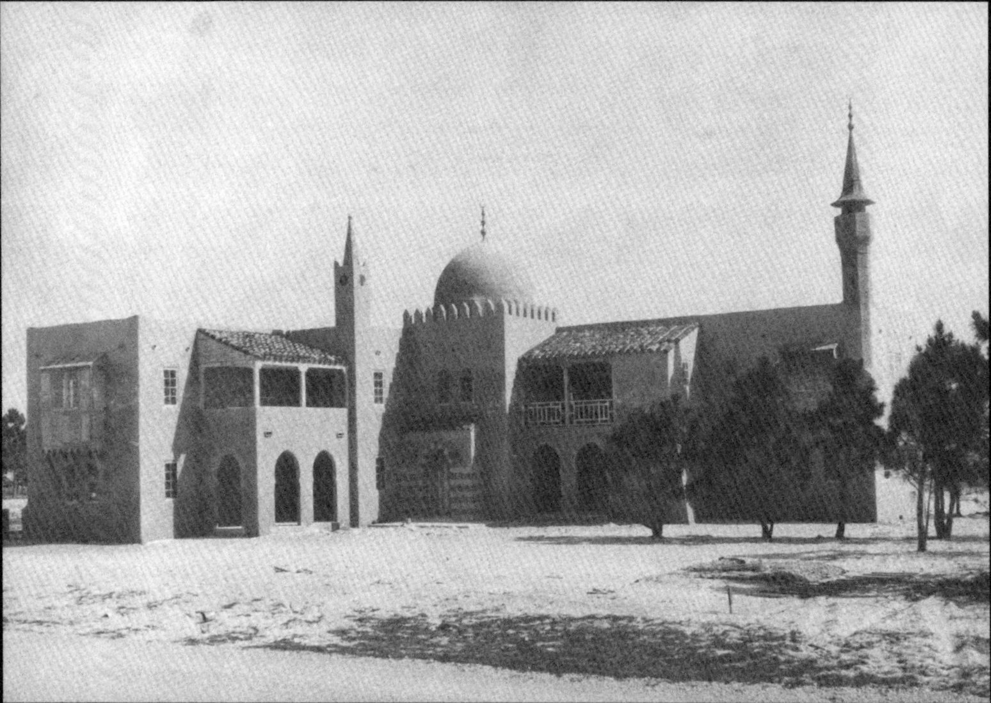

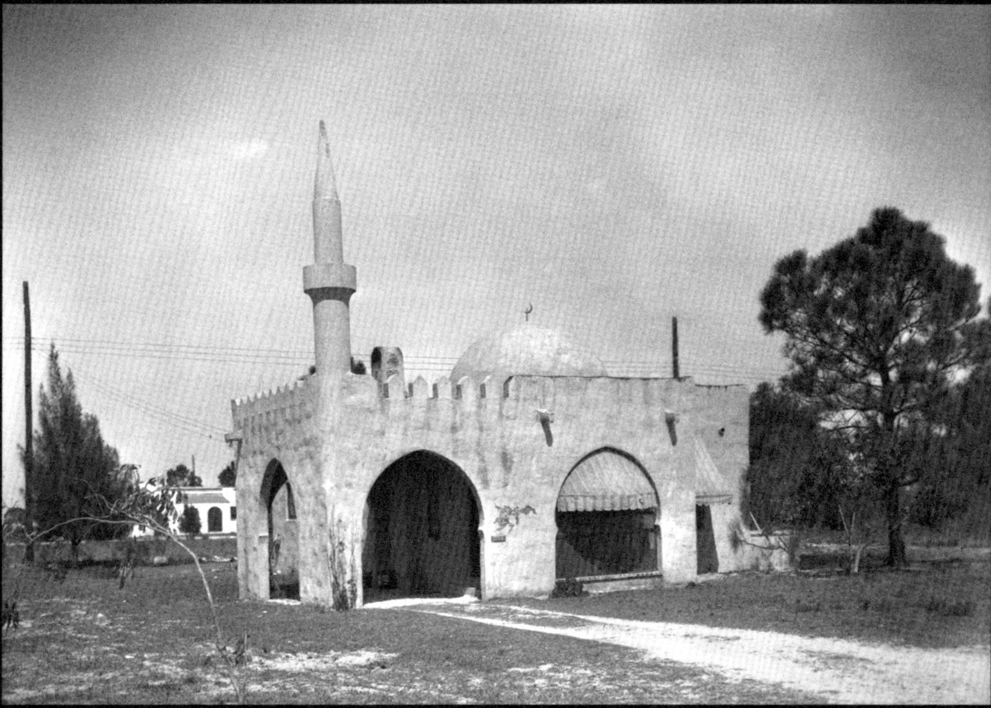

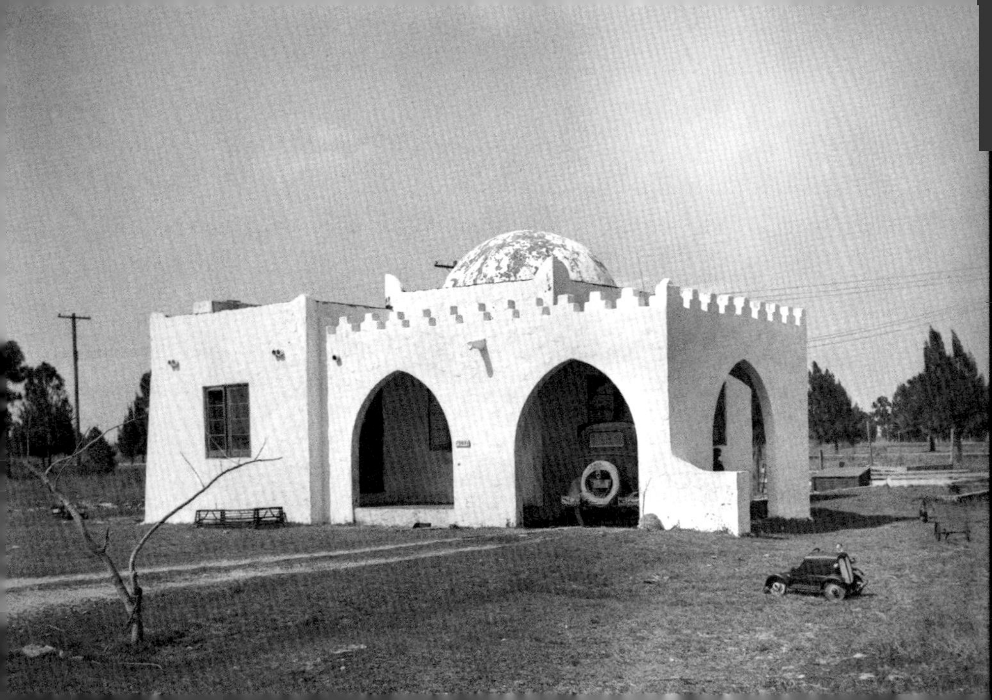

OPA-
TISHA-
WOCKA-
LOCKA

Anne Daems &
Kenneth Andrew Mroczek

MER. Paper Kunsthalle
Architecting

TABLE OF CONTENTS

ARCHIVAL PHOTOGRAPHS ....p. 3

A TALE TO BE RETOLD: 2006–2012
DEFINING PLACE, NAMING PLACE —
OPA-TISHA-WOCKA-LOCKA ....p. 29
The city of Opa-locka, Florida &
the architecture of Bernhardt E. Muller
By Kenneth Andrew Mroczek

MOORISH REVIVAL TIMELINE ....p. 38

SPECIFICATIONS ....p. 41
for the general construction of
a new residence building

BUILDINGS AND RESIDENCES ....p. 49

ANTHOLOGY ....p. 150

ARCHIVAL MATERIAL DESCRIPTIONS ....p. 174

ARCHIVAL NEWSPAPER ADVERTISEMENTS ....p. 181

A TALE TO BE RETOLD: 2006–2012 DEFINING PLACE, NAMING PLACE— OPA-TISHA-WOCKA-LOCKA

The city of Opa-locka, Florida & the architecture of Bernhardt E. Muller

By Kenneth Andrew Mroczek

Rolling up on 135th Street and onward to Opa-locka, we were in the back of the Maybach with our seats laid back, top open, curtains parted. The landaulet arrived and we cruised up to Chevron to pick up some local petrol and take a few pictures of the dome that seemed to suggest a new corporate identity faithful to the politics of its product.

"Opa-locka," you might ask, what kind of name is that? Like many American cities adopting Native American place names, such as "Manhattan," an Algonquian word meaning "isolated thing in the *water*," or "*Chicago*," *from the French transcription of shikaakwa* [garlic fields], "Opa-locka" is an abbreviation stemming from *opa-tisha-wocka-locka*,[1] from the Seminole for "high ground amid the swamp on which there is a camping place."

A hunting ground of the indigenous population up until the nineteenth century, Manifest Destiny brought a new destiny, deed and title were created, and the place ended up in the hands of the Curtiss-Bright Corporation (founded by James Bright, a cattle rancher from Missouri, and Glenn Curtiss, who had grown wealthy from his success in aeronautics). The first development of their 120,000-acre ranch land was Hialeah ("high prairie"), which centered on a Renaissance Revival horseracing track, Hialeah Park. The corporation's second wave of land transformation, Country Club Estates, the home to Curtiss's grand 21-acre winter estate Dar-Err-Aha,[2] was laid out around a golf course in a "Pueble Revival" style (the site is now an incorporated city called Miami Springs). The final city that the Curtiss-Bright Corporation was to construct in Dade County

1. "Not being versed in the Seminole or Creek Tongues, I must depend upon authority or tradition. In Opa-locka it has always been said that the name Opatishawockalocka meant "big island covered with many trees in the swamp," which is, of course, the definition of the Florida work hammock." Frank Scott FitzGerald-Bush, *A Dream of Araby* (Opa-locka, Florida: South Florida Archaeological Museum, 1976), 2.

2. "[Glenn Curtiss'] wife Lena named Dar Err Aha, a Persian phrase meaning 'house of contentment.' (Again one must wrestle with the myth-makers; it has long been said that Dar Err Aha is Seminole for 'chikee of Contentment,' knowing neither the Seminole nor the Persian language, I can only report that Lena Curtiss is the source of my version.)" Frank Scott FitzGerald-Bush, *A Dream of Araby* (Opa-locka, Florida: South Florida Archaeological Museum, 1976), 2.

was Opa-locka, designed and erected in the mid-1920s. Historically classified as "Moorish Revival," it is now considered by some to be the largest collection of Moorish architecture in the Western Hemisphere.

Mrs. Curtiss, a member of the Church of Christian Science, had a friend back up North whose son, Bernhardt E. Muller, himself a Christian Scientist, had recently designed their new church. Though little known, Muller had studied at the École des Beaux-Arts in Paris and was an independently practicing architect, registered with the AIA (American Institute of Architects) and maintaining an office at 527 Fifth Avenue in Manhattan. On the recommendation of his mother, Glenn Curtiss asked the young man to design Opa-locka.

Muller's original plan for Opa-locka echoed a Robin Hood/English Tudor cottage style, an aesthetic he had already exercised in previous projects. Interestingly, another such project, Grosvenor Atterbury's English-themed garden city, Forest Hills Gardens, had been begun in 1909 and was located in Queens, within Manhattan's periphery. (In 1925 Muller would design the First Church of Christ, Scientist, of Forest Hills.) Like Forest Hills Gardens, the winding streets of Opa-locka, laid out by Clinton MacKenzie, were those of a garden city. Opa-locka would advertise itself through the domestication of its landscape, holding gardening contests and offering community garden plots to residents.

But Opa-locka would not remain a mere English-style garden city in South Florida. A number of exotic influences had by this time been working on America for more than a century. One of the most important was the popularization of ancient Egypt, which began with Napoleon's arrival in/invasion of that country in 1798–1801, and in whose footsteps some 2000-plus scientists, scholars, and architects followed, documenting its culture. The accounts of their exploits would be mediated by publishers, who employed a series of new typefaces for the purpose.[3] Egyptomania reached an all-time high, just in time for Opa-locka, with the British Egyptologist Howard Carter's excavation of the tomb of Tutankhamen, in 1922. Two years later Carter was in to America to lecture to eager crowds.

Meanwhile, out West, the influential Frank Lloyd Wright, looking to define a suitable architectural style for California, was turning his attention toward the architecture and ornament of the Mayans when developing his pattern-block system, which he

---

3. Images and descriptions of Egypt were soon being disseminated in publications such as *Description de l'Égypte* (1809). Intense fascination with all things Egyptian led to suites of parlor furniture being produced which resembled that found in the ancient tombs. Multicolored woodblock-printed wallpaper could make a dining room in Edinburgh or Chicago feel like Luxor. Vincent Figgens in particular pioneered new typefaces which he called "Antique," of which specimens from 1815 and 1817 survive. Their growing popularity would eventually cause them to be referred to as "Egyptienne" by French and German type-founders; today they are commonly known as "slab serif." This style of typeface is widely used for advertising, posters, and flyers. There is, of course, no relationship between "slab serif" types and the ancient Egyptian system of writing. Either shrewd marketing or honest confusion led to them often being considered Egyptian, and many of the earlier ones bear Egyptian names: Cairo, Karnak, Memphis. http://en.wikipedia.org/wiki/Slab_serif as of 20 February 2013 [extracts, edited].

himself termed "California Romanza" (others have preferred to call the style "Mayan Revival").

At this juncture Glenn Curtiss decided to ask Bernhardt E. Muller for a revised plan for Opa-locka, adding an entirely new theme. This came at the urging of Mrs. Irene FitzGerald-Bush, the wife of Opa-locka's electrical contractor Frank Bush. Upon visiting the landscape where Opa-locka was to rise, she confessed to having been transported to a far-away land, to a scene from the *Arabian Nights*.[4]

Bernhardt E. Muller was not quite convinced of this sudden request for thematic revision, but soon began to imagine the city with great enthusiasm, drafting plans for far more structures than would be eventually realized. Muller, too, credits his wife with extensive research on Eastern architectural motifs for the project. Even so, as with a stage set, the many domes atop the houses built at Opa-locka express no interior volume, defeating the purpose of a cupola in a hot climate. Many homes were built with functioning fireplaces, lending the idea of coziness in a cottage up North—a somewhat incongruous feature for a subtropical environment.

The film *The Thief of Bagdad*, starring Douglas Fairbanks and premiering in 1924 at Sid Grauman's newly built Egyptian Theater in Hollywood, California, provided a cinematic image to complement the many books which had long illustrated the tales of the *1001 Arabian Nights*.[5]

Early advertisements for Opa-locka, which opened in 1926, exploited the collective imagination created through the media, directly referencing the film. One reads: "Of course you have seen Douglas Fairbanks' *Thief of Bagdad*, with its wealth of Oriental picturesqueness reminding one, indeed, of the famous illustrations to the Arabian Nights." By this time there had already appeared a slew of Moorish Revival synagogues, Masonic Shriners' temples (Ancient Arabic Order of the Nobles of the Mystic Shrine), movie theaters, and casinos in cities across the United States and Europe, and many more were to follow.

Beginning in the 19th century, World Expositions brought home the art and exploits of foreign cultures and colonial possessions to a wide public. For the visitors of these fairs, it was by and large their first encounter with "foreign" architecture. But the exhibits often represented a pastiche of styles formulated by Western architects. Similarly, "Oriental corners" could be found in 19th-century middle-class homes. Meanwhile the affluent were able to escape from a harsh winter to an "Oriental corner" somewhere in

---

4. "In her excitement, my mother turned to Mr. Curtiss, clapping her hands together, and exclaimed, 'oh, Glenn, it's like a dream from the Arabian Nights?' On the drive back to Country Club Estates, my father recalled, Mr. Curtiss was unusually silent, even for him. The next morning, before breakfast Mr. Curtiss went to his study and took from a shelf a volume of *The One Thousand and One Tales From the Arabian Nights*, illustrated with many watercolor drawings. He instructed his secretary to sent it at once to Mr. Muller; with it went a note from Mr. Curtiss saying, 'This is what I want Opa-locka to be like.'" Frank Scott FitzGerald-Bush, *A Dream of Araby* (Opa-locka, Florida: South Florida Archaeological Museum, 1976), 4.

5. *Robin Hood* (starring Douglas Fairbanks) was the first motion picture to premiere at Sid Grauman's Egyptian Theater in 1922.

the South, traveling in relative comfort by way of the emerging rail and, later, airline networks.

The Orange Blossom Special rail service would give a wink to Europe's Orient Express by making its inaugural journey via Opa-locka. There was even a mock hold-up by a band of hired thieves, played against the town's backdrop of crenellations, minarets, and turrets. (The event was reported in the following day's newspaper under the headline "Mob Stops Train in Opa-locka.")

This would mark just one of the many attempts of Opa-locka to actively promote itself by way of newspaper coverage and advertising. The city also began holding an annual "Arabian Nights Festival" and opened its own Miami sales office at 132 East Flagler Street, where visitors, prospective buyers, and tourists alike would be escorted to Opa-locka in company buses displaying the official municipal logo. Upon arriving, guests could inspect a model house, climb the stairs of an observation tower to choose a potential lot, or accompany their children to the zoo. Historian MaryAnn Goodlett-Taylor, who went to Opa-locka from Miami Springs to visit the animals when she was a child, recalls that the zoo remained until the mid-1930s.

Opa-locka had been conceived with eager optimism, during the real-estate boom that was to transform Florida's watershed of mangroves, oolitic limestone, muck and pinelands into themed, habitable landscapes. The hurricane of 1926 and the following great depression would slow the city's urgency. But after the premature death of Glenn Curtiss, Opa-locka's founder, in 1930, the newly incorporated city lost its funding.[6] In 1931 it was largely turned over to the U.S. Navy, which then proceeded to dismantle much of its civic infrastructure in 1938 while planning for an influx of 15,000 personnel.[7] Subsequently, the majority of the original hammock that was set aside as a park was destroyed. Although wartime was boom time, eventually the naval base was decommissioned and the city experienced the ghost-town effect felt by many company towns. It grew to be one of the most notorious, corrupt, and crime-ridden municipalities within Dade County. Opa-locka still struggles to recover: It has been Native Wars to World Wars to Cold Wars to Drug Wars.

With the increasing involvement of the United States of America in foreign conflicts, including, today, the ever-present War on Terror, it is curious to recall that two of the highjackers of 9/11 are known to have trained at Opa-locka Airport and lived in the adjacent community of Miramar (these facts are left out of official reports).[8]

6. "In 1926 a severe hurricane would impair the growth of the Curtiss-Bright Towns, Glenn Curtiss, an individual of principal, did everything he could, because he could, he felt, to help in the relief efforts. (It was to become apparent for another year that among the chief causalities of the storm was Opa-locka itself; the hurricane brought an immediate end to the already dwindling land boom in south Florida. But Mr. Curtiss refused to accept the fact. 'In times like this, Frank,' my father recalled Mr. Curtiss saying, 'it's men with capital who must keep things going. To hold back will bring on economic collapse.' Loyally, Mr Curtiss continued to build houses no one could buy, and my father followed his example. My father's investment was less, but unlike Mr. Curtiss's, it was total." Frank Scott FitzGerald-Bush, *A Dream of Araby* (Opa-locka, Florida: South Florida Archaeological Museum, 1976), 14.

7. Mr. Curtiss' last act on behalf of his city was to give the United States Navy the small airfield

of his Florida Aviation Camp, with the request that a naval reserve base be established to provide further employment. In January of 1931 the base was commissioned. In 1938 the small naval installation was enlarged, annexing the old golf course and the old hammock, including the sixty-acre portion of it set aside by Mr. Curtiss for a park. Bulldozers leveled the ancient oaks, destroying what had been one of the loveliest natural areas in the county.

8. See: http://www.browardbulldog.org/2011/09/fbi-found-directties-between-911-hijackers-and-saudis-living-in-florida-congress-kept-in-dark/(accessed 5 February 2013), and: http://www.historycommons.org/context.jsp?item=a091201shuckumsstory/(accessed 5 February 2013).

One hears that Opa-locka was known as the "Bagdad of the South" up untl 9/11, when the city distanced itself from the phrase. The celebrated Arabian Nights Festival has also been phased out. Some of the city's administration are concerned that imitative Arabic motifs could be viewed as mockery and that, with recent ethnic and cultural changes, it is time for the city to update its identity. Now, around holiday time, there is a Turkey Day when more than a thousand turkeys are given away to a long line of eager residents. But what does this have to do with that?

Perhaps it is meant as a day in memoriam of the city's erstwhile celebration of "Pioneer Days."

South Florida has been the scene of a curious architectural dialogue featuring historicism, modernism, and post-modernism, all mediated by the needs of war and enterprise. Thanks to the U.S. Army Engineering Corps, the dredging of Biscayne Bay gave birth to Miami Beach and the Venetian Islands, as the Everglades were being drained for agricultural land to expand habitable landscape in Southern Florida. With the success of newly platted suburbs such as Coral Gables, built in Mediterranean Revival style, Opa-locka with its Moorish Revival style would seemingly fit, while Miami Beach's leisure architecture signaled the desire for streamlined modernity. There, as consequence of thematic intervention, Art Deco would stylistically appropriate modernism, inflating its form and adding narrative motifs—an appropriation often viewed as theme-kitsch. It is as though a certain post-modernism (or historicism) preceded modernism in South Florida, and provided the reason for modernism's existence, which was then stylistically re-appropriated by post-modernism.

Mrs. Owens, a town resident, described Opa-locka as always having felt like a small, nice New England town, the type of town she left when she relocated with her husband in support of the marines, in the 1940s. The Owens family backyard of mangoes and citrus was removed when nearly all home-grown citrus trees were eradicated from South Florida's yards in fear of a spreading citrus canker. Later the action proved to be unnecessary. Nevertheless two mango trees are still there in that backyard, with fruit in full abundance. Another resident, Jackie, talked of times when the canals were still open to boats on Atlantic Avenue and Opa-locka's local fishermen would share the bounty and host fishfrys for the city folk. In the 1960s she and her cousin would dress up for the annual Arabian Nights Festival; the cousin, Charlotte, who now lives in New York City, remembers the lemons as being the size of grapefruits, with a strong, thick peel, and the smell of jasmine at night, its scent drifting through unlocked screen doors. Looking back, she credits having grown up in Opa-locka for her desire to travel and discover different cultures.

During the construction of Opa-locka Bernhardt E. Muller had remained largely in New York, drafting theme sketches; Carl Jensen and Paul Lieske were sent as project architects to oversee progress on the site. In 1959 Muller made a rare visit during the local Pioneer Days festival and was thoroughly discouraged with what he saw, with its regression. But after his visit the city adopted a strict odinance which mandates that all new constructions must incorporate Moorish details and adhere to an approved color-chart. This aesthetic ordinance is available from the municipal administrative offices, now housed in Town Center on Fisherman Street, a midrise office building with a large, arch-shaped tinted window, a feature which, in itself, recalls to mind Opa-locka's code revision.

The story behind Town Center is worth telling. It sits on surplus land that the city, hoping to find its way back to prosperity, sold for $1 per square foot to a developer; additional public funds were also secured to promote the site. When plans fell through with the biotech company which was thinking of becoming a tenant, the city moved its administrative offices here from the historic city hall and rents space to the tune of $600,000 a year. (It is Town Center LLC's largest tenant.)[9]

To improve a self-perpetuating "gangsta image," Opa-locka has adopted another ordinance banning the sagging of pants on municipal property. The legislation was offered by a well-dressed City Commissioner, Timothy Holmes, who can be seen jetting in and out of the newly built city hall on his electric motor cart. Timothy means well, expresses genuine respect for his community, and has supported another initiative to rename some of the streets after community leaders such as Irma B. Skiles, an early African American resident. Recently the city inaugurated Barack Obama Avenue—though Obama himself declined an invitation to campaign in Opa-locka.

By the look of some of the architecture in Opa-locka, it seems as if more people like to spend money on their cars, dressing them up in 22s, 26s, 28s, or ridin' high on 30-inch rims. Is it because more people own their own cars than a dwelling? Or is it the idea that while you can possess a car, you cannot really possess a piece of land. After all, in a country of eminent domain, you actually own nothing, nothing but the interest on it, secured through the taxes you pay. You pay taxes on a car, too, but you can take it with you— or rather, it can take you somewhere.

---

9. See: Jason Grotto "Biotech bid stung Opa-locka: Before he pitched a biotech park for Liberty City, developer Dennis Stackhouse wooed Opa-locka with a similar dream—and the city is paying," *Miami Herald*, 26 June 2007, http://www.miamiherald.com/multimedia/news/povped/part3/index.html (accessed 5 February 2013).

Some in these parts drive cars, but also some fly planes or are allowed to repose as passengers in them. In 1937 Amelia Earhart departed from Opa-locka Airport in her attempt to circumnavigate the globe, only to meet up with death. Seventy years later, Barrington Irving, piloting his own craft built out of donated parts, became at age 23 the yougest person yet to fly around the globe solo. He now heads Experience Aviation at Opa-locka Airport, an outfit which offers aviation opportunities to the youth of South Florida. Now and then, too, private jets arrive and depart.

Well, here we are: The new image of the horse-drawn carriage arrives, going slow, ridin' high, horses under the hood, up on the streets. Would that be a donk? And us in our Maybach, at the Chevron station. They spot us taking pictures of their shining cars whose reflections reveal countless hours of labor, of love. Someone yells out, "Fresh meat, what you taking pictures of?" I answer, "The cars and the architecture," and they answer, "Oh no you don't, we don't be takin' pictures round here." Showing respect and also maintaining focus, I turn about and take some more pictures of the domed petrol dispensary. At that moment one of the tinted windows of the car I had been taking pictures of rolls down and two fellows signal me over, asking what I am up to and what kind of music I listen to. They give me one of their compact discs, and ask me to tell them what I think of it—text me, twitter me up—and then one says: "Remember, there's a lot of niggas out here with no money and that camera you have is looking real nice and the CD I just gave you was free so remember that."

I talk to them about Opa-locka appearing in many songs on the radio, say thanks, take a couple more pictures, hop back in the Maybach, drop in the Eady/DCP (Dade County Plug), and go across the street to the McDonald's. It, too, flaunts a dome and a minaret atop its drive-thru, which does not seem so out of place with the usual festive McDonald's décor.

Driving around Opa-locka, listening to Eady/Dade County Plug, thinking about the lyrics: Like much of South Florida's hip-hop and rap music, Eady/DCP's lyrics are haunted by excesses of luxury and desperation, both of which are procured through the daily hustle. They emphasize a romantic image to provide a cinematic backdrop expressing glamor which is to document its own image.

So we continue conducting our research, shifting back and forth, sampling Miami's many intermittent free radio stations, taking note of all the artists who drop Opa-locka's name: Brisco, Rick Ross, Lil Wayne, Grind Mode, Yung, Quay & Shootemupbullet, Lil Rip, Mz. Opa-locka, Pit Bull, Bully Thunderbolt… The list is growing as we listen to that Maybach Music in the back of the Maybach.

BIBLIOGRAPHY

Berger, Ludwig, and Michael Powell, dirs. *The Thief of Bagdad*. London Film Productions, 1940.

Billings Stuard, Elizabeth. *Arabian Nights Stories*. Racine, Wisconsin: Whitman Publishing Co., 1923.

Chase, Charles E. Resourceful Rehab. *A Guide for Historic Buildings in Dade County*. Florida: Metropolitan Dade County Office of Community and Economic Development Historic Preservation Division, 1987.

Davies, J., T. Smith, N. Taylor, and W. Thompson. *Arabian Nights' Entertainments: Consisting of One Thousands and One Stories*. Vol. 1, London, 1787.

Demeulenaere-Douyère, Christiane. *Exotiques Expositions... Les Expositions Universelles et les Cultures extra-Européennes France, 1855–1937*. Paris: Somogy Éditions d'Art, 2010.

FitzGerald-Bush, Frank S. *A Dream of Araby: Glen H. Curtiss and the founding of Opa-locka*. Florida: South Florida Archaeological Museum, 1976.

George, Paul S. *The Dr. Paul George Walking Tour of East Little Havana*. Miami Florida: The Historical Association of Southern Florida, 1991.

Hannau, Hans W. *Tropical Flowers of Florida*. Miami Beach, Florida: Hannau Inc., n.d.

Maysles, Albert, and David Maysles, dirs. *Salesman*. Maysles Films, 1968.

Nicholas, Alwyn. *A Brief History of Opa Locka*. Miami, Florida: Just the Facts, 2005.

Said, Edward W. *Orientalism*. New York: Vintage Books, 1978.

Salkin, Alex. "L' Architecte Ernest Jaspar." *L'Art Belge*, Deuxième Année N° 11 (31 Décembre 1920): 6–8.

Scenic Florida. Tallahassee, Florida: Florida State Department of Agriculture, n.d.

Sherwood, Shirley. *Venice Simplon Orient-Express*. London: Weidenfeld & Nicolson, 1983.

Stockbridge, Frank P., and John H. Perry. *Florida in the Making*. Jacksonville, Florida: The de Bower Publishing Co., 1926.

The Arabian Nights' Entertainments. London: James Nisbet & Co., n.d.

The Arabian Nights. Chicago, Philadelphia, Toronto: The John C. Winston Company, 1924.

The Journal of Decorative and Propaganda Arts vol. 23 Florida Theme Issue, Miami, Florida: The Wolfsonian, Florida International University and the Wolfson Foundation Journal of Decorative and Propaganda Arts, 1998.

Walsh, Raoul, dir. *The Thief of Bagdad*. Douglas Fairbanks Pictures, 1924.

MOORISH REVIVAL TIMELINE

Orientalism advancing through exploitative trade and bourgeoisie curiosity in the eighteenth, nineteenth, and twentieth centuries

1787
BRIGHTON PAVILION, ROYAL RESIDENCE, BRIGHTON, ENGLAND — JOHN NASH (1752–1835), ARCHITECT

Built for George IV, Prince of Wales in an Indo-Saracenic style. The pavilion would later serve as an inspiration for one of America's first Moorish Revival residences: Iranistan.

1798
NAPOLEON'S EGYPTIAN CAMPAIGN, FORMATION OF THE INSTITUT D'ÉGYPTE

1809–29
DESCRIPTION DE L'ÉGYPTE

Description de l'Égypte [Description of Egypt] was a series of publications, appearing first in 1809 and continuing until the final volume was published in 1829, that offered a comprehensive scientific description of ancient and modern Egypt as well as its natural history. It is the collaborative work of about 160 civilian scholars and scientists, known popularly as "the savants," who accompanied Napoleon's expedition to Egypt from 1798 to 1801 as part of the French Revolutionary Wars, as well as about 2000 artists and technicians, including 400 engravers, who would later compile it into a full work.

1836
The Institut d'Égypte's activities continued in 1836 under the name The Egyptian Society, and supported work by French, German and English scholars. It was transferred to Alexandria in 1859, and its name changed again, this time to Institut Égyptien. The institute functioned under the auspices of Egypt's viceroy, Sa'id Pasha, and had several prominent members, notably the German botanist Georg August Schweinfurth, as well as Egyptologists Auguste Mariette and Gaston Maspero. Later members included Ahmed Kamal, Egypt's first indigenous Egyptologist, as well as Ahmad Zaki Pasha, a pioneering philologist. The institute returned to Cairo in 1880. Its previous name was restored by royal decree in 1918. Henceforth, it was directly under the Royal Palace's auspices.

1848
IRANISTAN, BRIDGEPORT, CONNECTICUT — LEOPOLD EIDLITZ (1823–1908), ARCHITECT

Iranistan was a Moorish-Revival mansion in Bridgeport, Connecticut commissioned by P.T. Barnum. The structure lasted only nine years before being destroyed by fire. The architect, Leopold Eidlitz, was a Jewish immigrant born in Prague, and one of the founding members of the American Institute of Architects. The mansion was influenced by a trip made by Barnum to the Brighton Pavilion.

1863
LE CASINO MAURESQUE D'ARCACHON — PAUL RÉGNAULD (1827–1879), ARCHITECT

A casino built for the city of Ville d'Hiver, a winter city comprising of an eclectic mixture of architecture styles, from Swiss chalets to English gardens, visited by those affected by tuberculosis and the wealthy.

1869
SUEZ CANAL OPENS

1872
CENTRAL SYNAGOGUE, NEW YORK, NY — HENRY FERNBACH (1829–1883), ARCHITECT

Fernbach was a German Jewish architect who immigrated to New York in 1855. He designed several synagogues in the Moorish Revival style.

1878
CLEOPATRA'S NEEDLE ERECTED ON THE BANKS OF THE THAMES IN LONDON

1881
CLEOPATRA'S NEEDLE ERECTED IN CENTRAL PARK

Gifted by Egypt as a tribute to the United States for remaining neutral while France and England sought to influence Egyptian politics. The monument was originally a pair of obelisks standing in Alexandria.

1882

The Battle of Tel el-Kebir/el-Tal el-Kebir was fought between the Egyptian army led by Ahmed Urabi and the British military, near Tel-el-Kebir. After discontented Egyptian officers under Urabi rebelled in 1882, the United Kingdom reacted to protect its financial and expansionist interests in the country, and in particular the Suez Canal.

1887
CASTLE WARDEN, ST. AUGUSTINE, FLORIDA

Built in 1887 as the winter home of William G. Warden, a business partner of John D. Rockefeller and Henry Flagler, the castle is a noteworthy landmark from the post-Civil War era in St. Augustine. The unique Moorish Revival architecture drew the attention of the city's visitors and was a focus for winter activity, for the Warden family through to the 1930s.

1888–91
TAMPA BAY HOTEL, TAMPA, FLORIDA — JOHN A. WOOD (1837–1910), ARCHITECT

Built by Henry B. Plant, a railroad and shipping magnate.

1889–90
PARK EAST SYNAGOGUE, NEW YORK, NY — SCHNEIDER AND HERTER, ARCHITECTS

The Park East Synagogue (Congregation Zichron Ephraim), with its richly decorated composed Moorish Revival facade, is located on East 67th Street between Lexington and Third Avenues. Its combination of Moorish and Byzantine architectural detail marks it as a late manifestation of the attempt to find a suitable expression for synagogue architecture, which accompanied the proliferation of new Jewish congregations after the Civil War.

1890–97
LES BAINS DUNKERQUOIS, DUNKERQUE, FRANCE — ALBERT BAERT (1863–1951), LOUIS GILQUIN (1827–1909), AND GEORGE BOIDIN (DATES UNKNOWN), ARCHITECTS

The construction of public baths in Dunkerque was initiated in the 1890s by Mayor Alfred Dumont, opening in 1897. Facilities included a hairdresser, a fencing room, steam baths, a bar-restaurant, and an oval basin filled with water at 25 degrees. In 1975 the baths closed permanently.

1891
LE TYPHONIUM, WISSANT, FRANCE — EDMOND DE VIGNE (1841–1918), ARCHITECT

Neo-Egyptian-style villa built for painters Adrien Demont and Virginie Demont-Breton.

1905
MODERN HELIOPOLIS, CAIRO, EGYPT — ERNEST JASPAR (1875–1940), ARCHITECT

The city was established between 1905 and 1914 by the Heliopolis Oasis Company, led by the Belgian industrialist Édouard Louis Joseph, Baron Empain, as well as Boghos Nubar, son of the Egyptian Prime Minister Nubar Pasha.

L'AEGIDIUM, ST. GILLES, BELGIUM — GUILLAUME SEGERS (DATES UNKNOWN), ARCHITECT

Art Nouveau Arabian-styled theatre.

1906

The Denshawai Incident is the name given to a dispute that occurred in 1906 between British military officers and locals in Egypt, believed to mark a turning point in the British presence in the country. Though the incident itself was a fairly small one in numbers of casualties and injuries, the British officers' response to the incident and its grave consequences led to the dispute's lasting impact.

1910
HELIOPOLIS PALACE HOTEL CAIRO, EGYPT — ERNEST JASPAR (1875–1940), ARCHITECT

1922

Grauman's Egyptian Theatre opens with the first "Hollywood Premiere," *Robin Hood*, starring Douglas Fairbanks.

1924

Thief of Bagdad, starring and produced by Douglas Fairbanks, premiering at Grauman's Egyptian Theatre, Hollywood, California.

1925
CITY PLANNING OF OPA-LOCKA, CLINTON MACKENZIE (1872–1940), URBAN PLANNER

1926
OPA-LOCKA, FLORIDA — BERNHARDT EMIL MULLER (1878–1964), ARCHITECT, CURTISS-BRIGHT COMPANY, DEVELOPER, GLENN H. CURTISS (1878–1930), JAMES BRIGHT (1866–1959), FINANCIERS

SPECIFICATIONS

For the general construction of a new residence building to be erected on lot 18, block 132, City of Opa-Locka, Fla., for The Miami Daily News and Metropolis, in accordance with the accompanying plans and these specifications, prepared by Bernhardt E. Muller, architect of Opa-Locka, Fla.

PRELIMINARY
All contracts shall be as per the standard form of the American Institute of Architects. These specifications are intended to embrace the furnishing of all labor and material required for the full and complete erection and finishing of the building on the supposition a general contractor will furnish and build and take charge of the entire construction; provide temporary privy, removing same with accumulations on completion of the work. Also a storage shed for tools and drawings. Keep all excavations free from standing water by temporary drainage connection, maintain night lights for all materials placed so as not to obstruct streets or sidewalks, making good any damage to this or adjoining property, or to pavement, walks or curbs caused by the building operations. Conform with all requirements of the City and State building codes, taking out all building permits as required. Remove any trees or obstructions encumbering the site, leaving the lot practically level; also shall take care of all foundation debris, drains, or other obstructions in such a manner that the building operations can properly proceed. Establish all finished lot grades and the location of the building. The owner shall pay for all engineering service required to establish lines and level. All trees or shrubbery on lawn to be protected and boxed up during construction of the building.

EXCAVATIONS
Stake out the building accurately according to plans, establishing all lines, stakes and levels; excavate for footings, and foundation walls making all excavations level. All excavations to be sufficiently wide for the proper erection of all work. On completion of building fill in around outside of all walls to finished grade level on lot, tamping all earth and removing from the lot all earth not needed for grading and filling. All leveling of lot and finished grading to be according to the directions of the owner.

MASON WORK
Perform all mason work for fireplace, cement block work, concrete and cement work in the best manner, using only first class materials. Build all erection scaffolding and forms and do all bracing of walls and frames and assisting other mechanics by doing such cutting as the nature of their work demands such aid.

CONCRETE WORK
Build all footings for foundation walls 16 inches wide by 8 inches deep as shown on plans, of one part .... Portland cement manufactured by .... to two parts sharp sand and four parts crushed rock, all machine mixed with fresh water and well poured and spaded and left level on top surface. Tamp all earth well and firm before laying any concrete and confine same within board forms securely wired and braced and stakes driven in. A wet mixture of concrete not containing too much water to readily flow is advised. Insert three-eighth inch round reinforcing bars as shown on plans. Bend bars around corners at least two feet. Also all anchors for sill plate spaced four foot centers. Any concrete failing to set properly to be removed and the work redone satisfactorily to owner. All cement to be kept dry until used and no re-tempered cement permitted. Provide vents in all walls as indicated on plans. Use eight inch cement block laid with holes horizontal. Place copper screen in back of all vents.

CEMENT BLOCKS
The contractor for this part of the work shall furnish, deliver, and erect all material required for chimney, fireplace and vents, as indicated on plans, of hard tested cement blocks, manufactured by .... capable of resisting eight hundred pounds per square inch in direct compression, together with all necessary special shapes required at corners. All cement blocks shall be true and regular in size, manufactured of such design that all webs and shells are in direct compression when laid in the wall. All block to offer a good surface for the stucco and plaster finish. Block cracked or broken will not be acceptable under this specification. All block shall pass City Engineer's test. Laying – All block used in chimney and fireplace must be laid with the holes or voids vertical in the wall, in order to develop their full strength. Care must be taken that the tops of all unfinished walls are thoroly covered or protected against stormy weather.

Mortar – All mortar used for laying up the blocks shall consist of .... Portland cement, manufactured by ...., and clean, sharp sand in the proportion of one part cement to three parts sand, well mixed to a smooth moderately stiff mortar. Lime, not to exceed ten per cent of the cement by volume, will be allowed in the mortar.

CEMENT WORK
All cement and tile floors to have a rough concrete base in proportion to one part cement, two parts sand and four parts broken stone. Cement floor in front porch, bathroom and fireplace to be a three inch rough concrete floor. Front porch to have inlaid broken tile of variegated color. All finish cement floors to be coated with .... waterproof hardener. All steps to be of cement work with red brick inserts.

BRICK WORK
Brick work on exterior steps and mantel in living room shall be of hard burned pressed brick manufactured by .... of color and texture selected by the Architect. All brick work to be laid up in cement mortar, manufactured by .... in color as selected by the Architect. All joints to be finished as directed. Joints to be one-half inch wide. All fire brick to be laid flat side vertical for hearth, with joints not more than onefourth inch wide.

DAMPERS
Damper for fireplace to be a cast iron damper manufactured by .... of size required, property set in place with mortar.

41

CARPENTER WORK

Execute all framing, fitting and finished work in a substantial and workmanlike manner, doing all cutting, blocking-, patching and furnishing wood centers, grounds, etc. as may be required in the construction of the building. All framing timber to be No. 2 Douglas fir. Take all measurements for finished work at the building and verify all measurements on drawings before proceeding with the work.

JOISTS

Frame all floor joists, ceiling joists and roof joists to properly carry out the required construction of the building. All joists to have at least four inch wall bearings and bearing on girders carefully made and joined. The crown of all joists to be up, double for headers and trimmers and under partitions parallel to span of same. Anchor every four feet and cross bridge all floor joists, ceiling joists and roof beams with 2 × 2 or 1 × 4 bridging; cut in and nailed with two nailings at each end of each piece, with one row of bridging for every span of twelve feet or less. Frame for trap opening where directed. All joists to be as follows: First floor joists: 2 × 8–16 inches on centers Ceiling joists: 2 × 6–18 inches on centers Roof beams: 3 × 4–16 inches on centers, braced to ceiling beams.

GIRDERS

Built up girders to be well spiked and bolted together. All ends of girders to have a level bearing. All girders must be of best dense Douglas fir, selected for strength.

STUDDING

All studding to be 2 × 4, space 16 inches on centers, except where soil stack occurs use 2 × 6 inch studding, space 16 inches on centers. Set flat way all studding for closets where no bearing wall. Provide floor and ceiling plates and set plumb and bridge with 2 × 3 or 1 × 4 cross bridging and 2 × 4 flat bridging once in the height of first story. Form trussed heads over all openings and double stud jambs of all openings. All corners to be diagonally braced with continuous piece halved at studding.

SHEATHIHG

Cover entire roof with a seven-eighths by six inch sheathing D&M or ship-lap with tight joints, double nailed, end all cuts made over bearing a. Entire exterior of building shall be covered, with 1 × 6 square edge sheathing, laid diagonally and four inches apart. Hail at each stud with 28d. nails.

FLOORS

Cover all floors with a seven-eighths by six inch square edge Douglas fir flooring or shiplap laid diagonally and close; and all joints made over joists. Finish floor for entire house to be edge grain clear Douglas fir 21/4 inch face D&M, blind nailed and smoothly scraped and sanded, leaving no inequalities. Bathroom to have tile floor. See elsewhere for this finish floor. All floors to be machine sanded.

WINDOW FRAMES

Provide all rough frames of Douglass fir for windows as per details shown on plans. Interior frames to be of same finish as rooms; all frames to have moulded wood stops. All door frames to be well anchored in walls with two anchors per jamb and all set plumb. Prime all frames before setting in place. DOOR FRAMES & DOORS All exterior door frames to be of Douglas fir, one and three quarters inches thick with staff bead on outside. Exterior doors to be Laminex Doors, manufactured by Wheeler & Osgood, one and three quarters inches thick with glazed panels and wood muntins and with wood glass stops. All interior frames to be clear No. 1 Douglas fir sanded, well mortised, with moulded stops. All interior frames to be one and oneeighth inches thick. All interior doors one and three-eighths inches thick. Closet doors which shall have turned spindle grills at top for ventilation, all to be No. 29 Laminex doors, manufactured by Wheeler & Osgood, and free from warps, scratches or plane marks. All exterior woodwork and screens to be of Douglas fir; screen wire to be of copper. Thresholds for exterior doors to be of quarter sawed white oak.

SASH

Sash for entire building to be of Douglas fir 3/8 inches thick with muntins as shown on plans. All sash to be hinged at sides to swing out. All sash to swing to meet S. E. winds where possible. All sash to have operators as specified elsewhere.

SCREENS

Screens shall be of Douglas fir placed at all windows on inside and hinged at sides. Window screens shall be the width of the sash adjacent thereto. Door screens shall be hinged with heavy spring outts and holdpasts. All screens shall be seven-eighths inches thick. Use copper wire for all screen work and rigidly brace all corners to make screens substantial.

IRONING BOARD

Ironing board in kitchen to be as manufactured by .... recessed in wall and properly anchored in place.

INTERIOR FINISH

All stock for inside wood finish to be select Douglas fir, smoothly sanded made with tight miters and joints, with no splicing allowed in length for any trim or casing. Take all mill measurements at the building as the contractor will be responsible for all work fitting in place. Window stools to be one and one-eighths inches thick with returned ends and aprons; base-board three-quarters by three end three quarters inches, with molded shoe at floor level. Provide picture moulding three-quarters by one and three-quarters inches at ceiling for living room, dining room and all bed rooms.

HAT STRIP

Provide hat strips in all closets. Strips to be of molded Douglas fir three-quarters by three inches, securely fastened to wall with hooks spaced ten inches apart. Also provide fourteen inch shelf and hanger rod in each closet.

WAINSCOT PAP

Provide in kitchen a wainscot cap; cap to be neatly molded, designed about three inches wide, placed four feet six inches from the floor and securely fastened to the wall. Bath room cabinets, as specified elsewhere to be built in wall by carpenter.

OABIMET & REFRIGERATOR

Cabinet and refrigerator in kitchen to be as manufactured by .... set in place where shown on plans.

ANCHORS

Furnish one end one-quarter inches by onequarter inch Standard strap anchors, tieing joists with holes punched in same for nailing to joists every 4'-0". Provide all anchors, stirrups, ties or bolts as may be required to properly construct the building. Rafter plates to be anchored to mason wall.

BATHROOM FLOOR AM WAINSCOT, FRONT PORCH AND HEARTH FLOOR

To be finished with a layer of tile furnished and laid by .... in design and color to suit architect, applied as directly by manufacturer. Tile wainscot four feet six inches high. Base to be six inches high, also provide cap all flooring and wainscot to be done in a neat and workmanlike manner and entirely satisfactory to Architect. Tile in front of fireplace and front porch shall be a hard burned clay tile of design and color selected by the Architect.

WIRE LATH
The entire exterior of building shall be covered with National Steel Fabric, stype P 214, as manufactured by the National Steel Fabric Co. All sheets shall be properly nailed to sheathing as directed by manufacturer.

STUCCO
The stucco shall be a waterproof stucco as manufactured by .... All stucco should be applied immediately after being mixed; no re-tempered stucco shall be used. All stucco work shall be thoroly wetted down until cement has set, in hot or dry weather, as too rapid drying will cause cracking. The block surface shall be free from all foreign material and shall be thoroly wetted down before the first or scratch coat is applied. The first coat shall be applied with force so as to key properly, also to prevent air bubbles or holes and shall be thoroly scratched to insure proper bond with the next coat. The second coat should be applied as soon as the prior coat has sufficiently set to allow working soon same and should be straightened with darby and straight-edge, then floated with cork or wooden float to prevent waves showing on the finished wall. Should it be impossible, to apply the last coat as soon as the former coat has become thoroly set, wet down the coat already applied before applying others, to give a, better bond between successive layers. The finish coat of Pattern approved by owner as far as possible should be applied to the entire area, of one structure at the corners at one operation. The material must have a total thickness of not less than one inch. Finish coat of stucco is to be waterproof.

PLASTERING
All side walls, partitions, to be plastered with a hard mortar as manufactured by ...., sanded by the plasterer, using sharp, sifted sand, applied well and followed at once with a brown coat before first is dry, doing such rough scratching as necessary and rodding all work smoothly with straight-edge. When bone dry, apply the finish coat of white lime putty, white silica sand, leaving a sand finish, except for living room and dining room which shall have a. special finish as directed by the Architect, leaving all of walls plumb, all angles sharp and with no scratches or catfaces visible. All lath for walls to be sound Douglas fir lath laid with broken joints, and all nailed and keyed to form proper clinch. Use expanded metal, as manufactured by.........................., well stapled and placed at all intersections of frame and masonry and all angles in rooms. Kitchen, a white hard wall, to be plastered with cement as manufactured by ...., to a height of four feet six inches. All Keene cement finish to be blocked off to imitate tile in a neat manner 2 × 5 inches.

SHEET METAL
Provide copper flashing where required on roof to make roof an absolutely water-tight job.

COMPOSITION ROOFING
To be a five ply roofing as manufactured by ....and guaranteed for five years. All flashing to be done by roofer and guaranteed an absolutely water-tight job. All roofing to be done according to manufacturer's specifications.

PAINTING
Prime all door and window frames, sash and all exterior wood work with a coat of paint manufactured by .... All outside doors shall be primed likewise. Do all needed puttying and sanding, giving two coats of paint as directed. Unless directed otherwise paint all window frames and sash a light cream color and exterior wood work old Arabian tints. All interior plastered walls and ceiling and woodwork including inside of entrance doors shall be painted. Unless otherwise instructed give all plaster and wood finish two coats of paint and finish with a dull gloss enamel in color to suit Architect. Make this a complete first-class job. Painter must not paint any finish that is not clean and well smoothed and sanded and in proper condition for painting. All plaster to be sized before painting. All floors to receive two coats of thin shellac. Wainscot in kitchen to receive two coats of paint and one coat of enamel in color.

GLASS
Glaze all windows with D.S.A.A. glass; all glass to be free from scratches, waviness or discoloration and must be satisfactory to the owner. All window glass to be properly fastened and puttied on the outside. Glass for bathroom windows to be frosted obscure or colored glass as may be selected by Architect. Front door to have plate glass.

HARDWARE
Furnish all rough hardware such as nails, spikes, screws and anchors that may be required for the proper construction of the building; also all bolts, stirrups and other rough hardware as may be required to properly complete the building. All finished hardware for doors and windows to be as manufactured by ...., to be of solid sheet bronze. All doors to have mortice lock with glass knob and escutcheon. Front entrance door to have cylinder block. All exterior doors to have 5 × 5 Stanley sheradized butts, three per door and bronze knobs on outside. All other doors (interior) to have two hinges 3 × 3 inch steel butts, finish same as other hardware. Provide coat hooks for closets spaced about ten apart. Provide door bumpers with rubber tips for all doors. Provide a spring floor hinge for D. A. door.

PLUMBING
Install a first-class sanitary plumbing system with all fixtures set ready for use in full accordance with all rules and regulations of the City Building Code, the State Board regulations and all inspectors having legal jurisdiction over this work. All work and materials to be of the quality and kind required by such supervision, but in no case inferior to what is herein specified, even if satisfactory to the State and local inspectors. All fixtures to be left clean and in perfect condition, and all plumbing installation fully tested before completion and acceptance by the owner. Perform all excavation for all drains, sewers and piping, both inside and outside of building, refilling all trenches after work has been laid and tested with filling well tamped. Do all shoring of walls necessary and use pipe cleeves where pipes or drains pass thru walls.

SUPPLIES
Make connections with City water supply running in a pipe of size demanded by the Water Company. Provide and set the meter and shut-off where directed to control entire building. Run branch supplies to bath room, water closet, bath tub, lavatory, to sill cocks where directed. Kitchen sink and heater with independent cut-off for each. Supplies for water closets to be not less than 1; lavatories, sinks and heaters to be one-half inch. Run three-quarter inch lines to all sill cocks where directed by owner. All supplies to be galvanized pipe, screwed up tight, red lead joints. Connections between lead and iron to be with brass soldering nipples wiped to lead or screwed to iron.

SOIL PIPE

All pipe to be cast iron, free from defects and coated inside and outside with asphaltum. Support by hangers and make complete with bends, offsets and reducers with joints cork tight with oakum and lead and with cleanouts with brass screw cap at base and all vertical stacks in accessible places. Vertical stacks shall extend one foot above roof with roof opening made water tight with heavy sheet lead flashing and extending over too or hub of nine. All connections of lead and wrought iron into cast iron with brass thimbles, corked and soldered to lead or screwed to iron. Connections to water closet made with heavy lead bends. All water drains outside building to be four inch vitrified glazed pipe connected with septic tank. All soil and drain lines below grade to be laid as shown on foundation plans. All sewer lines inside of building to be extra, heavy cast iron pipe.

SEPTIC TANK

To be of size three feet deep and three feet wide by six feet long placed where directed. Top to be twelve inches below grade. The contractor shall construct a tank to accomodate soil lines of the building. Tank shall be constructed of re-inforced concrete walls, floor and cover. Provide two man holes in top cover and inlet and outlet to be cast in place. Drain from septic tank to field to properly drain all water. Keep this drain tile as close to top of ground as possible, leave one-fourth inch between tiles and place a sheet of roofing paper on top of joints before filling in earth. This tank shall be to the entire satisfaction of City and State Sanitary Departments. This tank shall be constructed at same time as the foundation of building.

BATH TUB

All plumbing fixtures to be as manufactured by .... Provide and set a sixty inch enameled front bath tub as selected, fitted with nickel plated compression bath cock with four ball china index handle, one-half inch supply pipe and nickel plated waste and overflow, with chain and rubber stopper. Provide door in wall for access to pipes.

WATER CLOSET

To be enameled in and out syphon jet bowl, Sloane valve, top lever, china handle, nickel plated supply pipe, one inch angle stop and nickel plated offset, flush connection with nuts, ivorite seat (split) with bolts and china bolt caps.

LAVATORY

To be enameled round front lavatory, with integral back and rear outlet over bowl, supported on concealed wall hanger to be fastened to studding, fitted with nickel plated compression faucet with china index handle, nickel plated three-eights inch wall supply pipes, nickel plated 1. inch P trap and waste plug, china stay, chain and rubber stopper. Lavatory to be 10. inch by 14. inch bowl with eight inch back. Outside of lavatory to measure 18 × 21 inches. All lavatories to have hot and cold water supplies.

MEDICINE CABINET

Place in bath room over lavatory a steel cabinet (medicine) white enameled baked on; enameled steel shelves with turn catch and handle and hinges. Size of glass 14 × 18 plain plate mirror. Size of cabinet 31 × 33 outside dimensions. Cabinet to have open space at bottom. Kitchen sink to be an enameled sink with wide apron front and back and end, all to be in one niece as selected by owner. Sink to be set up complete with all necessary fittings for hot and- cold water.

HEATER

Place in kitchen an electric water heater neatly finished, and furnish complete with all necessary fittings, supplies, bibs, etc. Connect heater with a twenty gallon steel storage tank set on suitable supports. Tank to be covered with two inch thick asbestos covering. Connect to all bath tub, lavatories and sink.

ELECTRIC WIRING

Furnish all labor and materials required to install the electric wiring-system complete, known as flexible conduit, to all outlets shown on plans and as herein specified in accordance with the Rules and Regulations of the National Board of Fire Underwriters and the local Electric Company from which service is obtained, and according to all provisions of the Florida building code or city building code. Furnish certificate of inspection and acceptance of the work by the proper local or State inspector bureau. No lamps or fixtures are embraced in this contract. All wiring to be left operative and ready for service. Use sleeves where conduit passes thru masonry walls. Do all cutting or wood framing and all patching in an approved manner, repairing any damage to plastering; all outlet boxes to be flush with finished plaster. Cut out box to be safety metal cabinet installed where directed. Run service wire from point on outside wall in a conduit to the main cabinet. Switch control for cutting off all service to building, and with meter attachment to meter furnished. Provide a special power circuit for all units requiring same. All rooms to have outlet and independent toggle switches as shown on plans. Place service outlets base plugs and power outlets where shown on plans. All electric lighting fixtures to be furnished and installed by ....

GREASE TRAP

To be constructed of eight inch thick poured concrete walls of size three feet in diameter and four foot deep with five inch re-inforced top slab one-half inch diameter rod six inch o.c. and three-eights inches diameter tempered bars eighteen inches o.c. cat in a man hole of same thickness. Re-inforce bottom slab in same way. Inlet and outlet to be set prior to pouring.
The following items are not included in the general contract and will be let separate by the owner:
    Landscape (including walks)
    Awnings
    Shades
    Draperies and curtains
    Electric range

City of Opa-Locka
Building Structure Color Code
Approved Colors for All City Structures

TRIM

Sweetheart	Kink's Canyon Grey	Woodrose	Mayflower Blue	Sun Kiss
Chatam Tan	Surrey Beige	Enchantment	Cancun Blue	Forum Green
Serengeti Plain	Spinnaker	Black	White	

Before Purchasing Paint For Any Structure Please
Provide Our Office With A Sample Of The Desired
Color. Once The Color Is Approved Only Then Can You
Obtain A Permit

City of Opa-Locka
Building Structure Color Code
Approved Colors for All City Structures

BASE

Stone White	Champagne Sparkle	Blue Silk	Lemon Ice	Pink Bauble
Stonington Beige	Welsh Green	Honey Moon	Siesta Key	Sassafras Tea
Pinky	Toasty Grey	Sea Swell	Blue Bow	Quiet Nest
Wispy Peach	Rose Mallow	Sand White	Fresh Cut	Empress Mauve
Storytime	Pastorale Jade	Apricot	Fairytale Pink	Bone White
Italianate Villa	Cherry Blossom	Pastel Sage	Colorado Dawn	Peach Puff

Before Purchasing Paint For Any Structure Please Provide Our Office With A Sample Of The Desired Color. Once The Color Is Approved Only Then Can You Obtain A Permit

City of Opa-Locka
Building Structure Color Code
Approved Colors for All City Structures

BASE

Burmee Beige	Spirea	Simply Taupe	Limoges Blue	Prickly Pear
Pale Orange	Pink Parfait	Indian Painting	Boudoir	Naughty Neutral
Inheritance	Pink Tiger	Seashell Pink	Autumn Haze	Newborn
Eternity	Billowing Clouds	Jonquil Yellow	Touch of Nectar	Cotton Blossom
First Light	Fountain Mist	Costa Mesa	Peach Medley	Summer Haze
Coconut Milk	Citron Ice	Coral Flower	White	

Before Purchasing Paint For Any Structure Please Provide Our Office With A Sample Of The Desired Color. Once The Color Is Approved Only Then Can You Obtain A Permit

480 ALI BABA AVENUE *TRAIN STATION*

432 OPA-LOCKA BOULEVARD *HURT BUILDING*

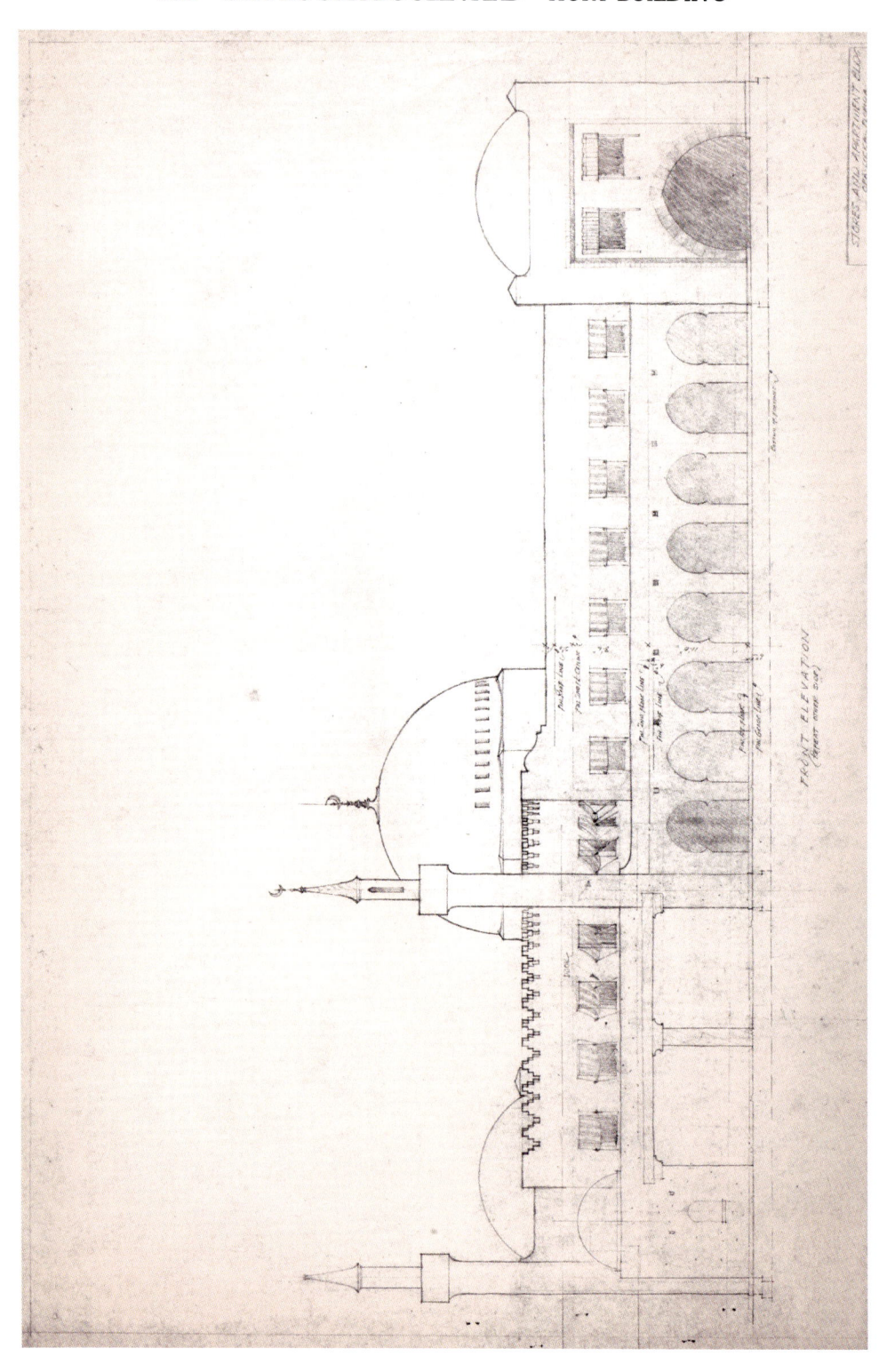

51

777   SHARAZAD BOULEVARD   *CITY HALL*

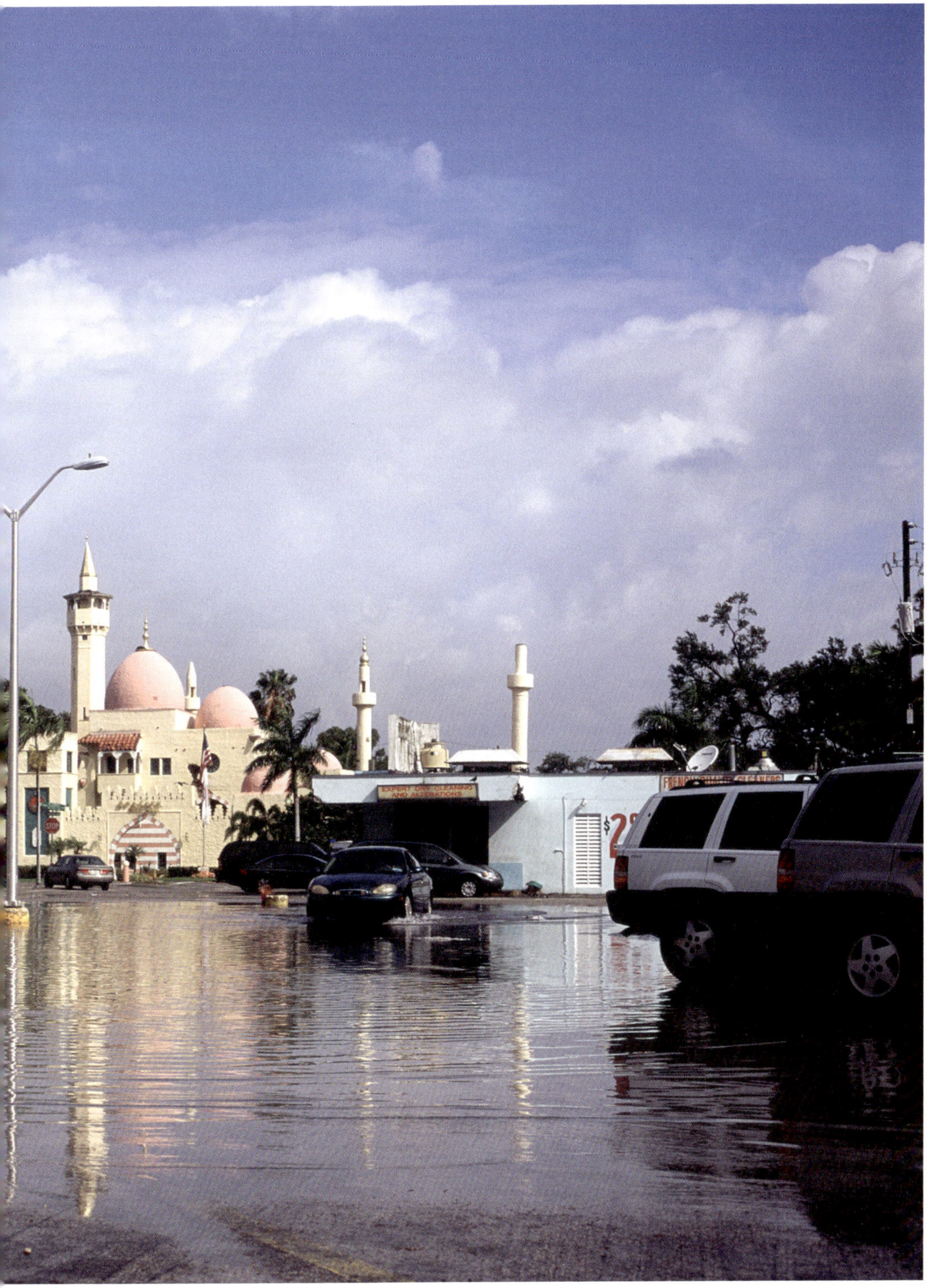

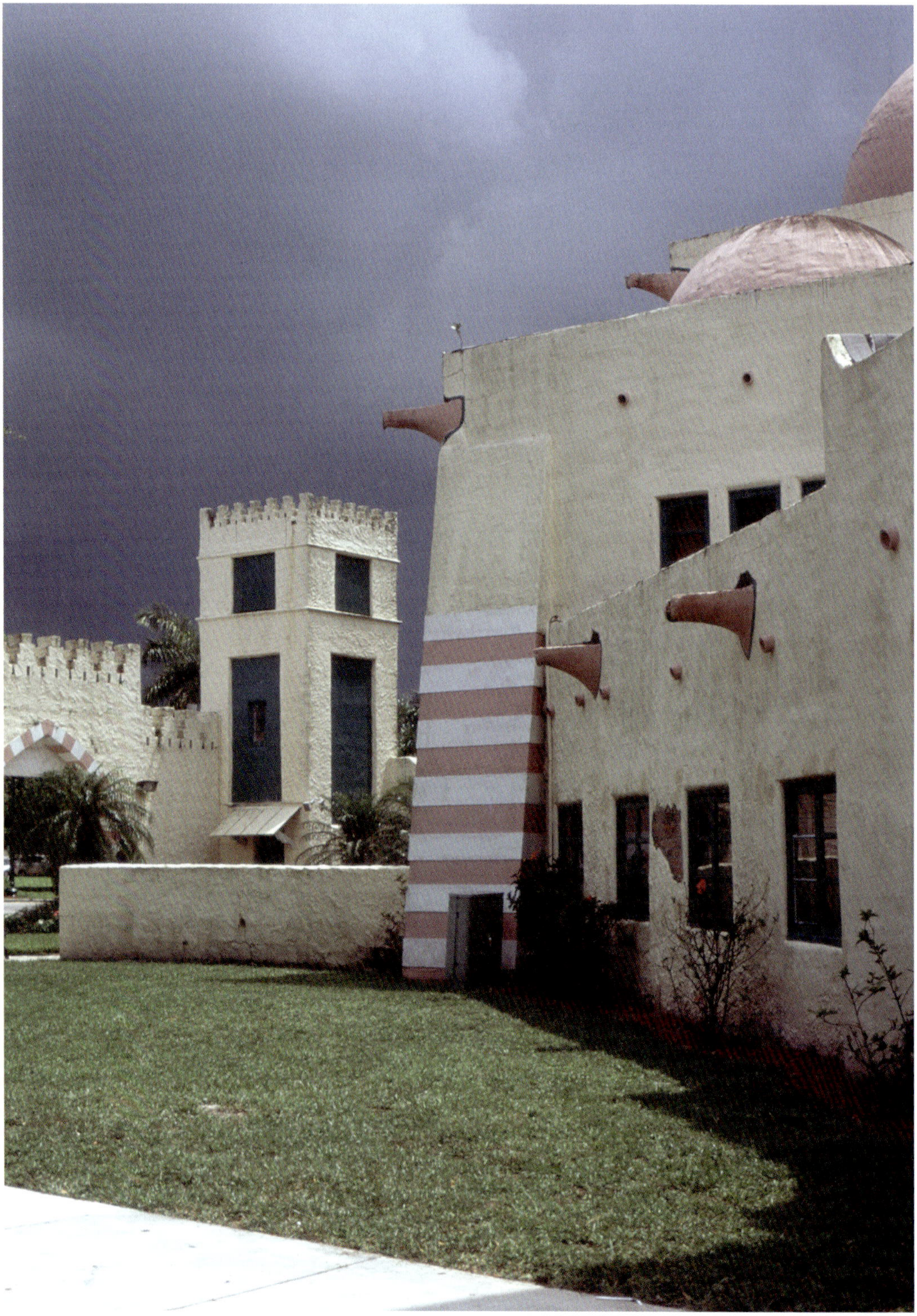

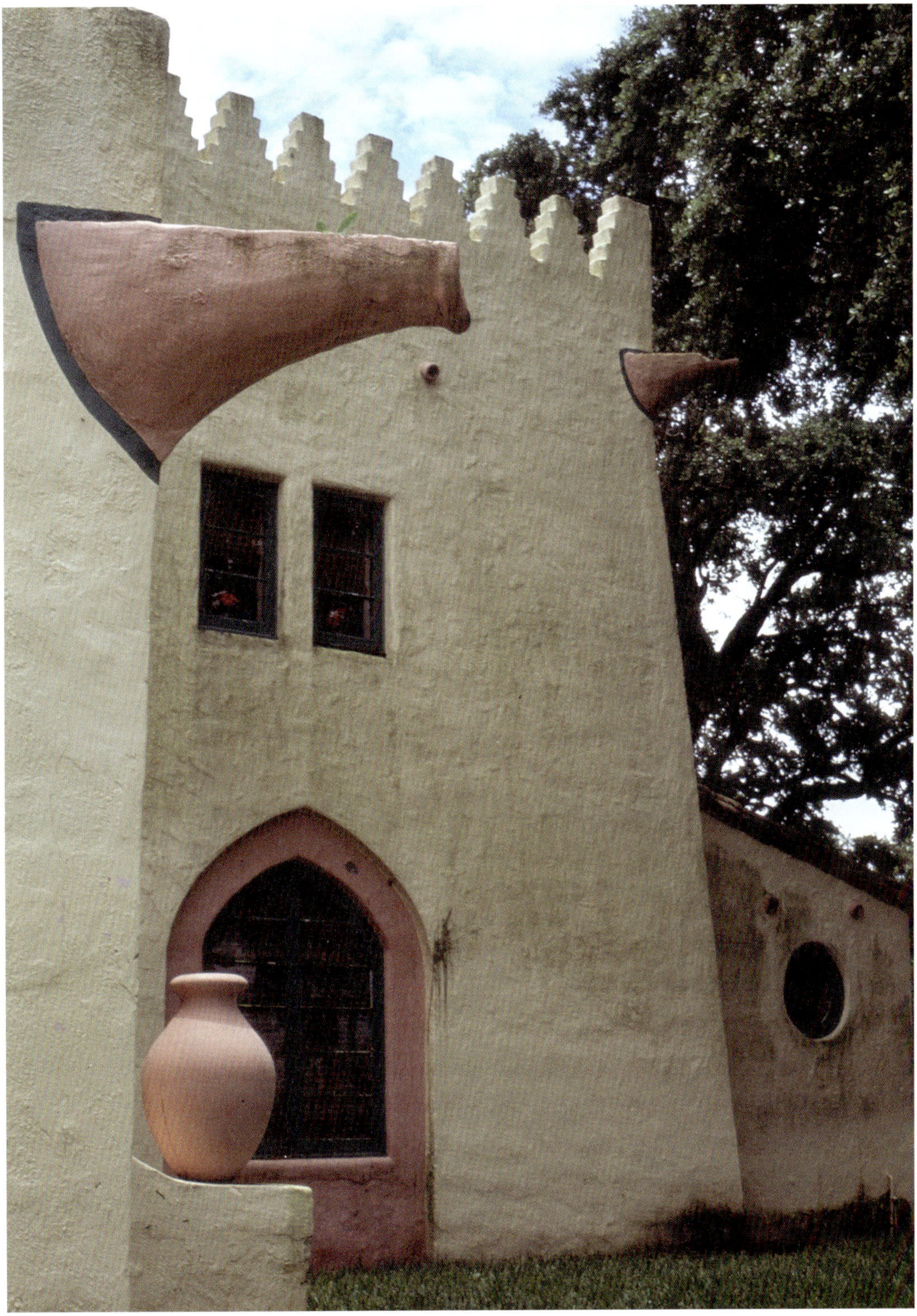

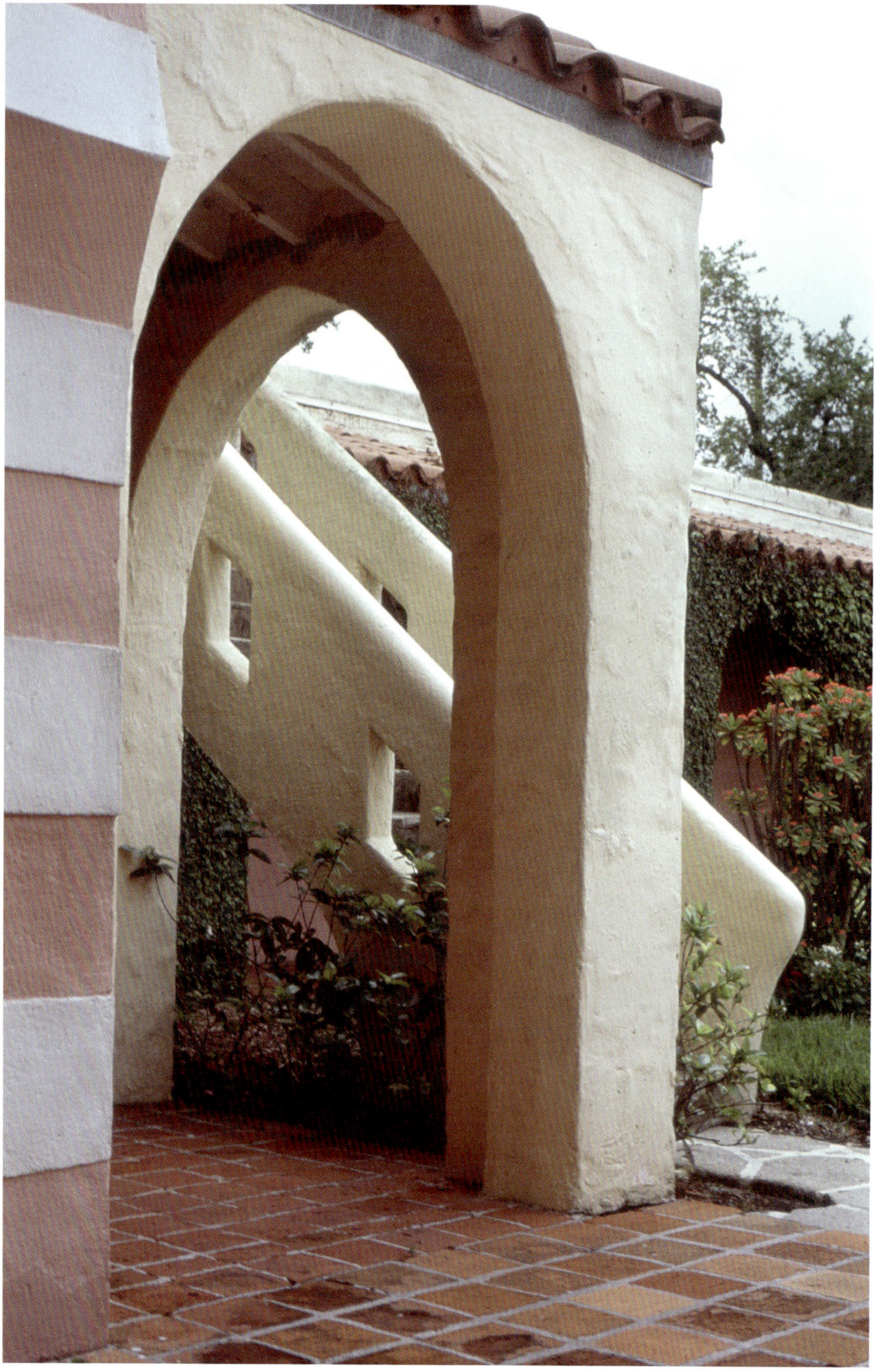

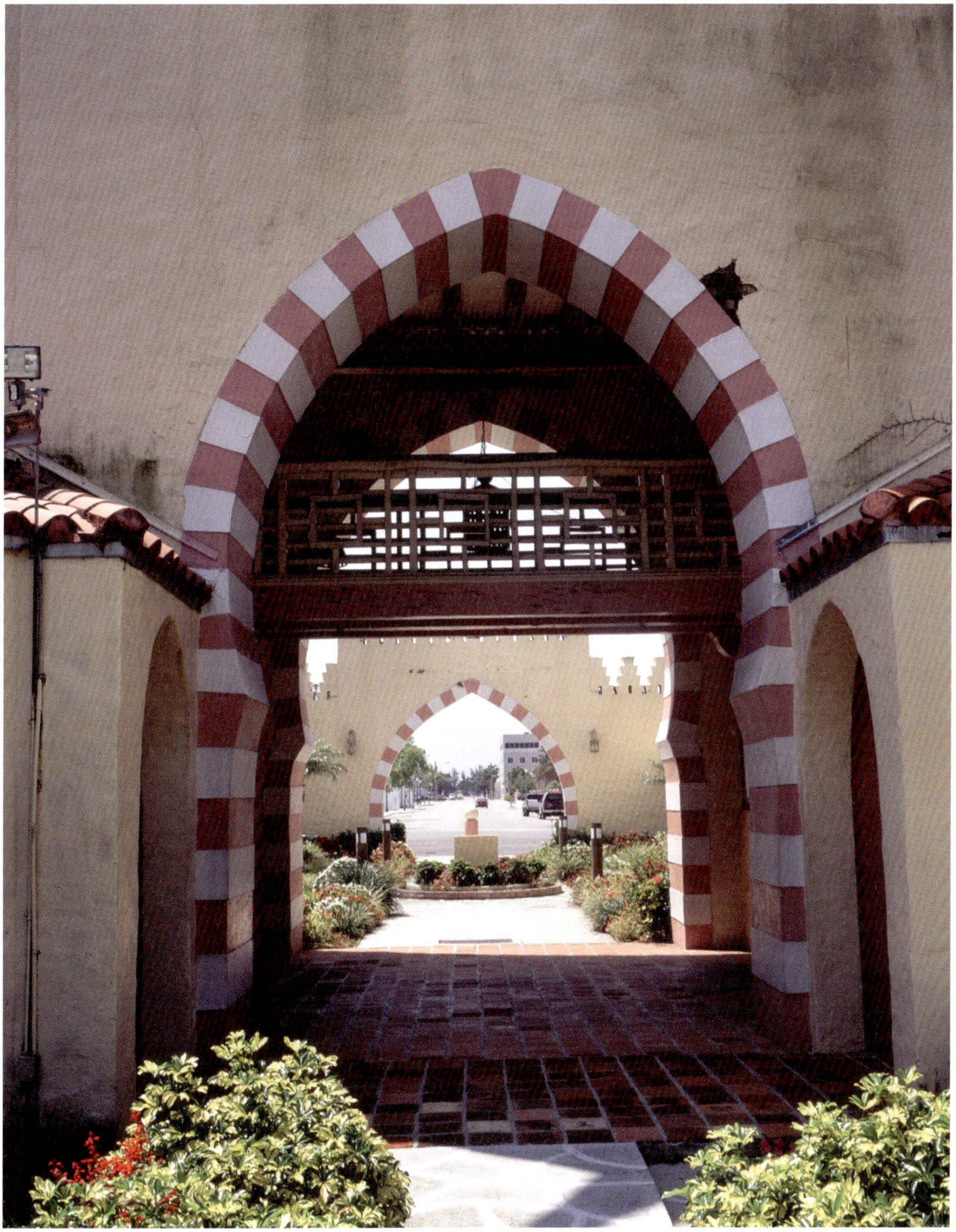

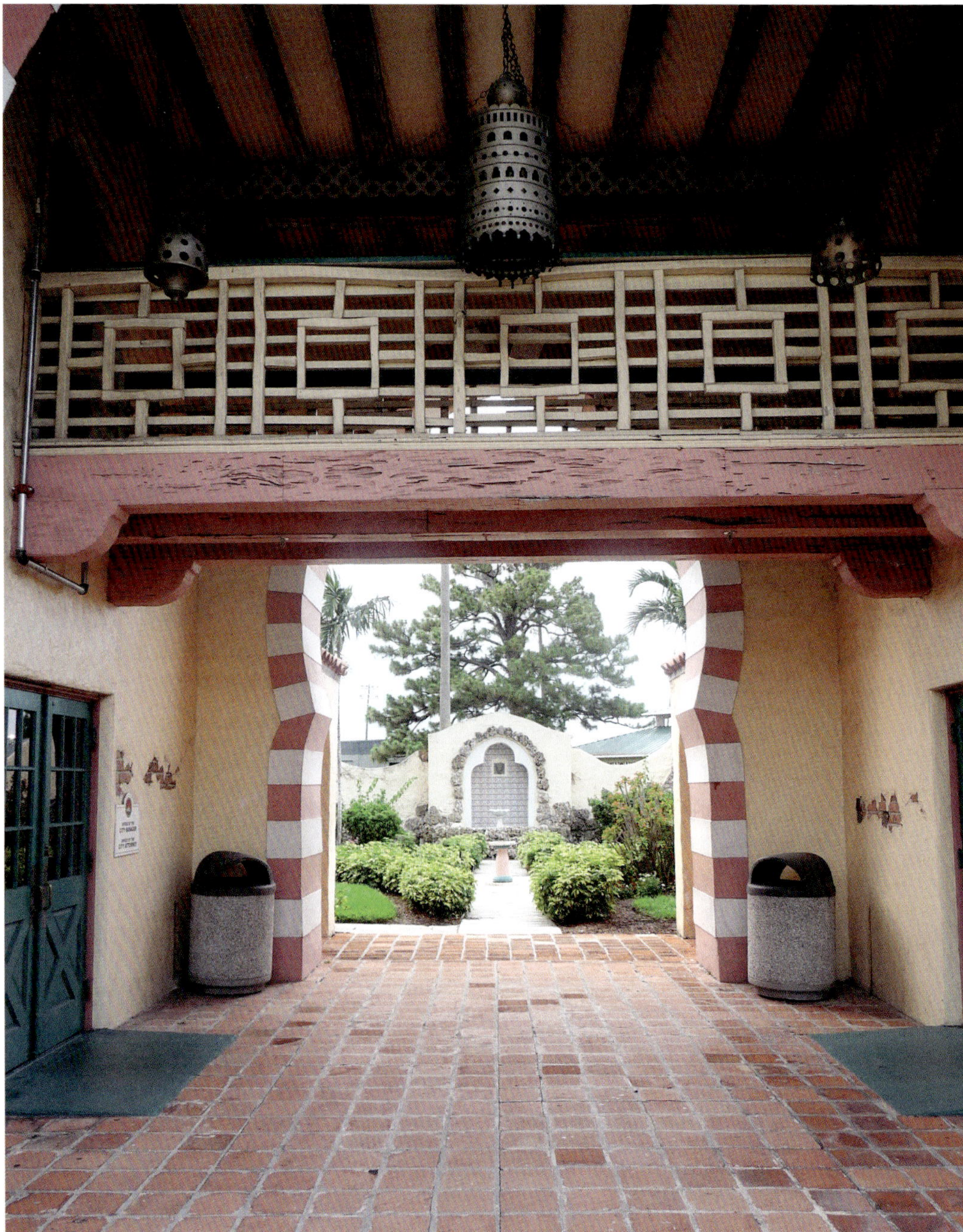

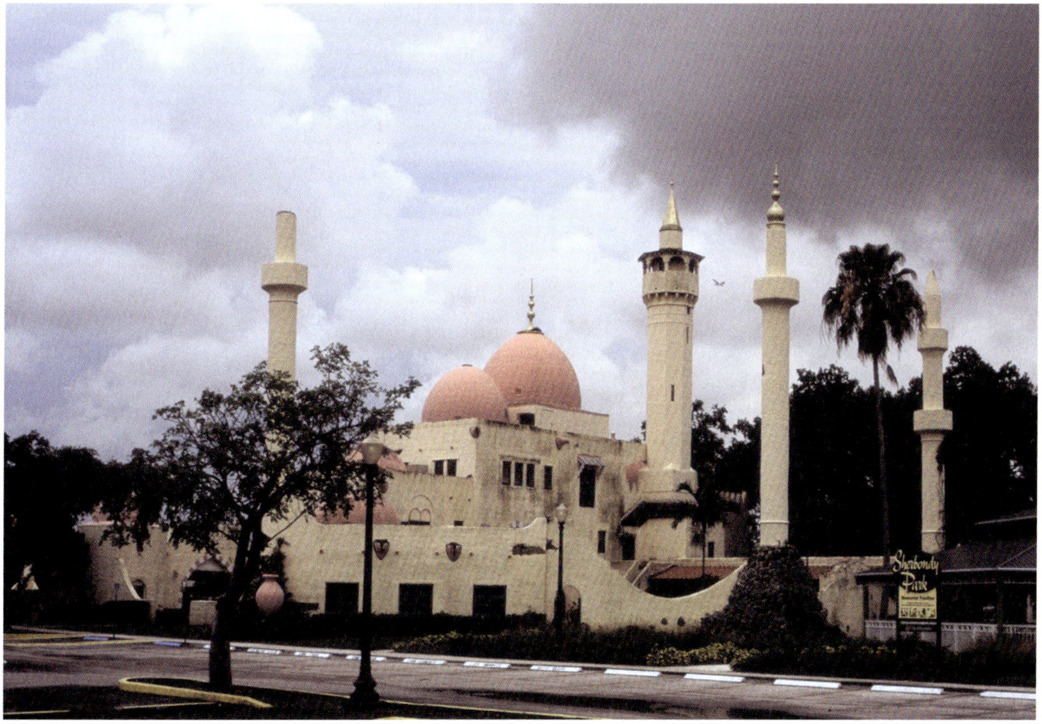
Sherbondy
Park

117 PERVIZ STREET   *ROOT BUILDING*

124 PERVIZ STREET   *FIRE AND POLICE STATION*

613 SHARAR AVENUE *LONG HOUSE*

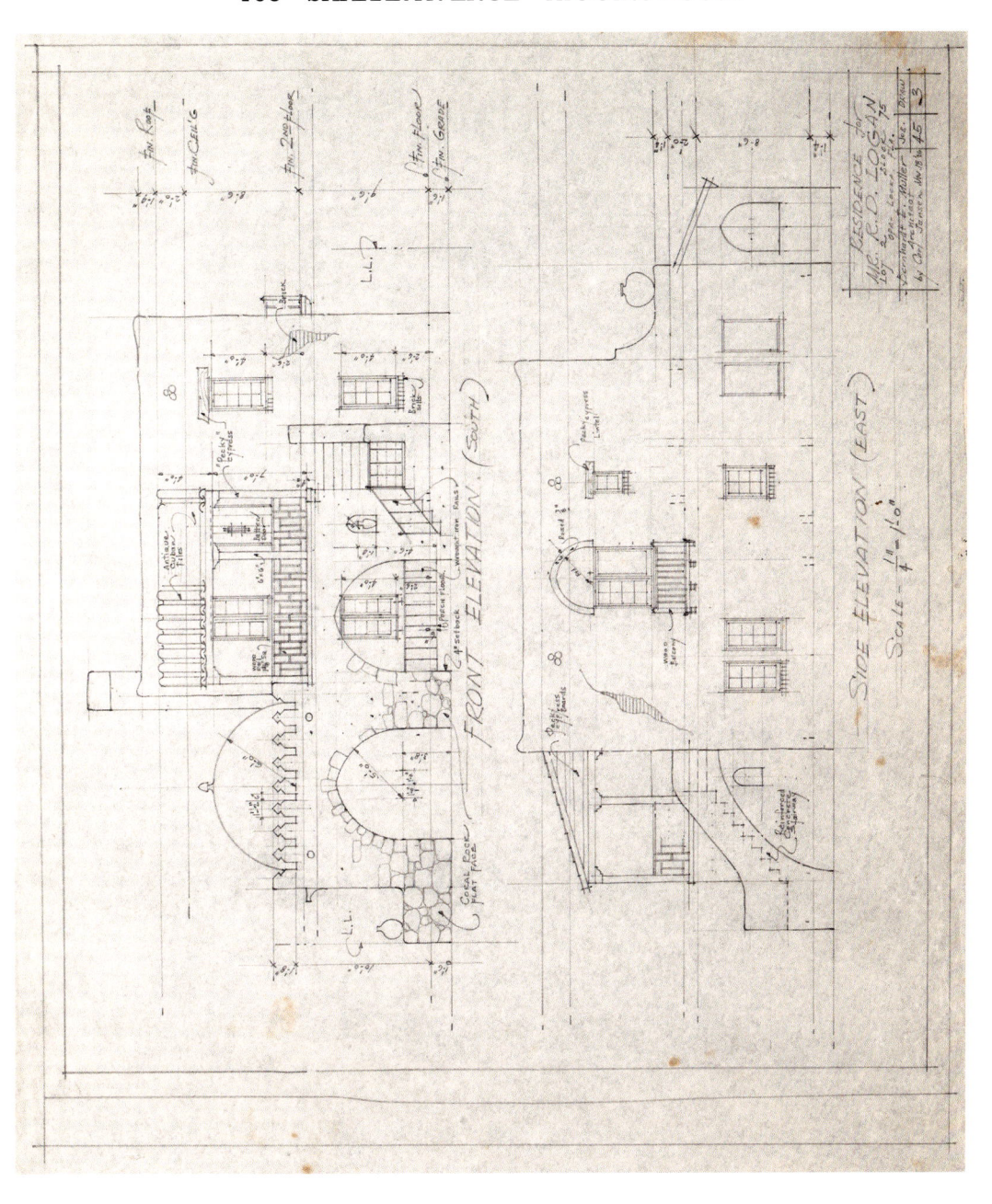

705 SHARAR AVENUE *HIGGINS HOUSE*

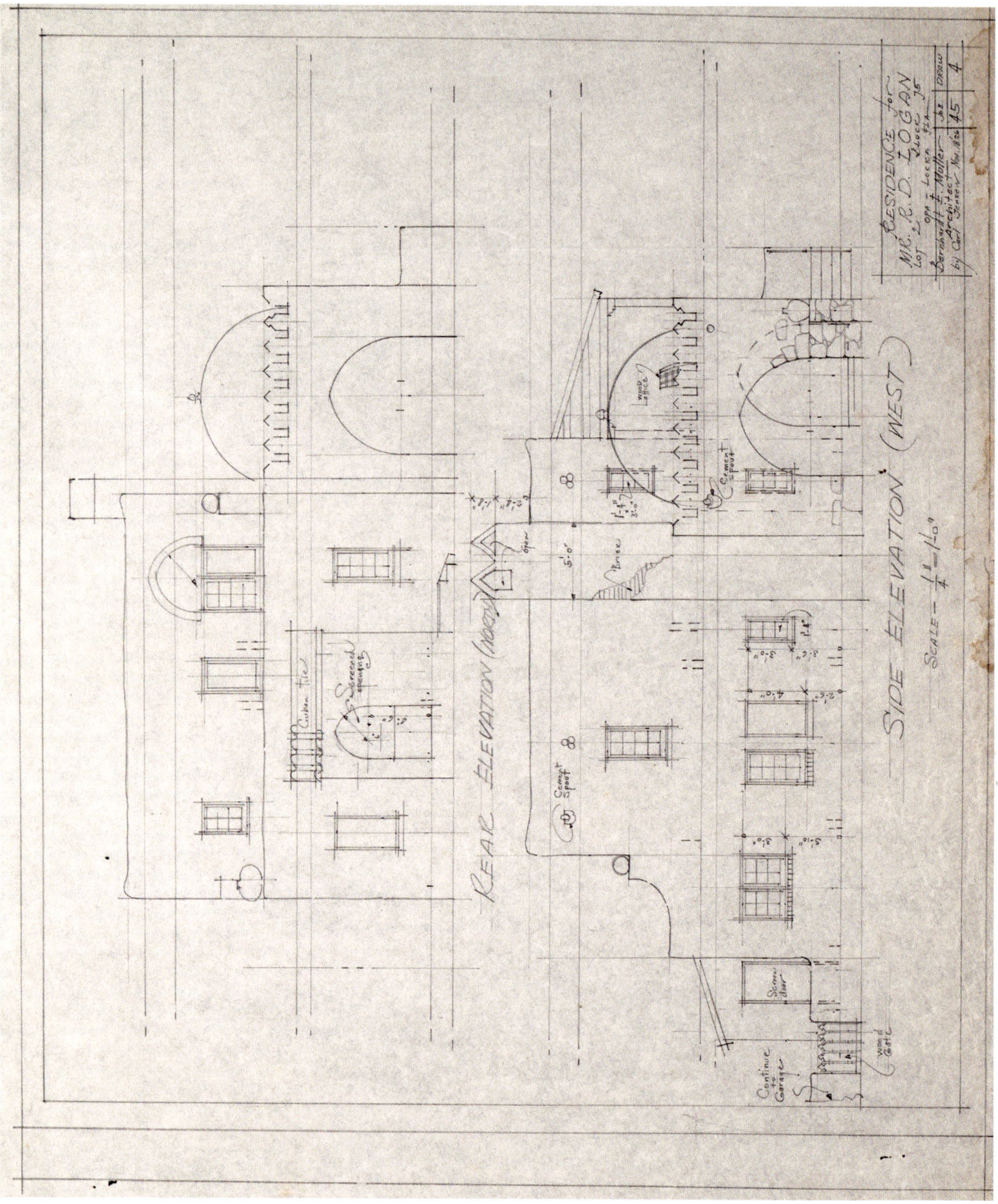
REAR ELEVATION (NORTH)
SIDE ELEVATION (WEST)
RESIDENCE for
MR. R. D. LOGAN
Cement spout
Brick
Screen door
wood gate
Continue to Garage

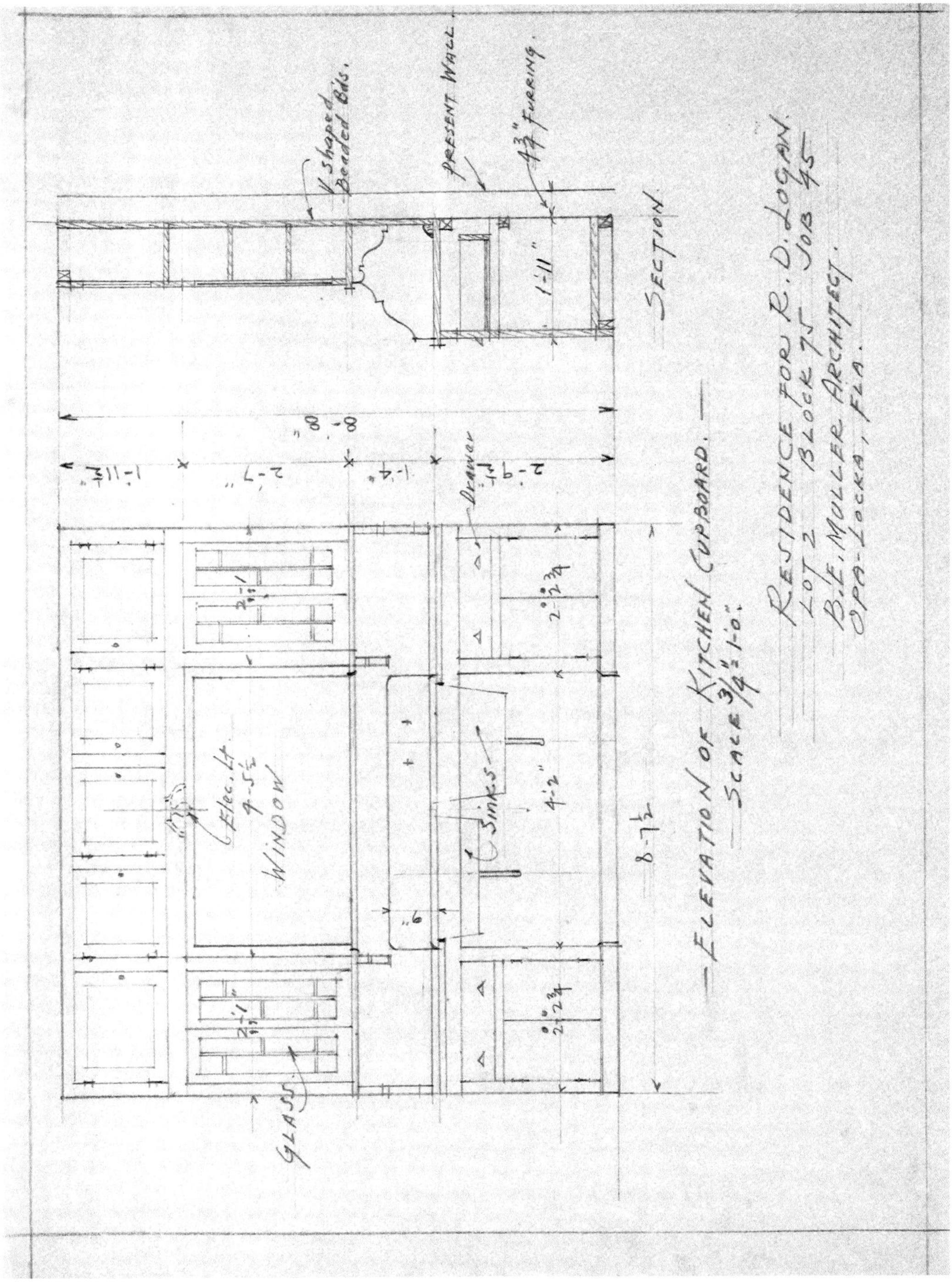
ELEVATION OF KITCHEN CUPBOARD.
SCALE 3/4" = 1'-0"
RESIDENCE FOR R. D. LOGAN.
LOT 2 BLOCK 75 JOB 45
B. E. MULLER ARCHITECT.
OPA-LOCKA, FLA.
SECTION
V shaped Beaded Bds.
PRESENT WALL
4 3/4" FURRING.
WINDOW
GLASS
Sinks
Elec. Lt.
Drawer

Detail of Fireplace.
Scale 3/4" = 1'-0"

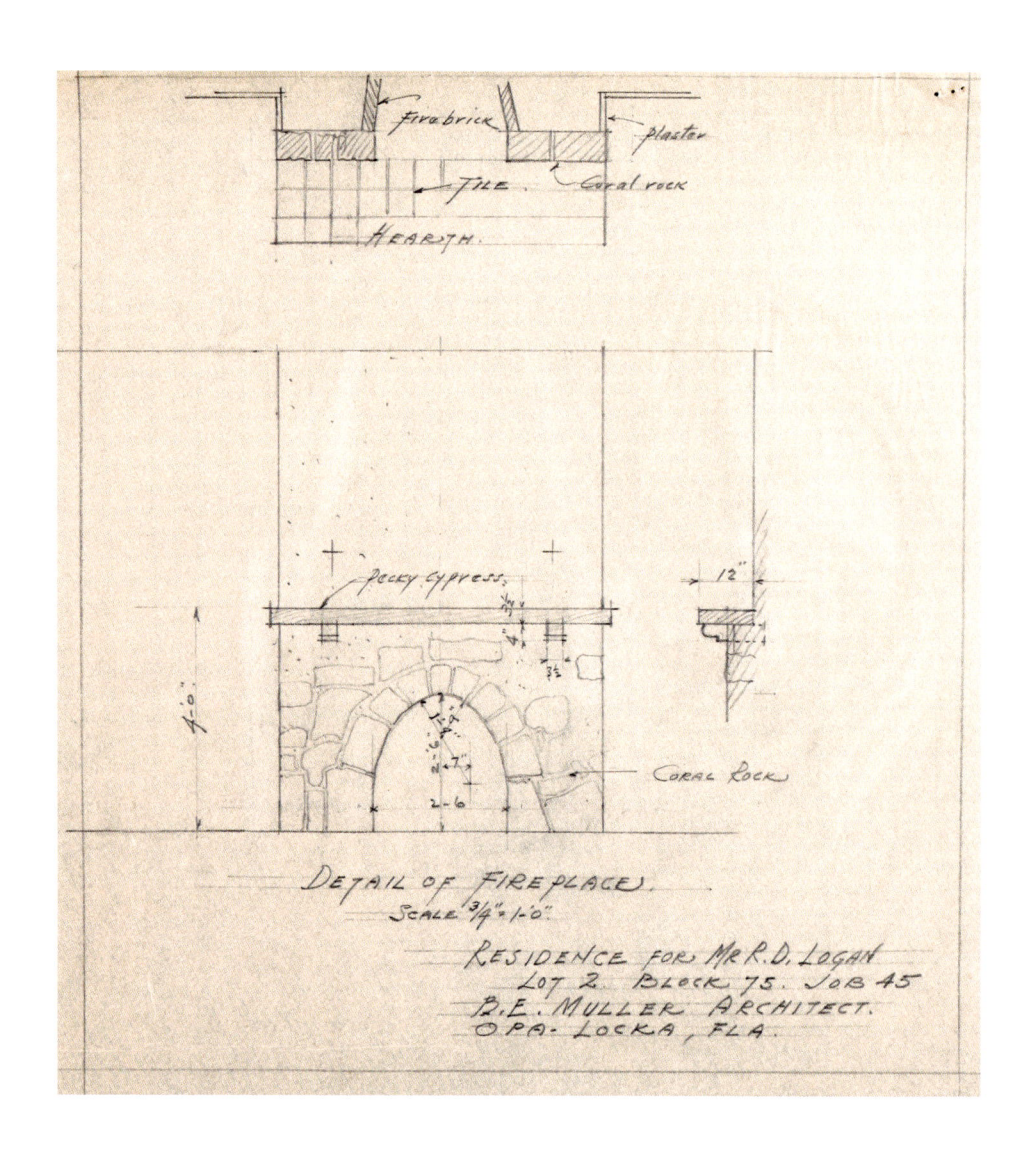

Residence for Mr. R. D. Logan
Lot 2, Block 75, Job 45
B. E. Muller Architect.
Opa-Locka, Fla.

FRONT DOOR
CLEAR CYPRESS

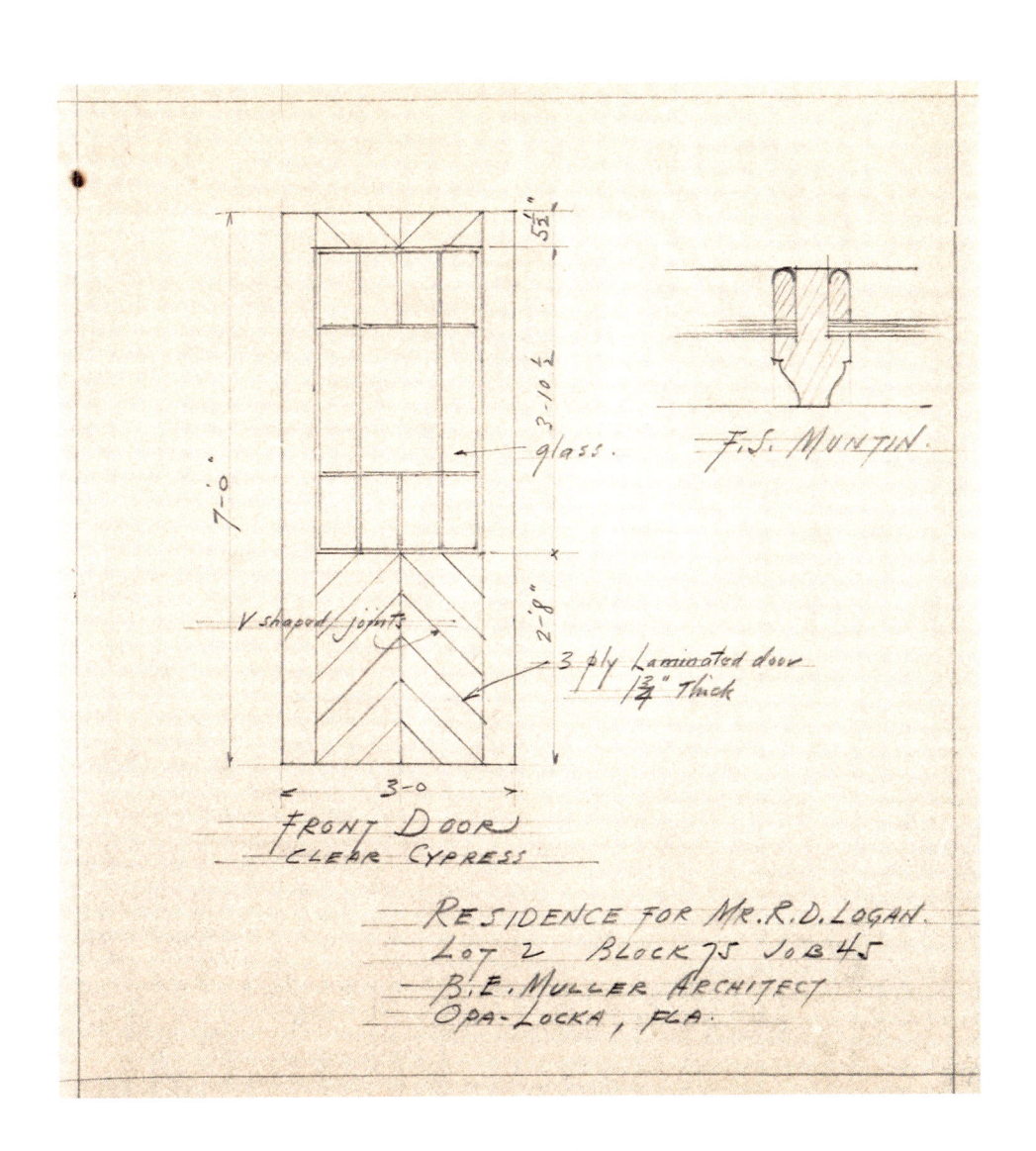

F.S. MUNTIN.

glass.
V shaped joints
3 ply Laminated door 1¾" Thick

7'-0"
5½"
3'-10½"
2'-8"
3'-0"

RESIDENCE FOR MR. R.D. LOGAN
LOT 2 BLOCK 75 JOB 45
B.E. MULLER ARCHITECT
OPA-LOCKA, FLA.

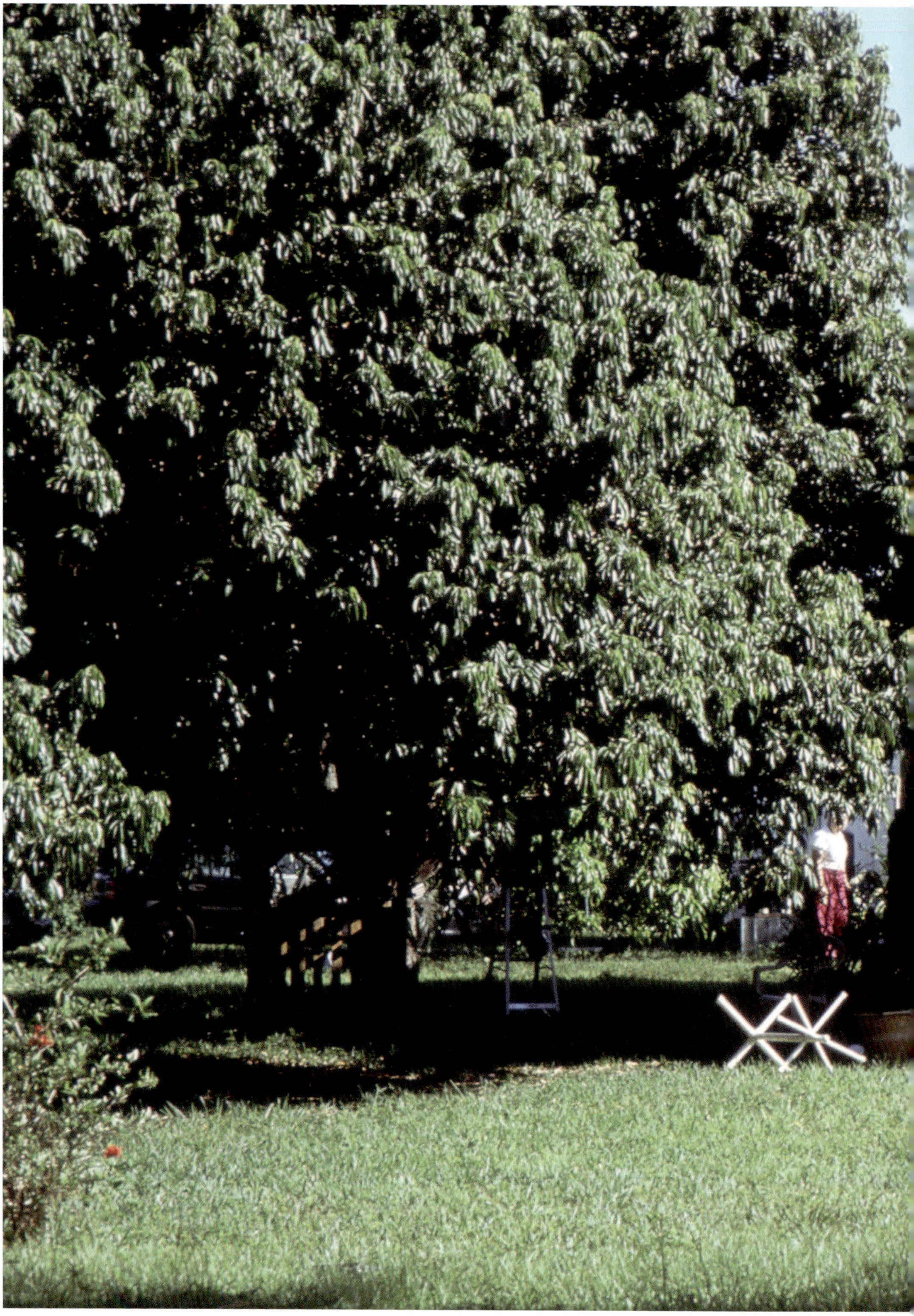

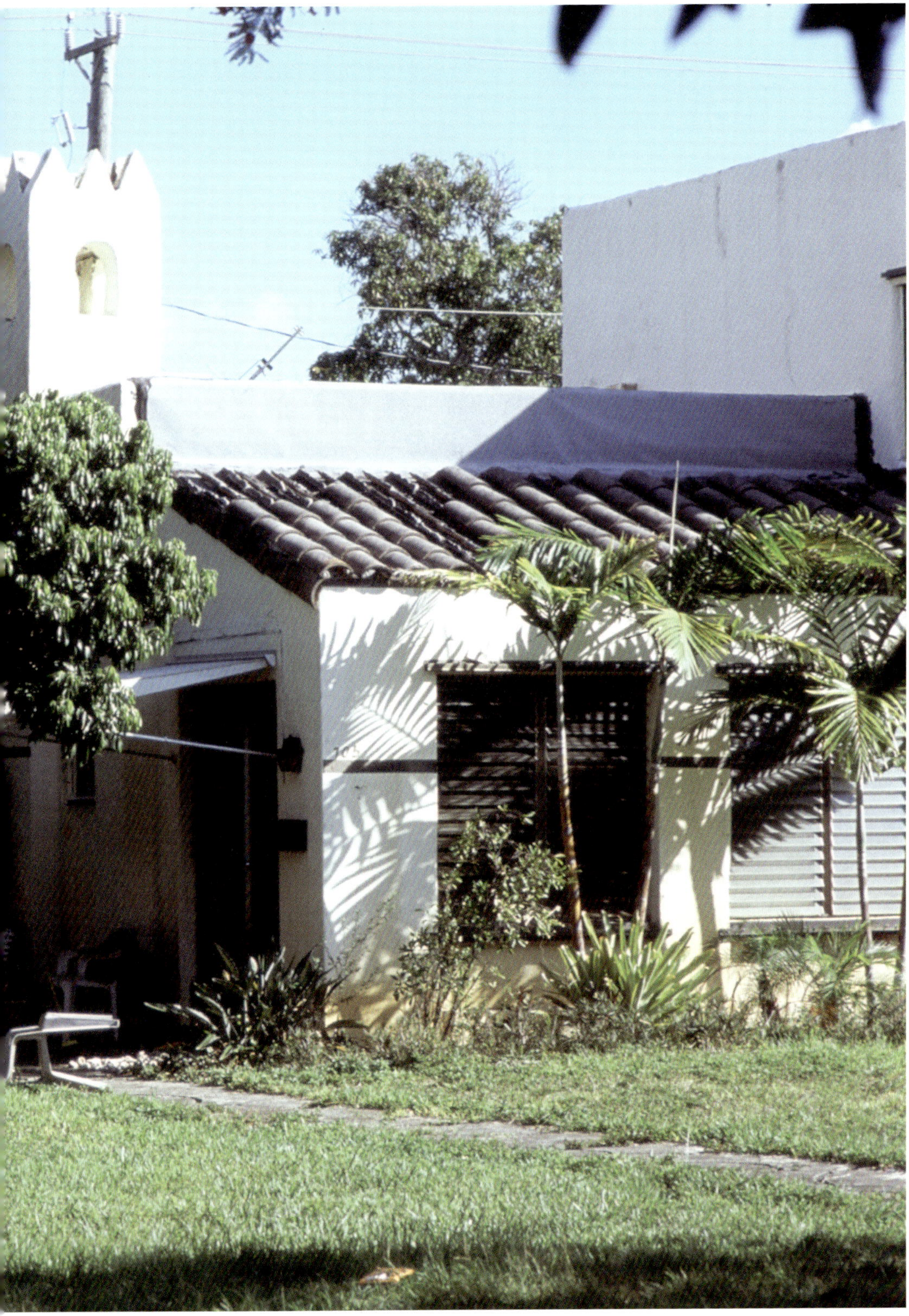

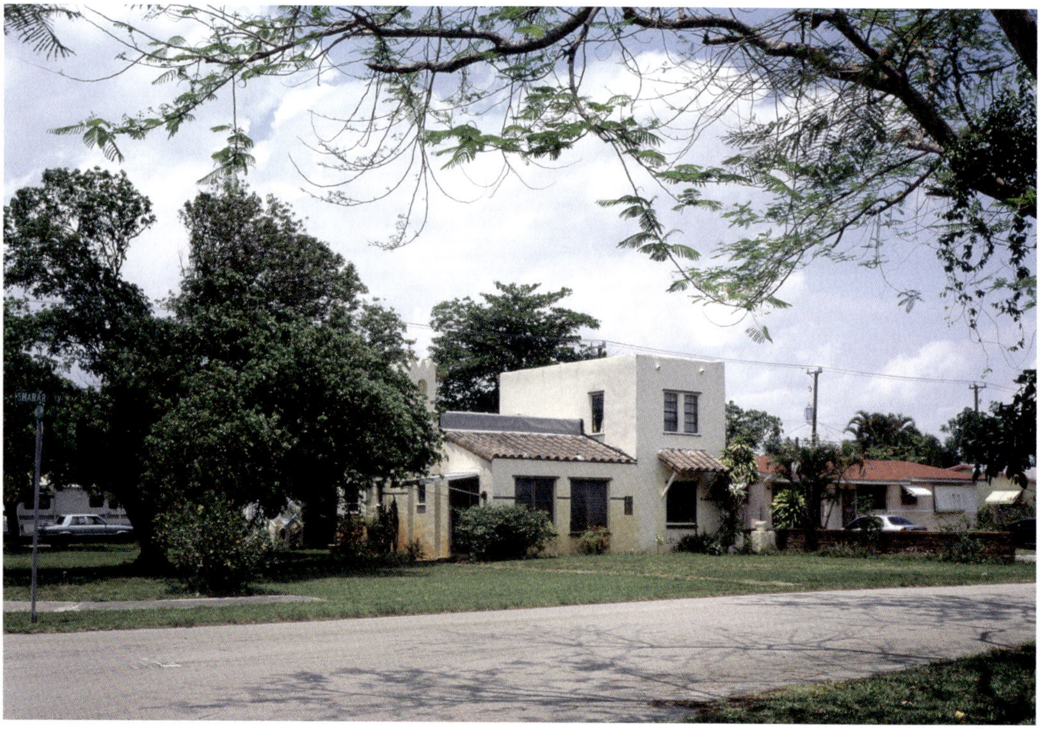

721 SHARAR AVENUE *HELMS HOUSE*

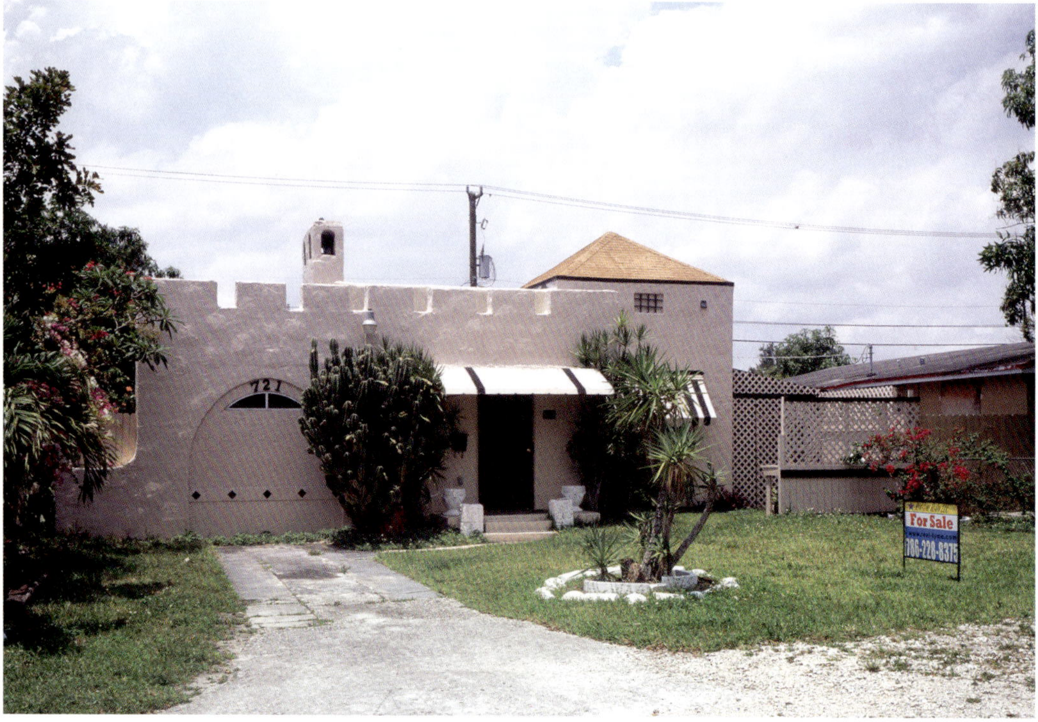

915 SHARAR AVENUE *ETHEREDGE HOUSE*

1006 SHARAR AVENUE   *KENDRIK HOUSE*

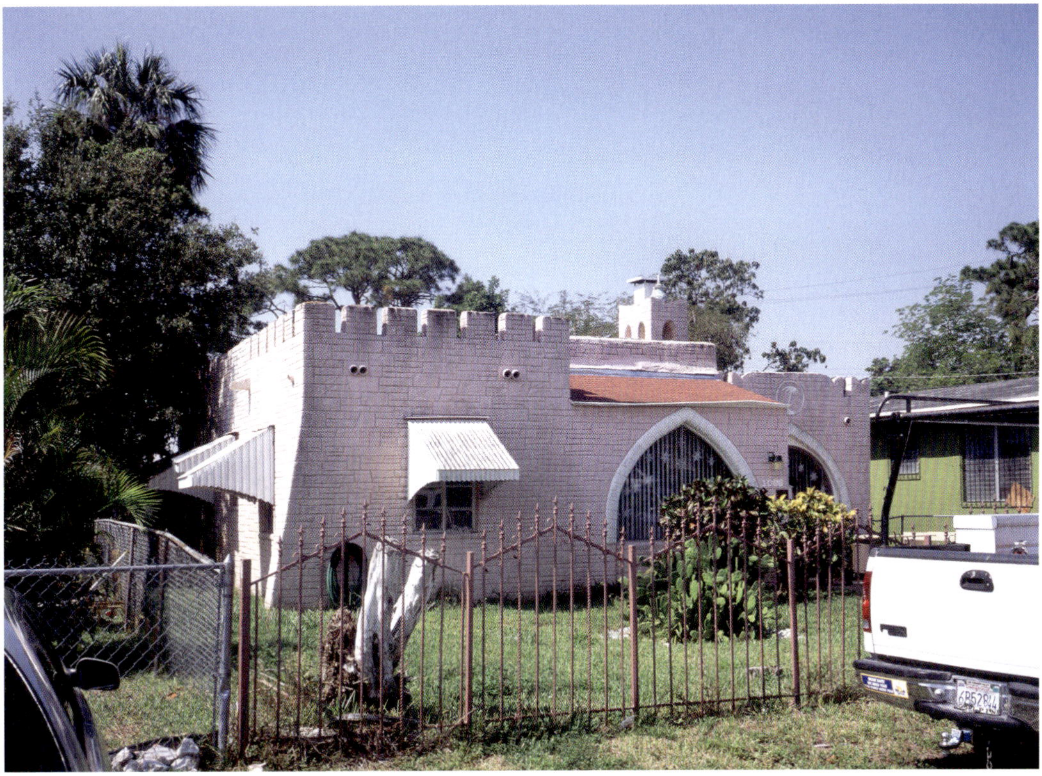

1010 SHARAR AVENUE *BOSTIK HOUSE*

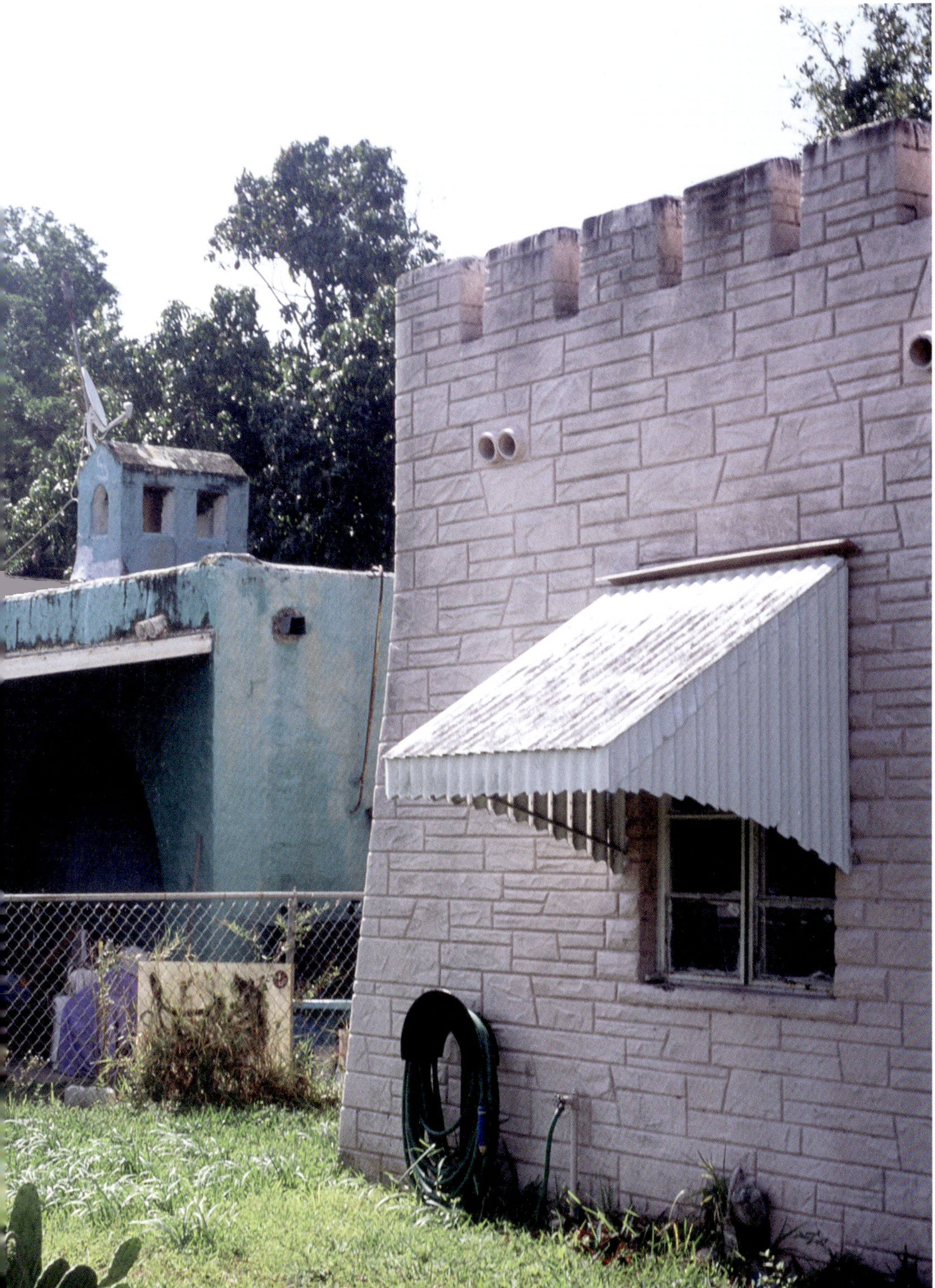

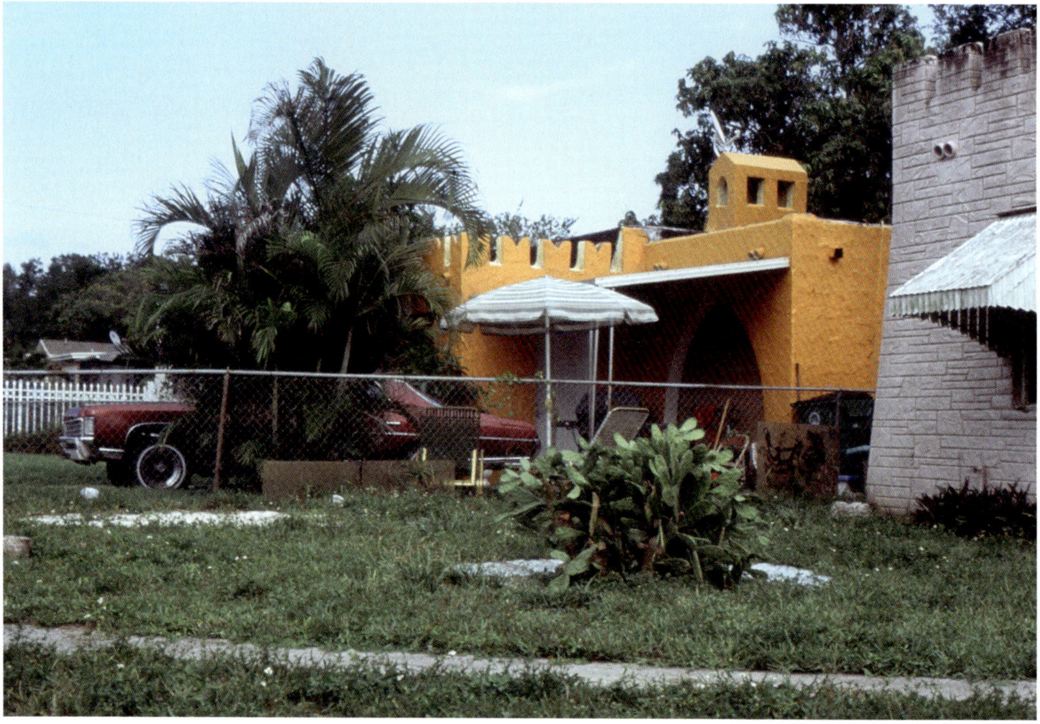

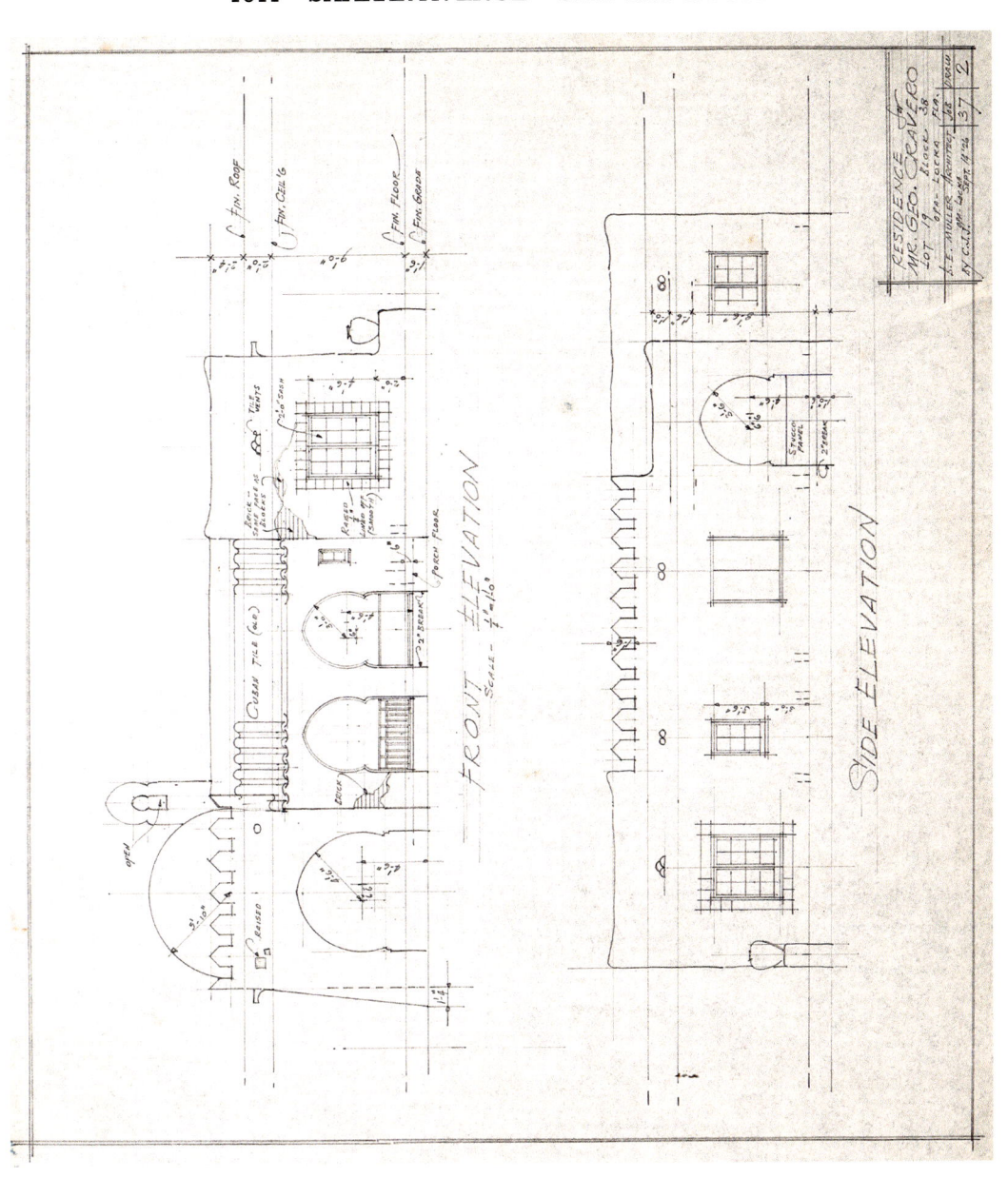

1011 SHARAR AVENUE *CRAVERO HOUSE*

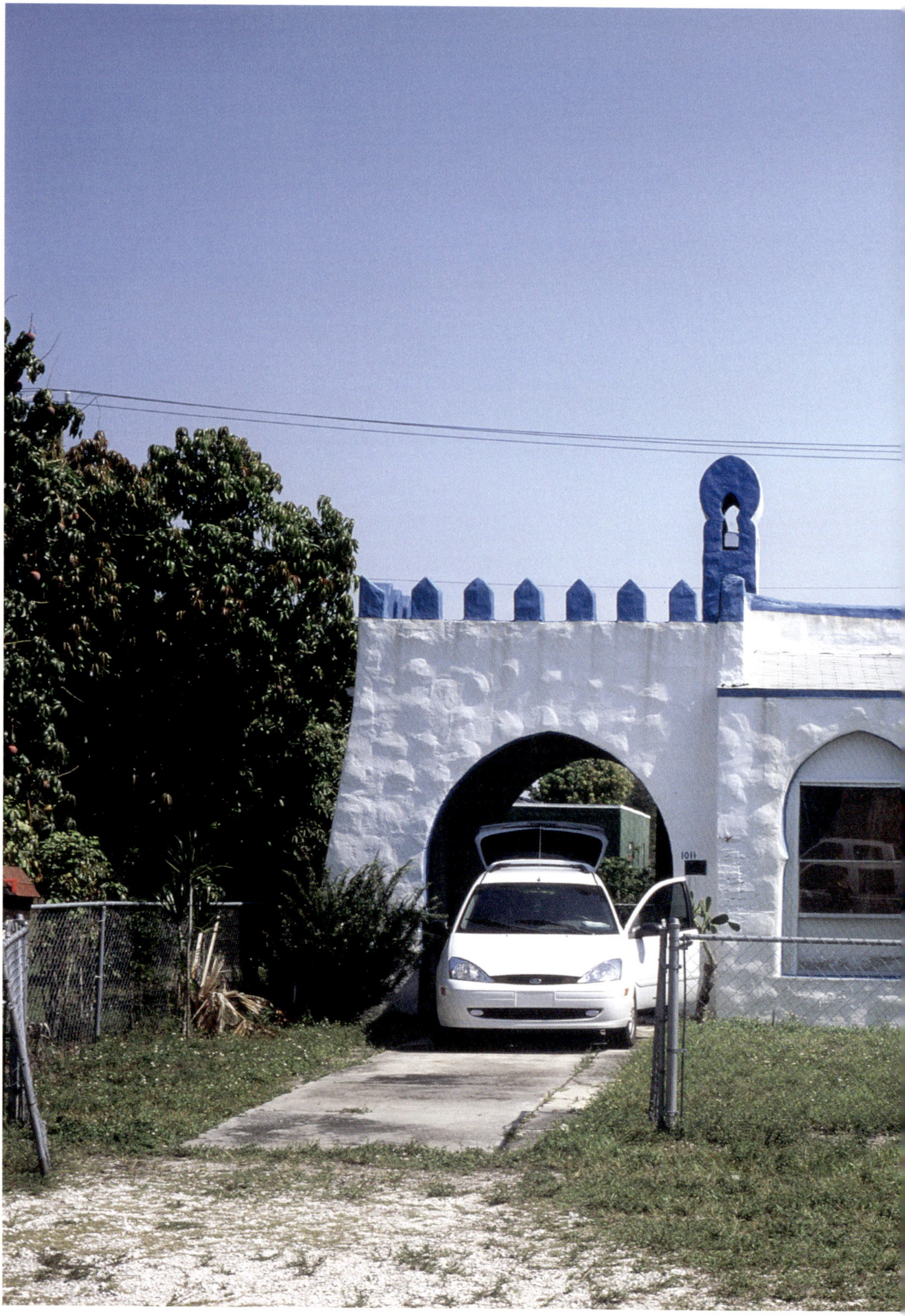

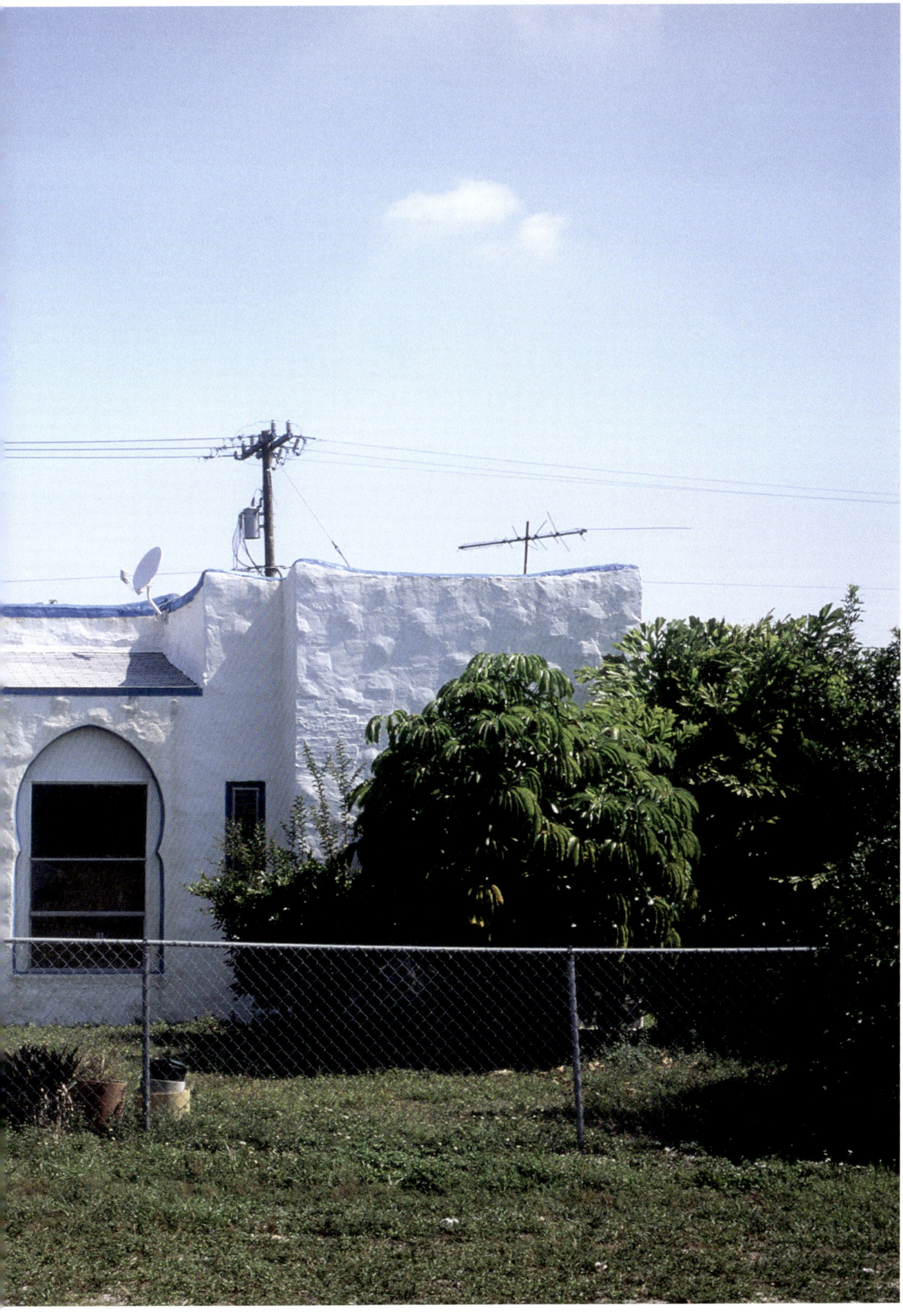

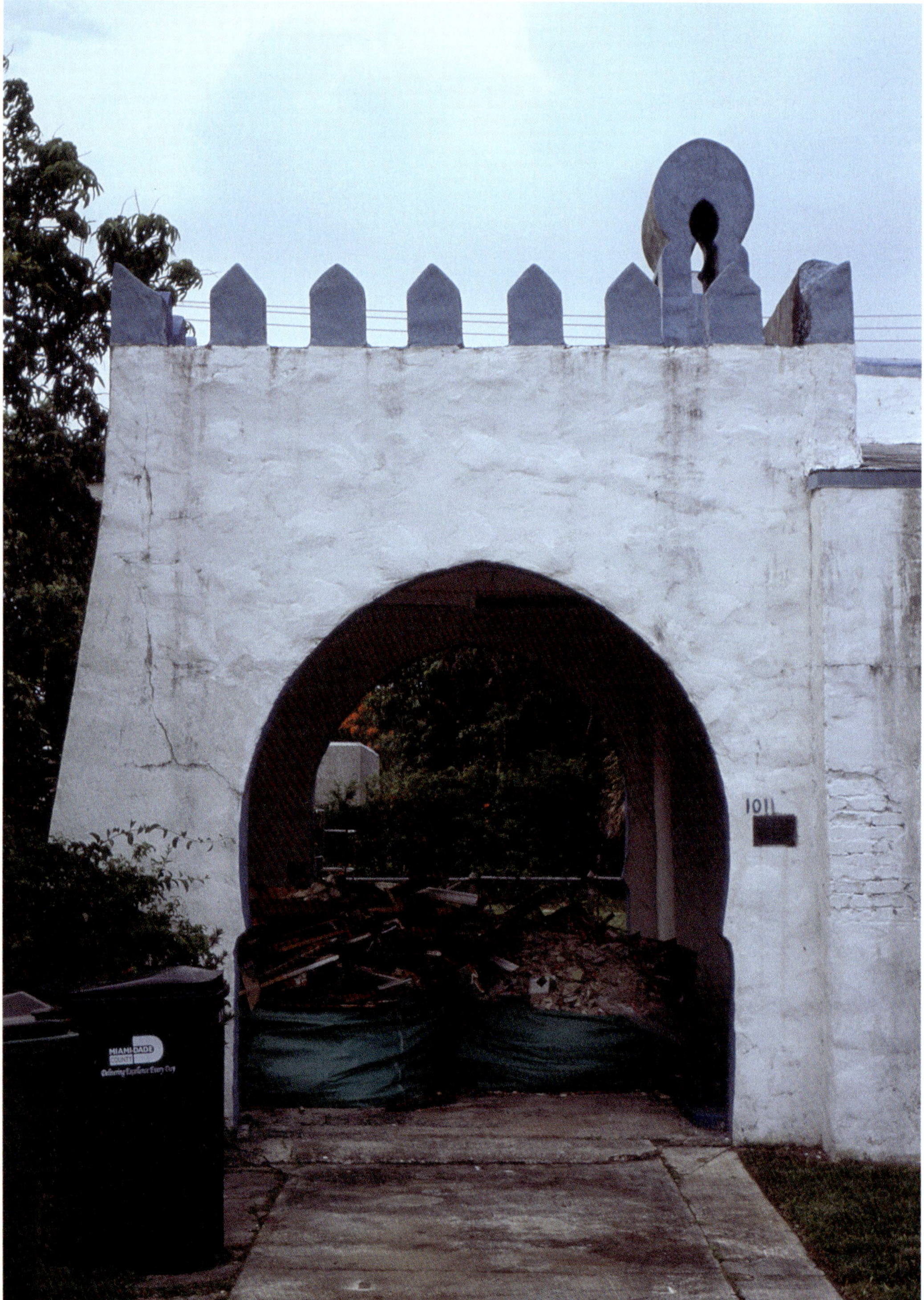
1011
MIAMI-DADE

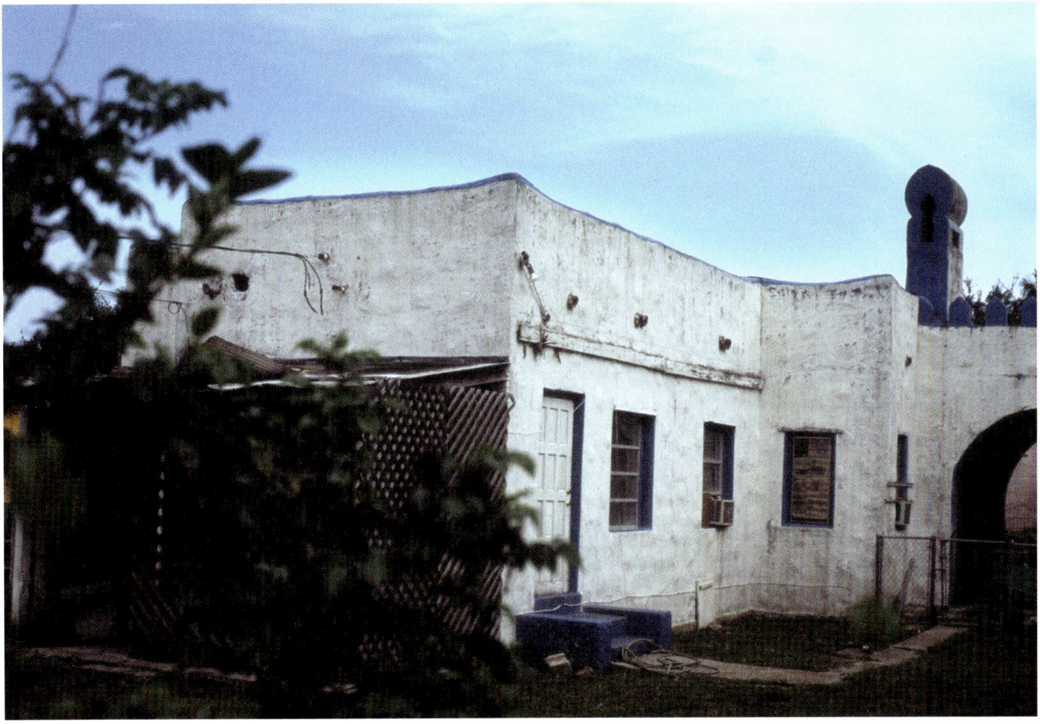

1145 SHARAR AVENUE   *SHUCK HOUSE*

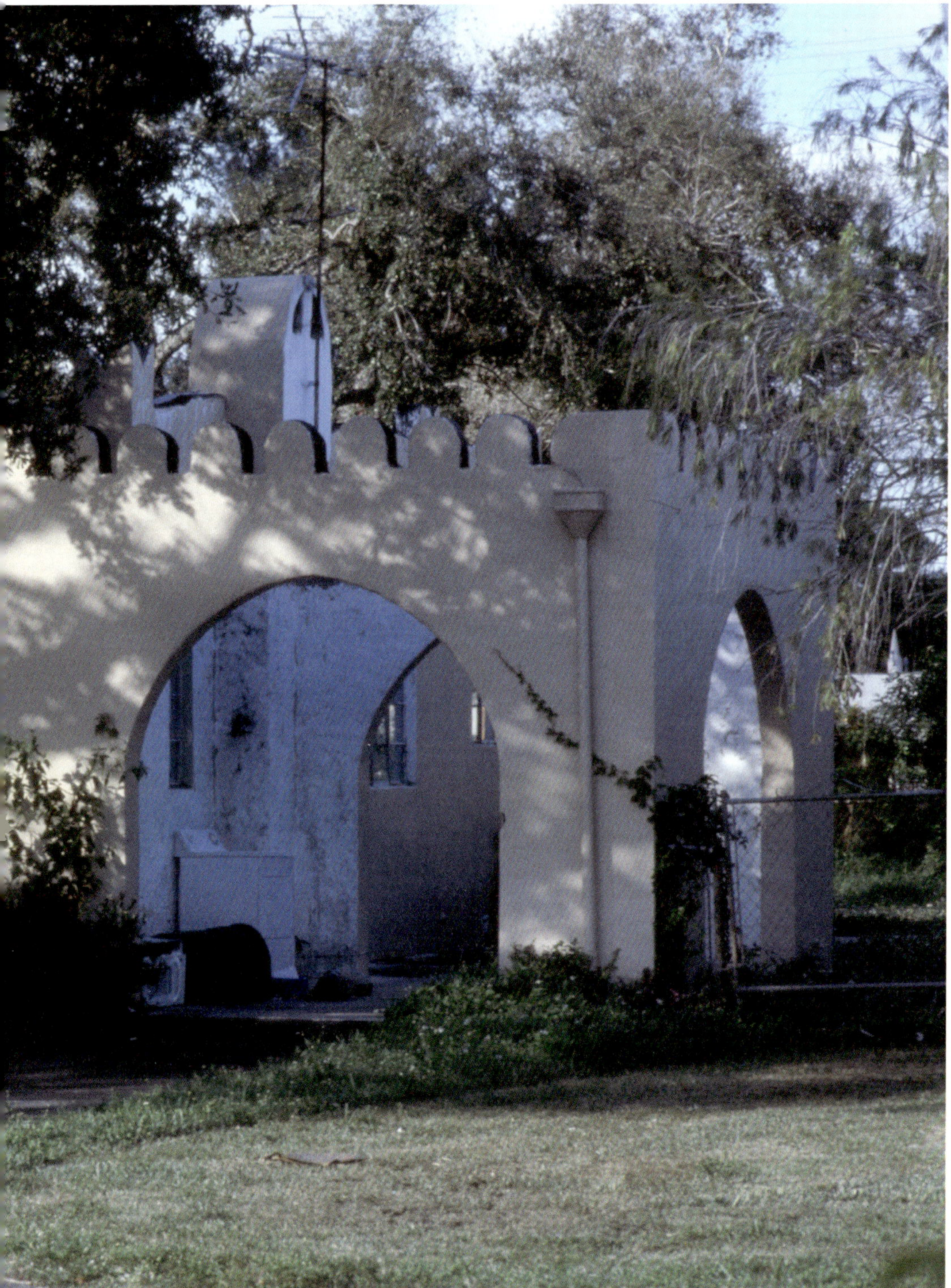

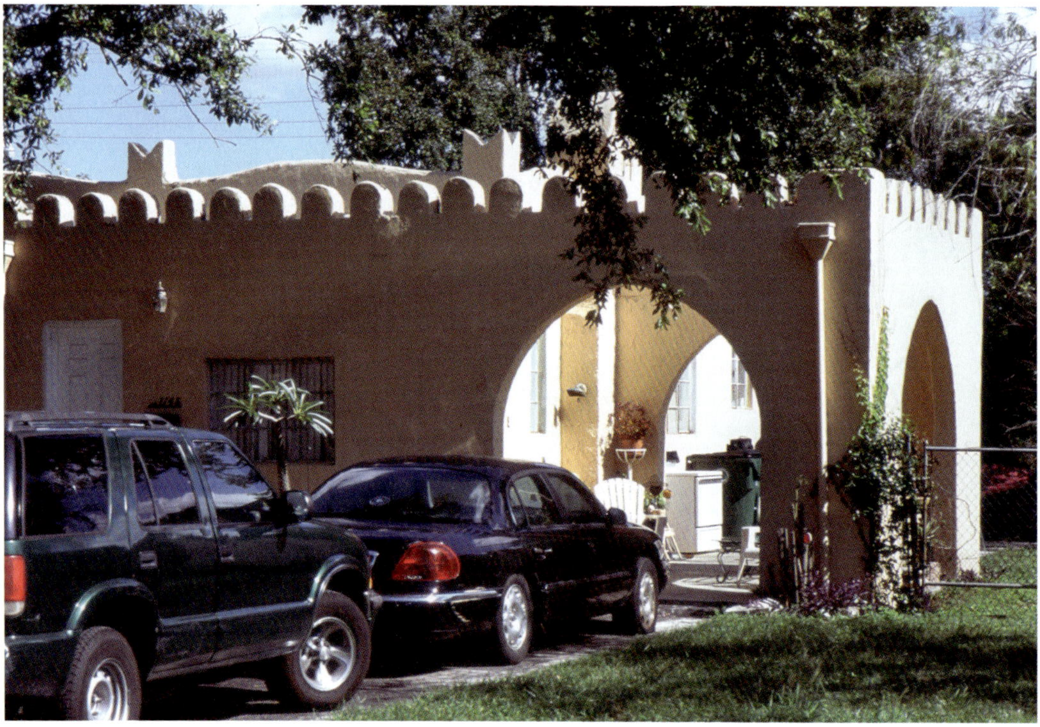

1301 SHARAR AVENUE *(NAME UNKNOWN)*

1110   PERI STREET   *TINSMAN HOUSE*

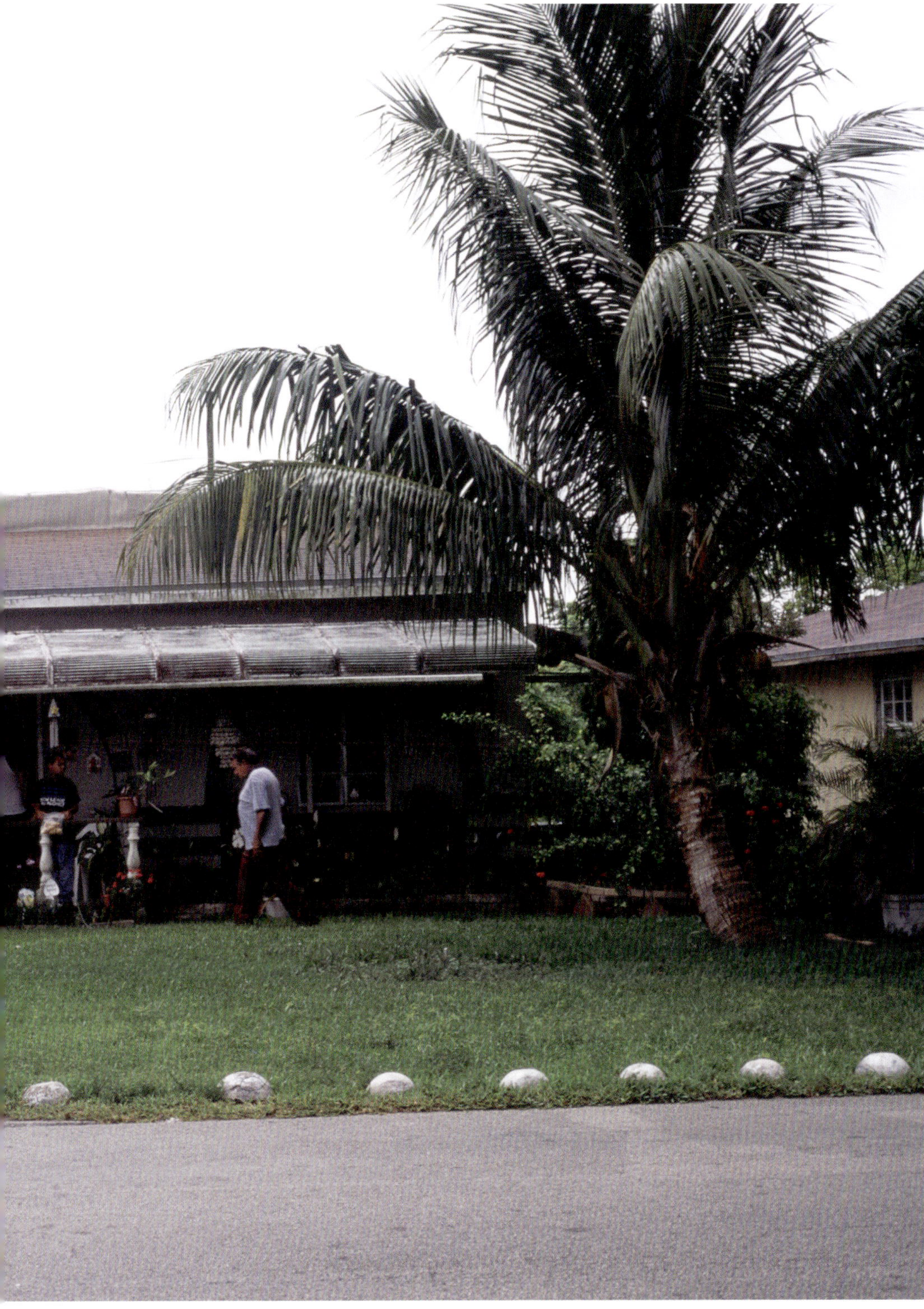

90

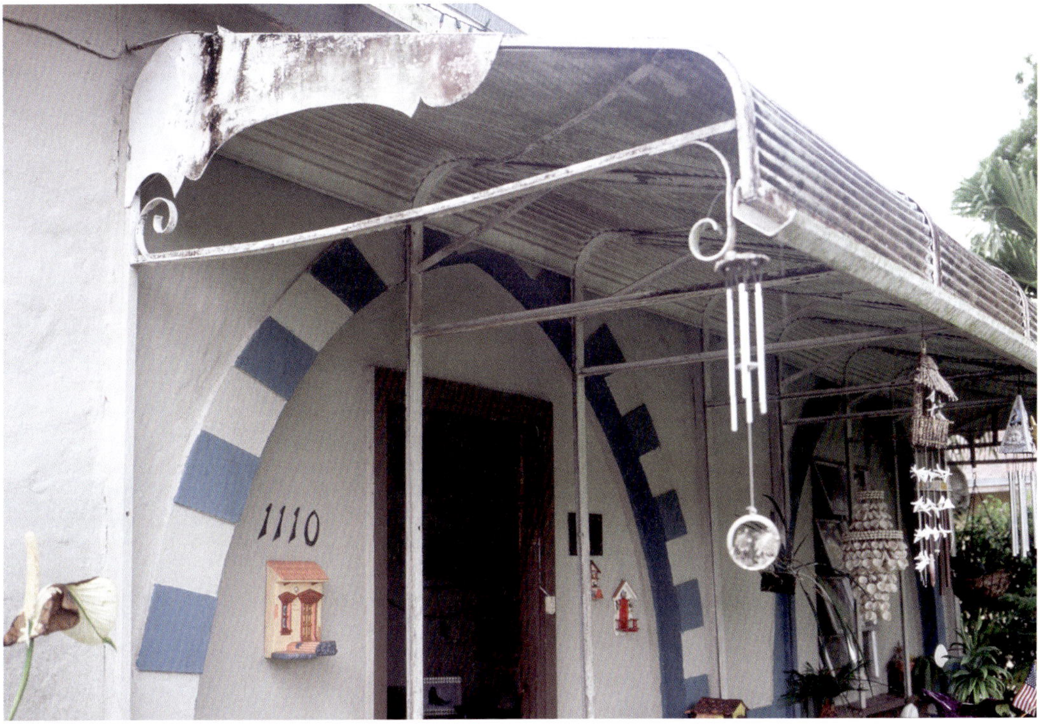
1110

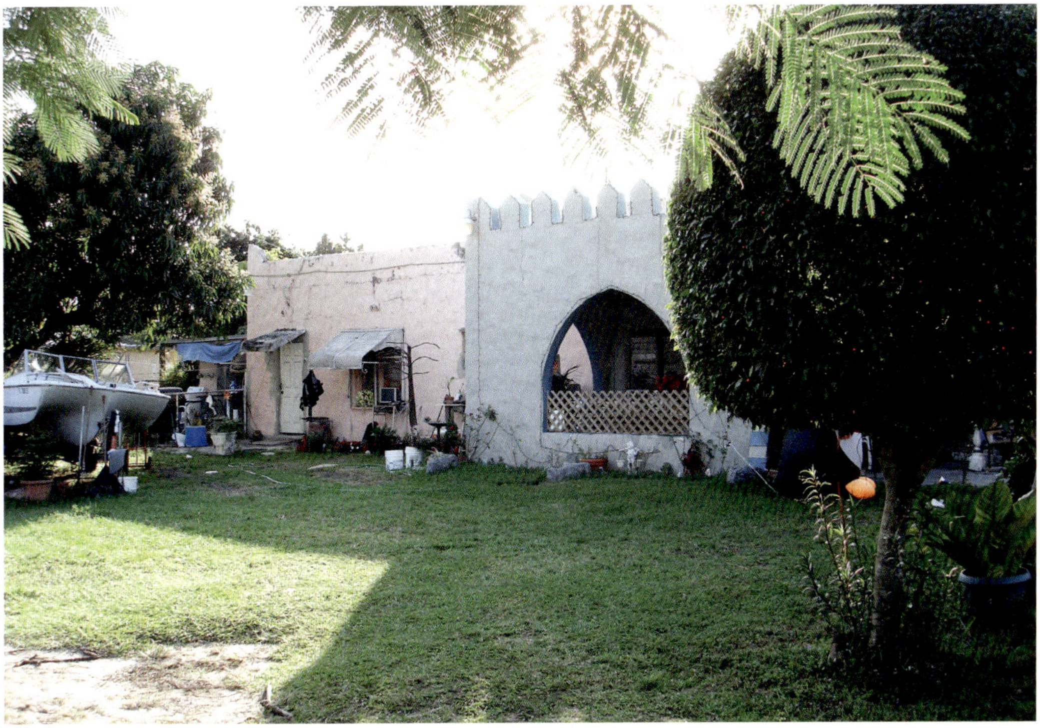

1145   PERI STREET   *(NAME UNKNOWN)*

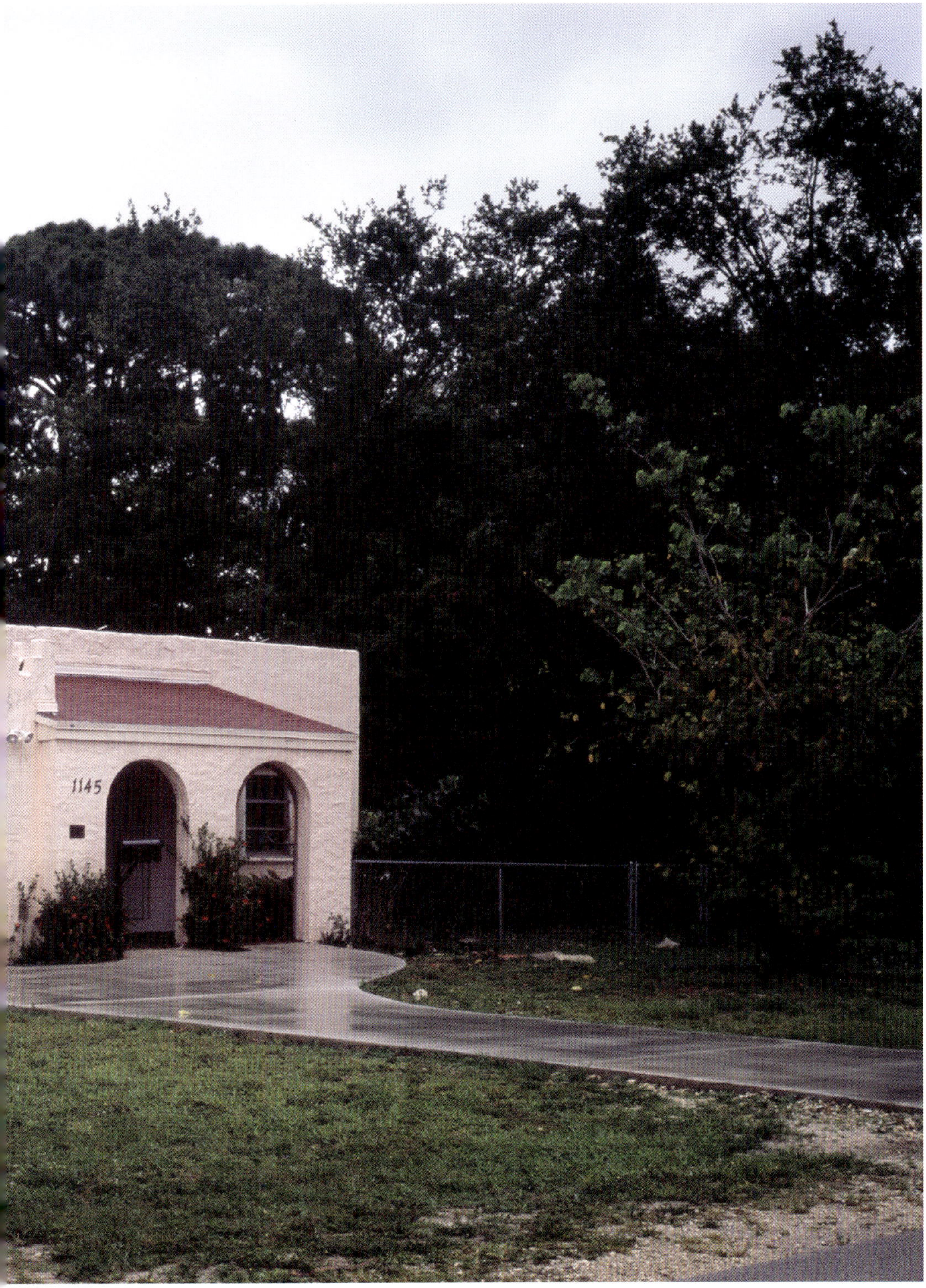
1145

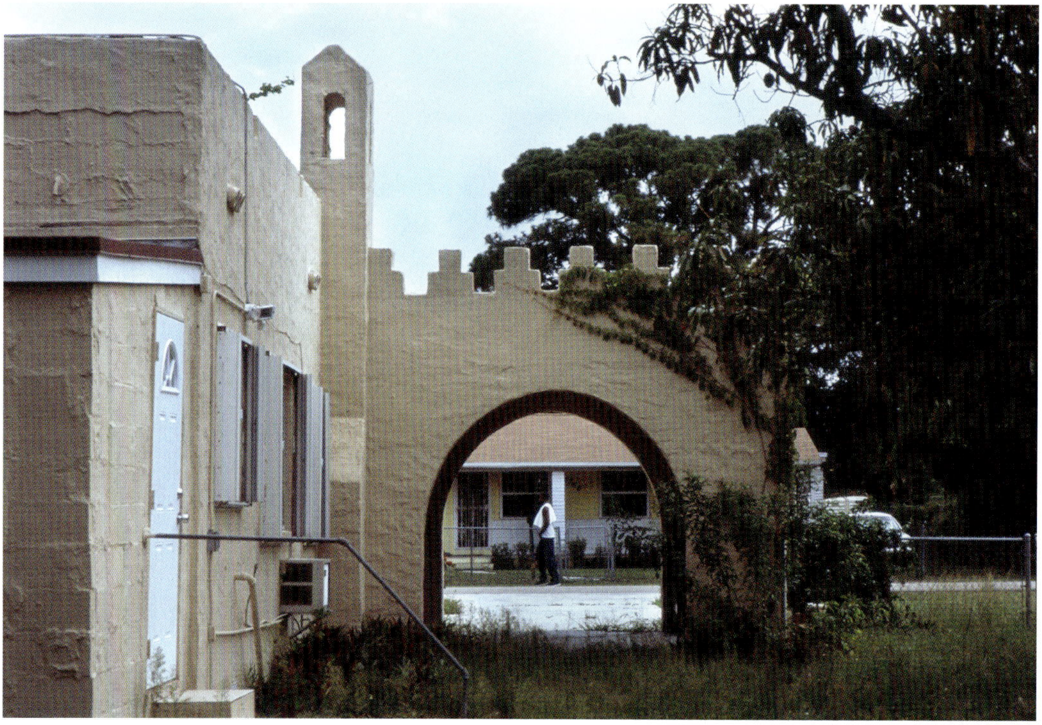

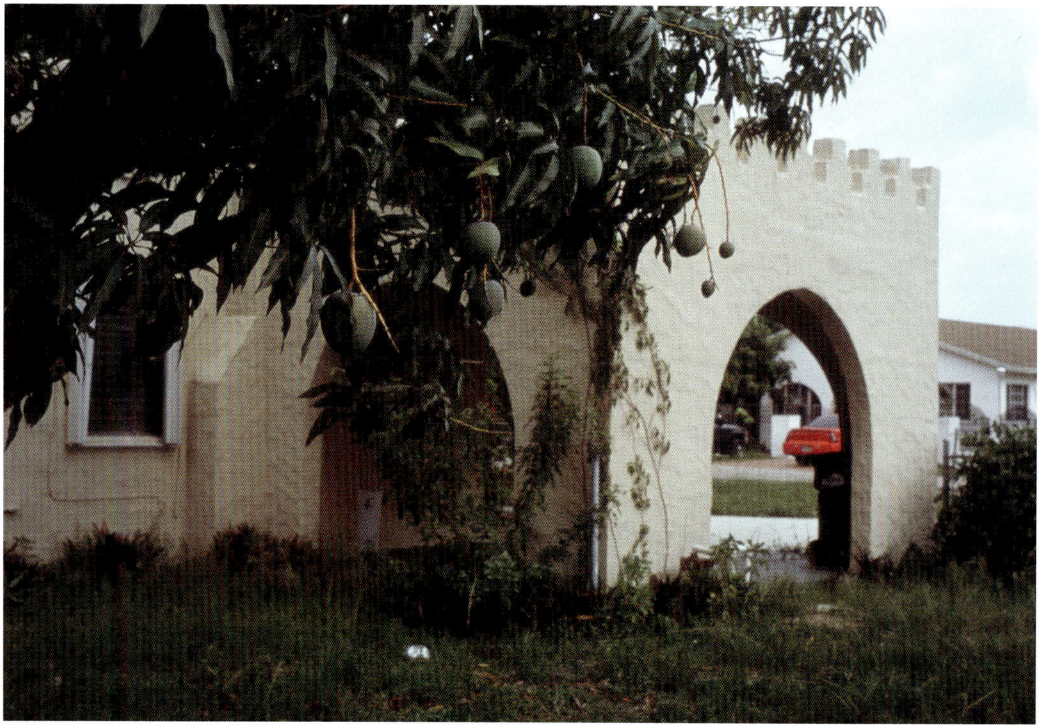

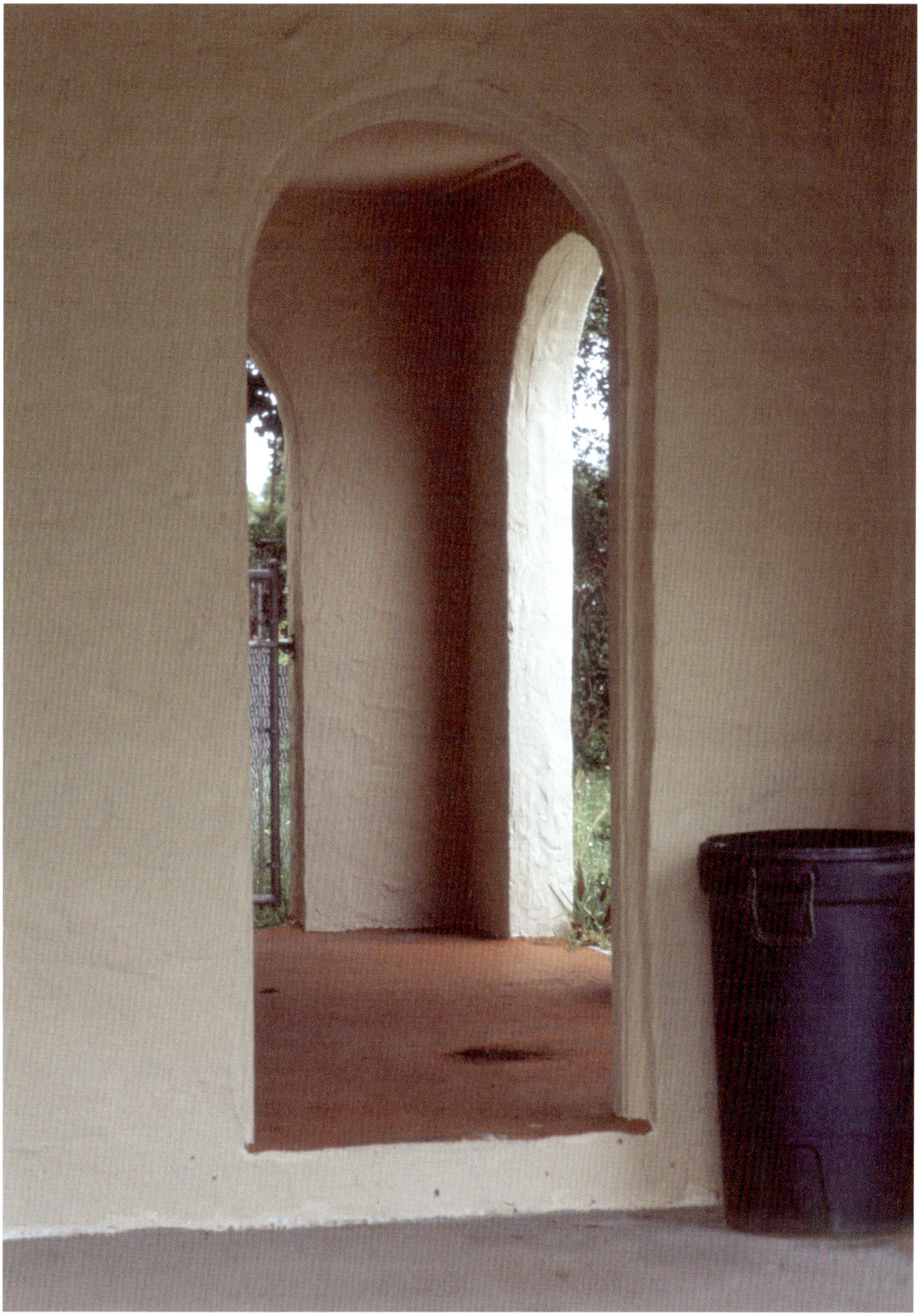

1156 PERI STREET *CROUSE HOUSE*

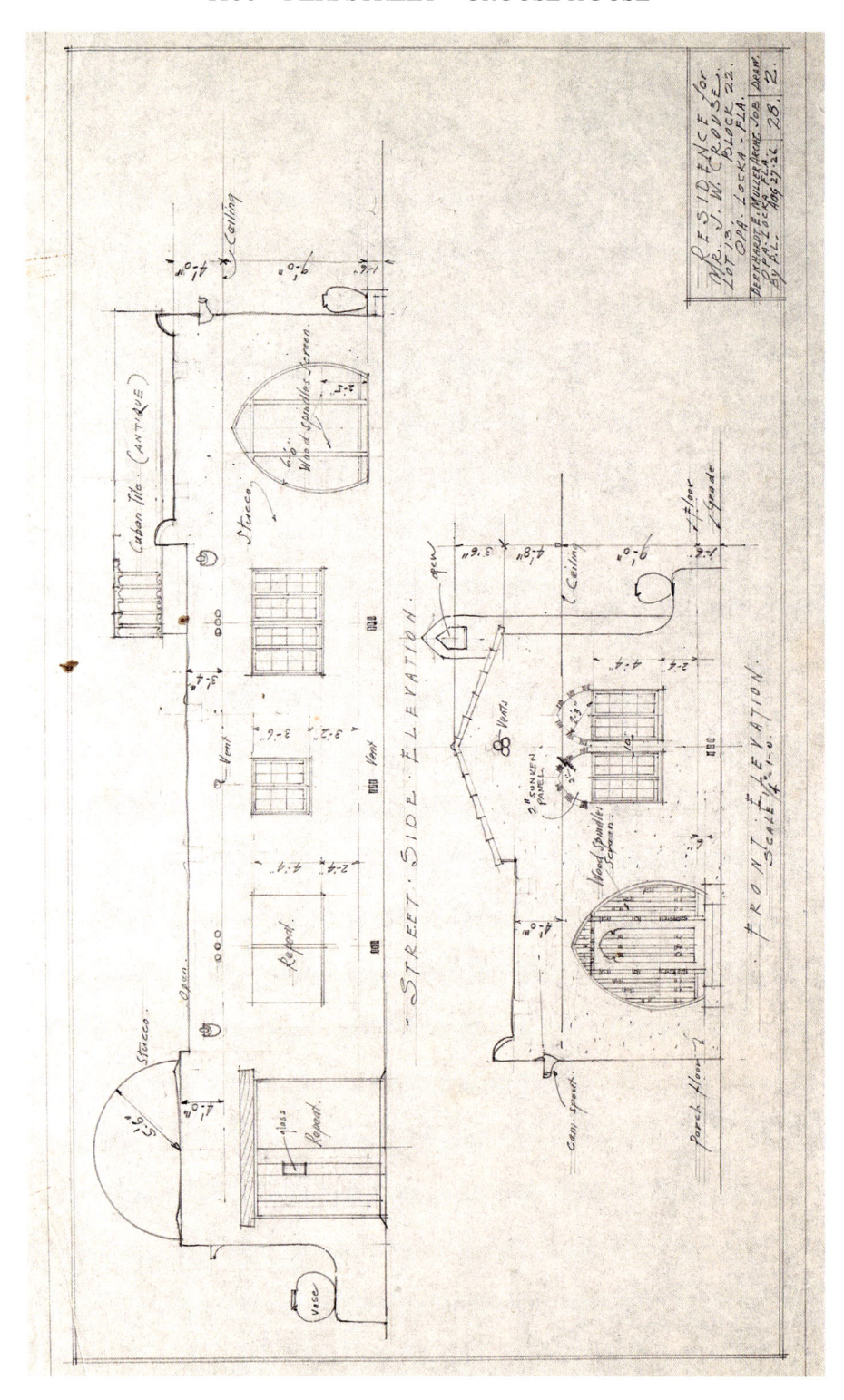

97

1211 PERI STREET *HELMS HOUSE*

1340   PERI STREET   *BUSH HOUSE*

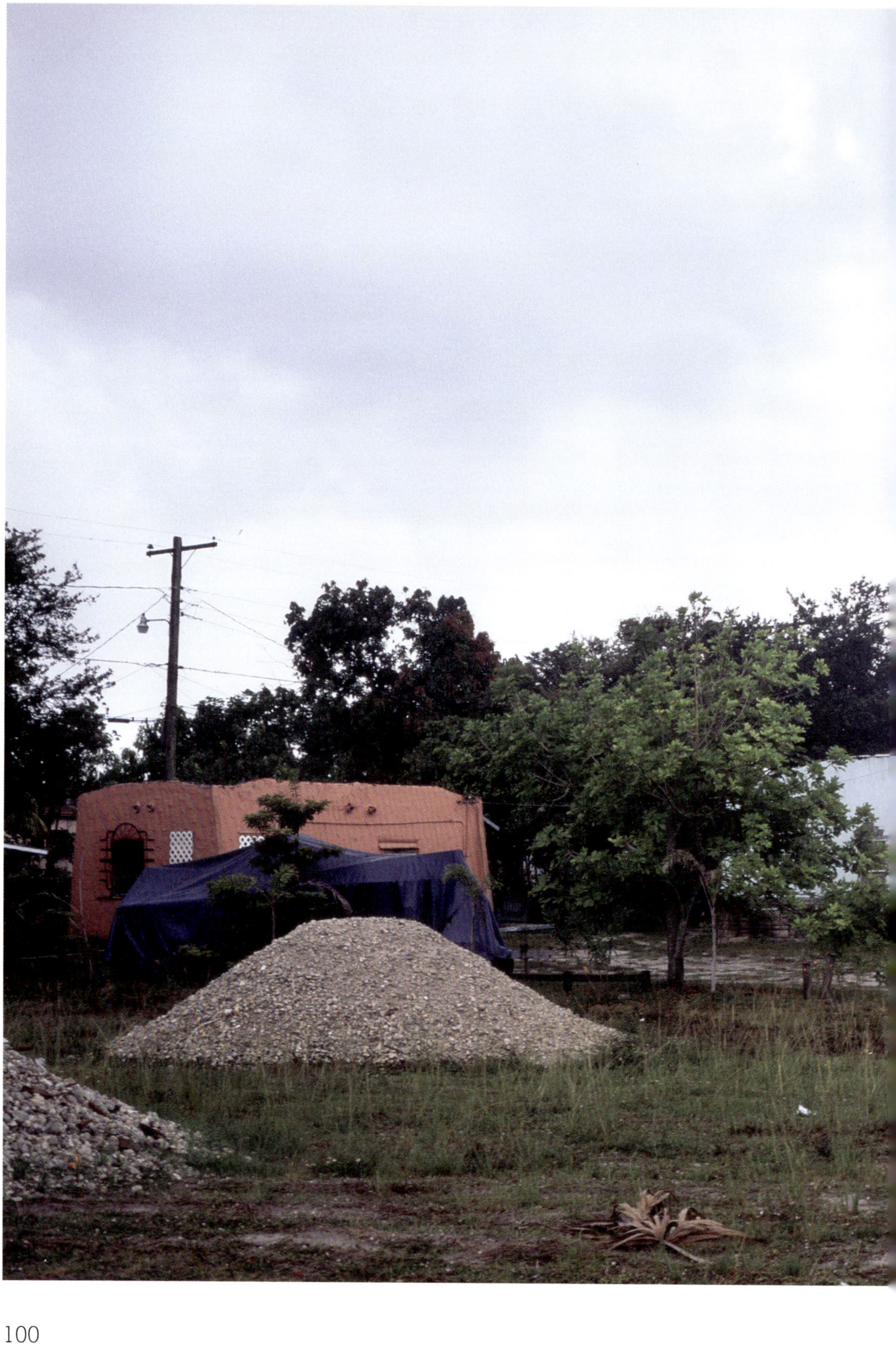

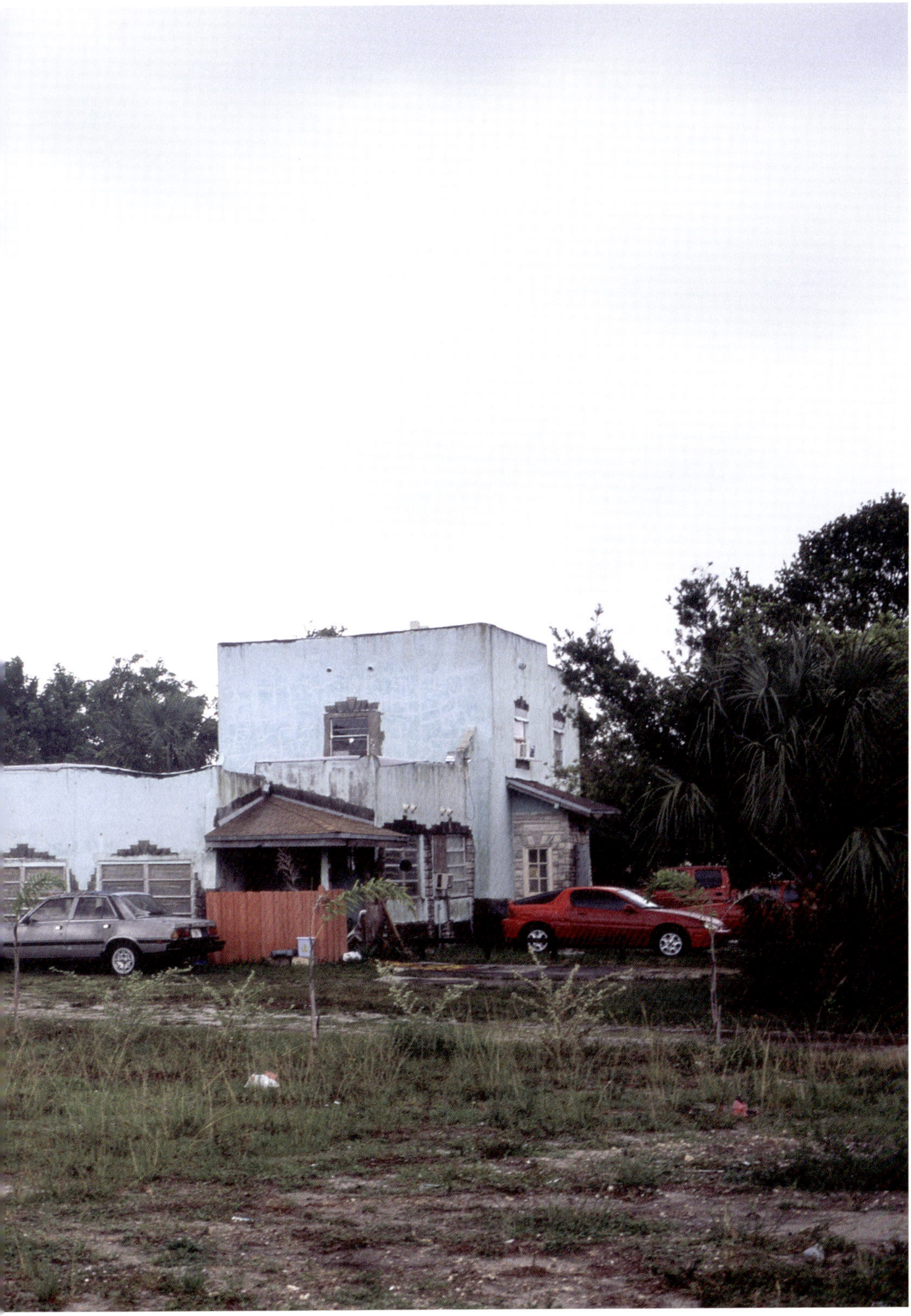

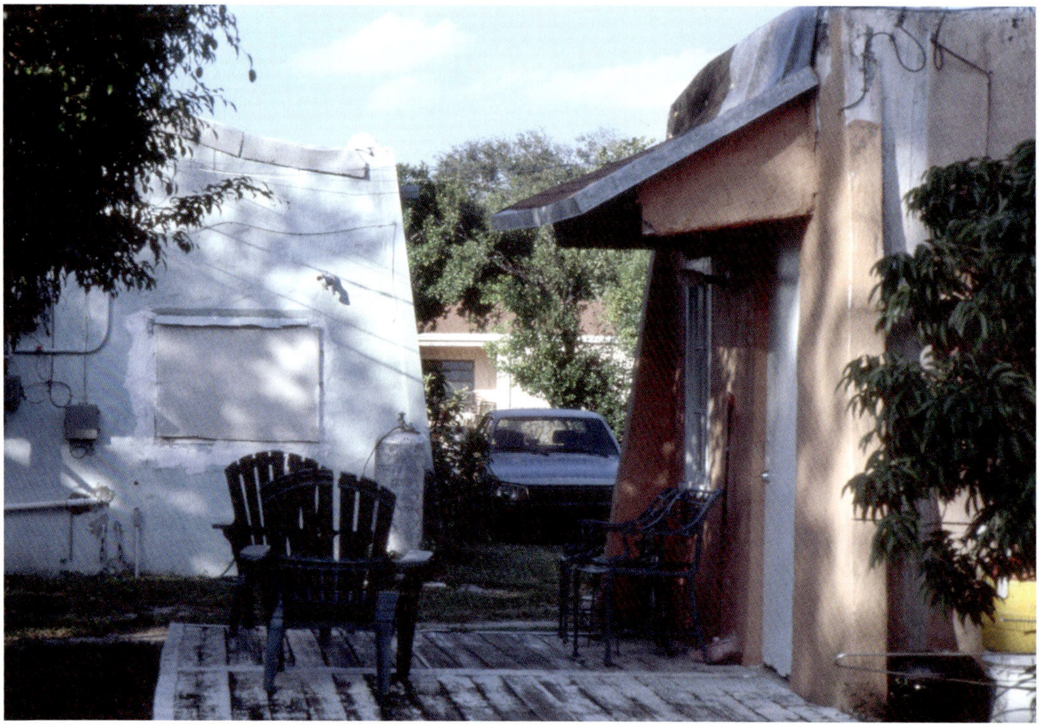

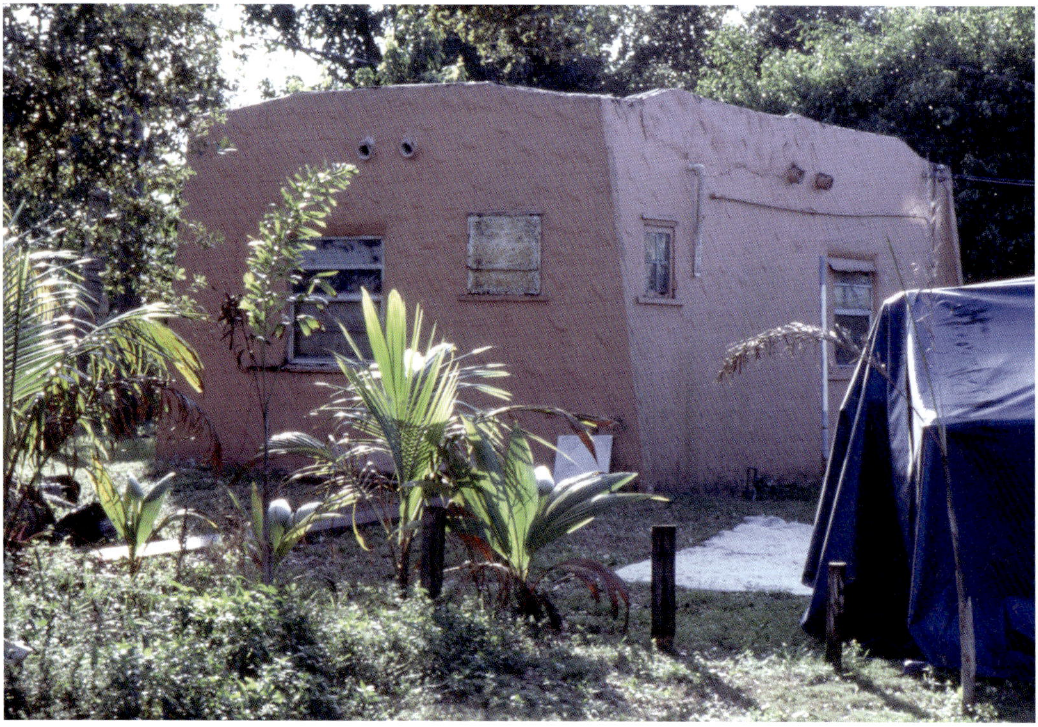

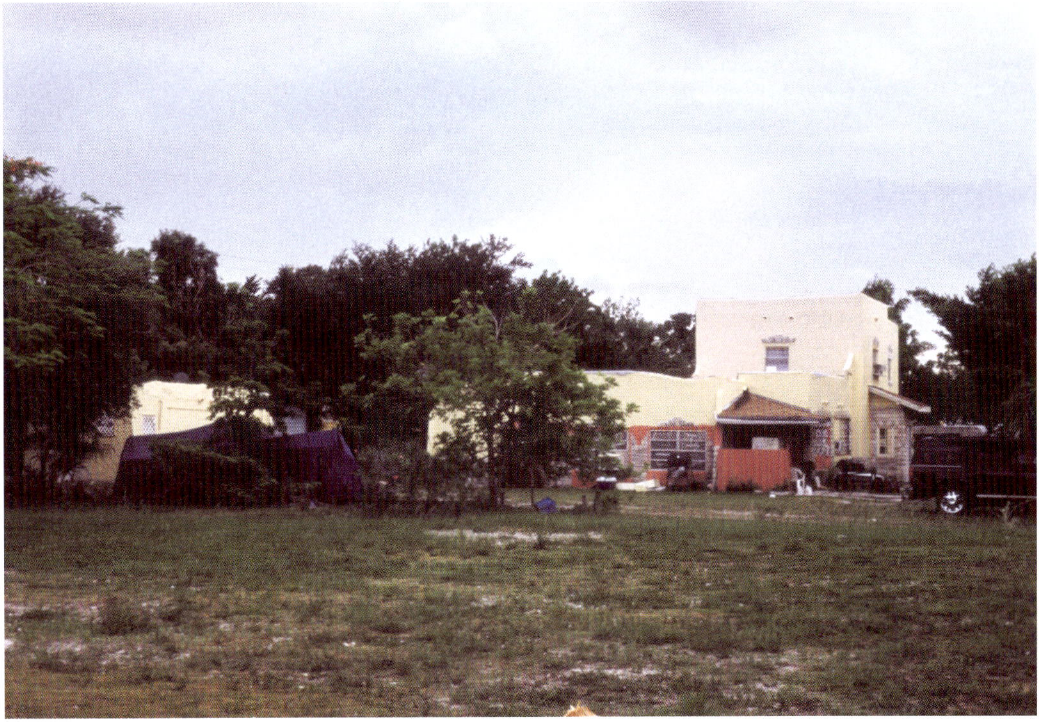

401 DUNAD AVENUE *BAIRD HOUSE*

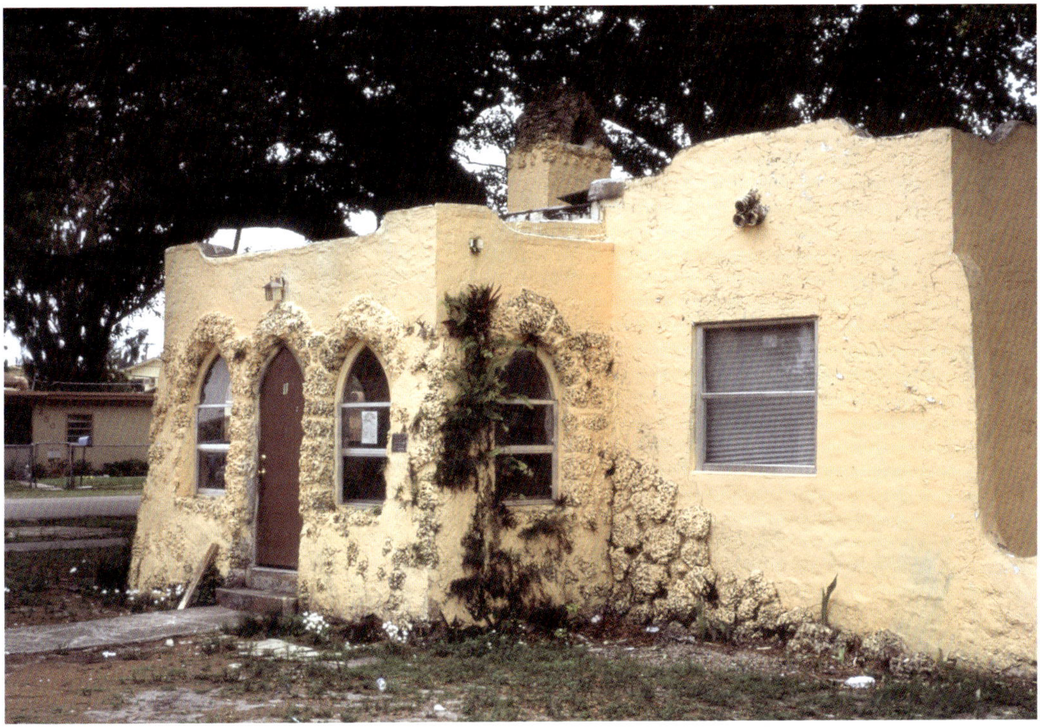

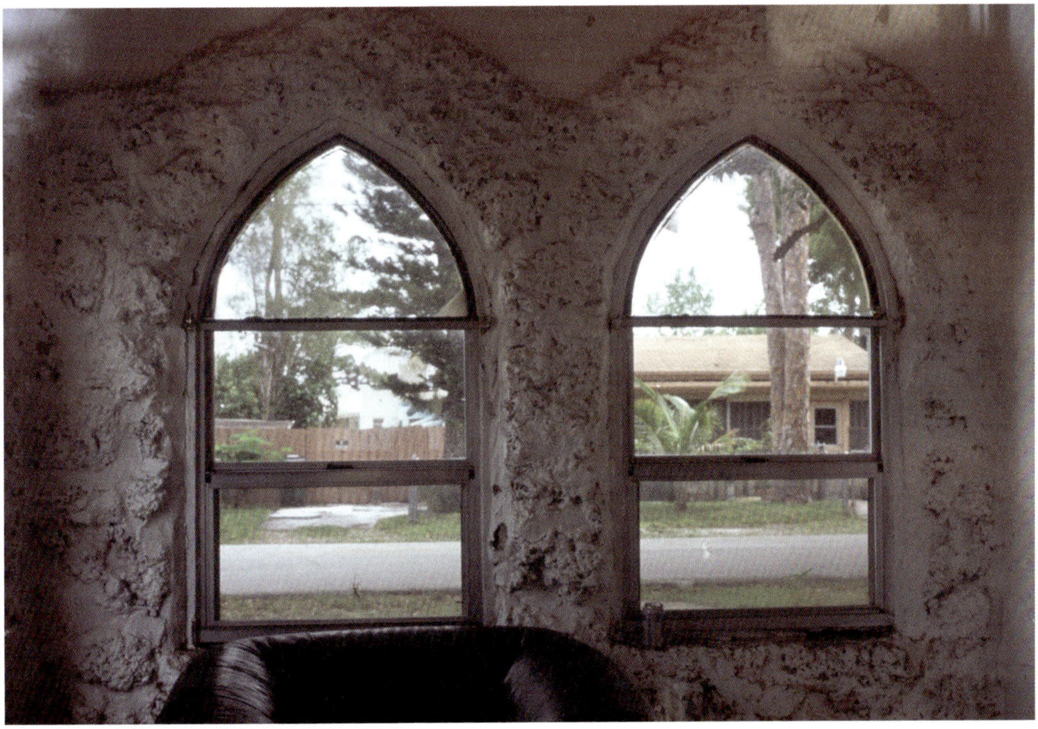

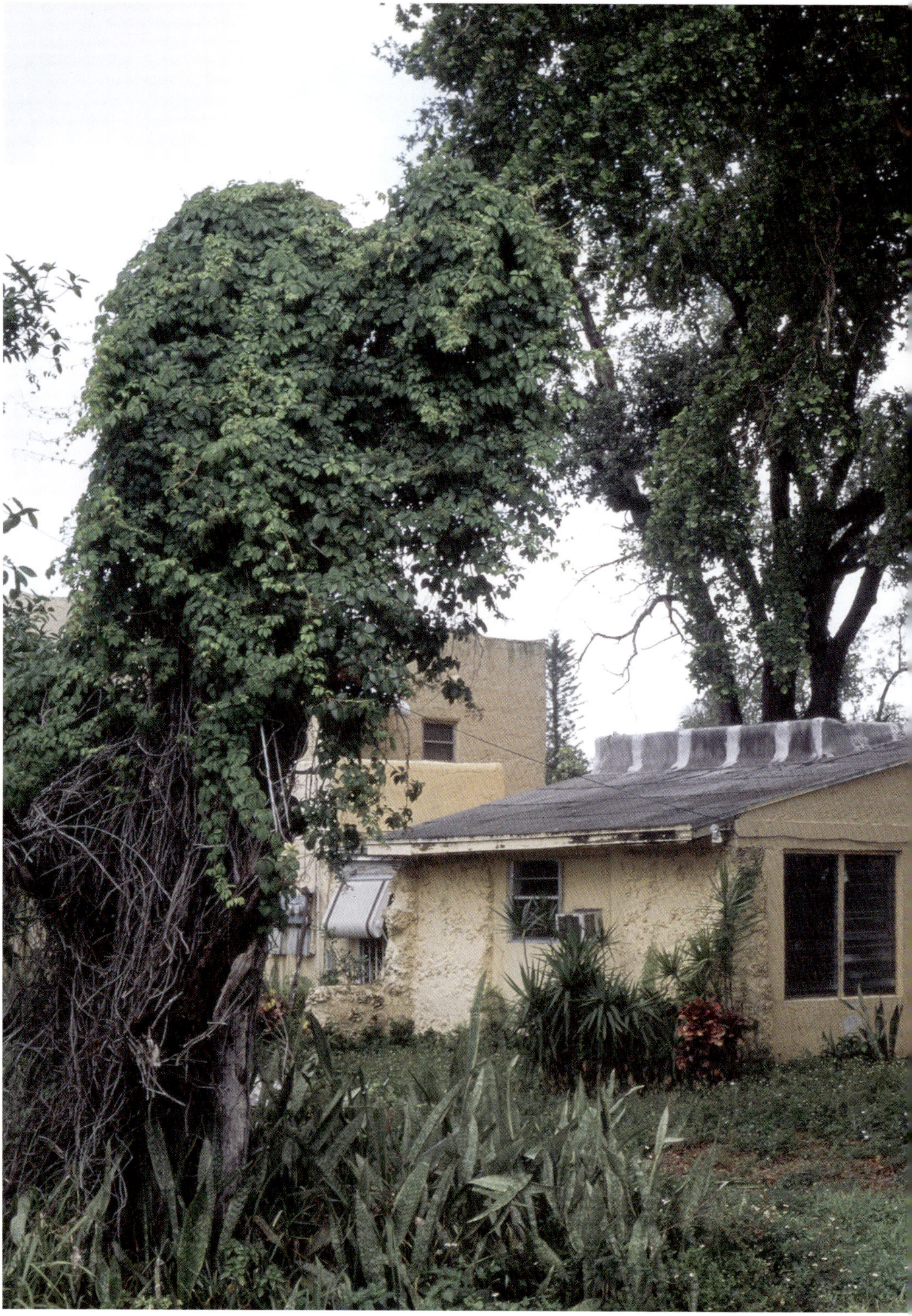

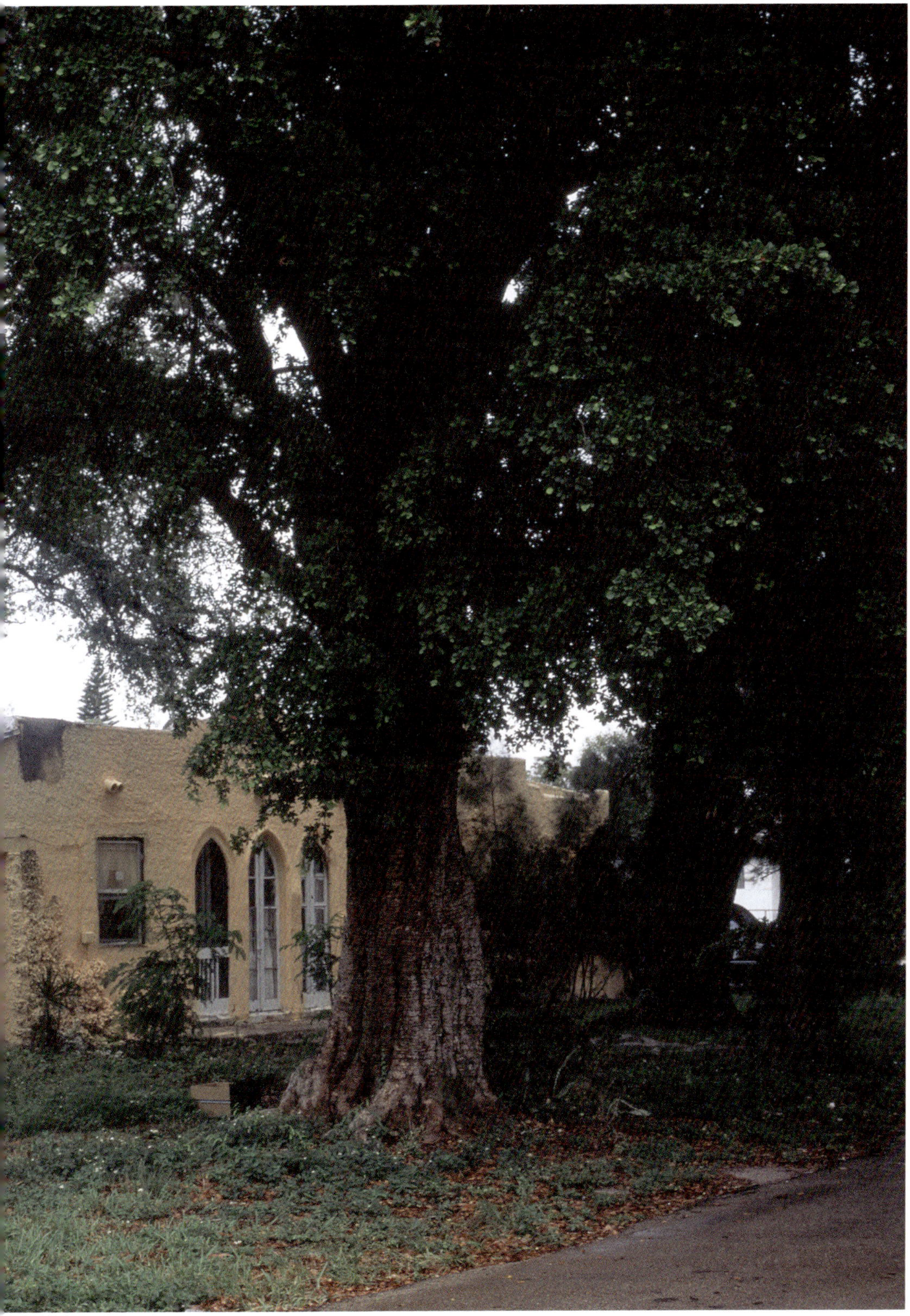

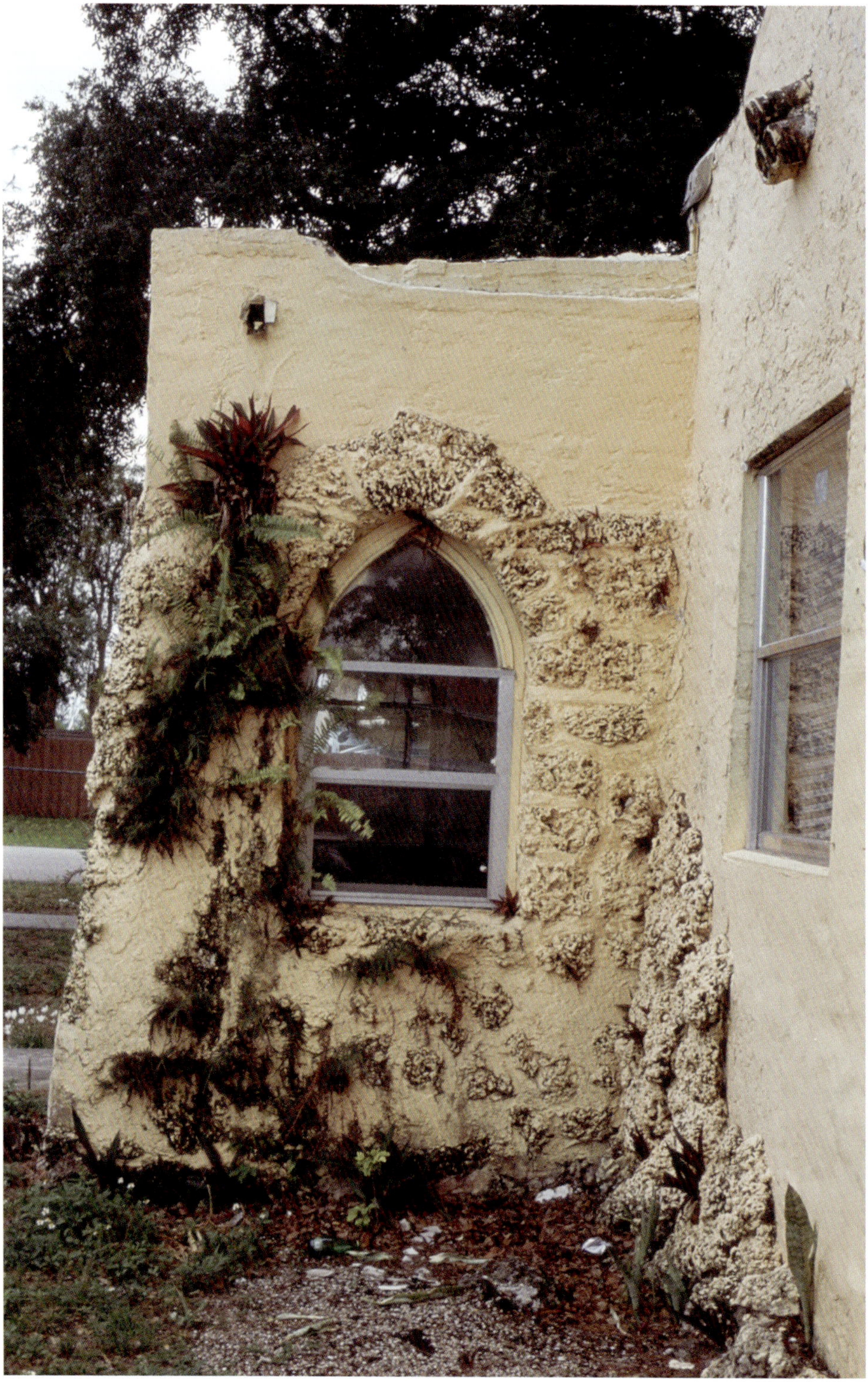

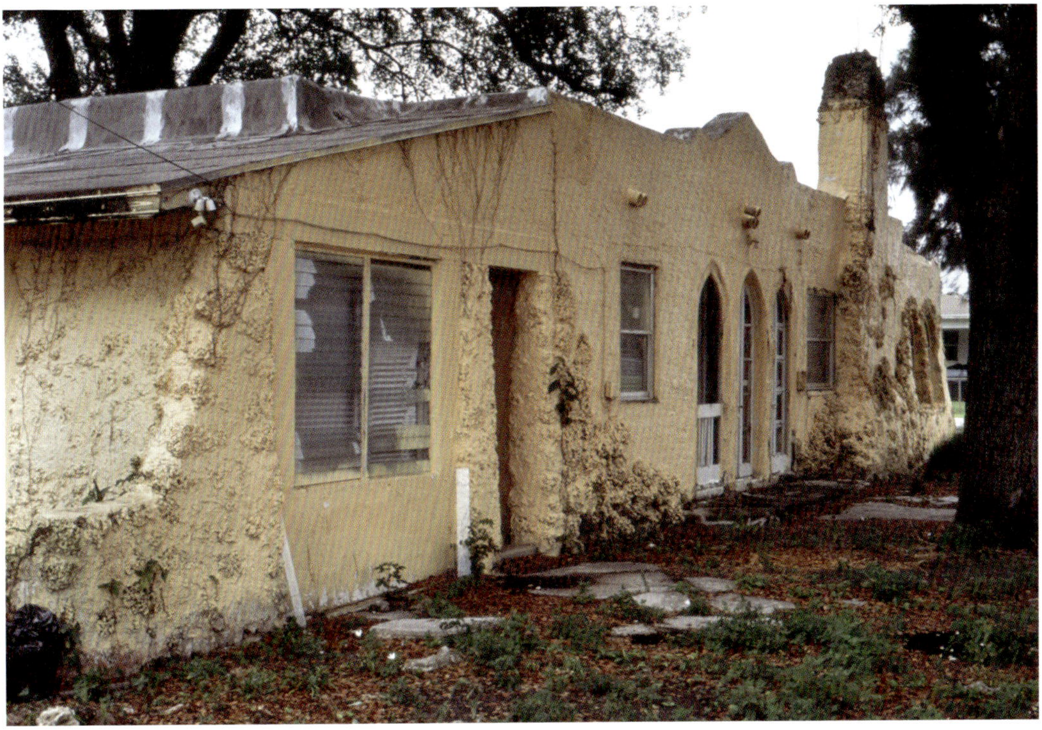

811 DUNAD AVENUE *TOOKER HOUSE*

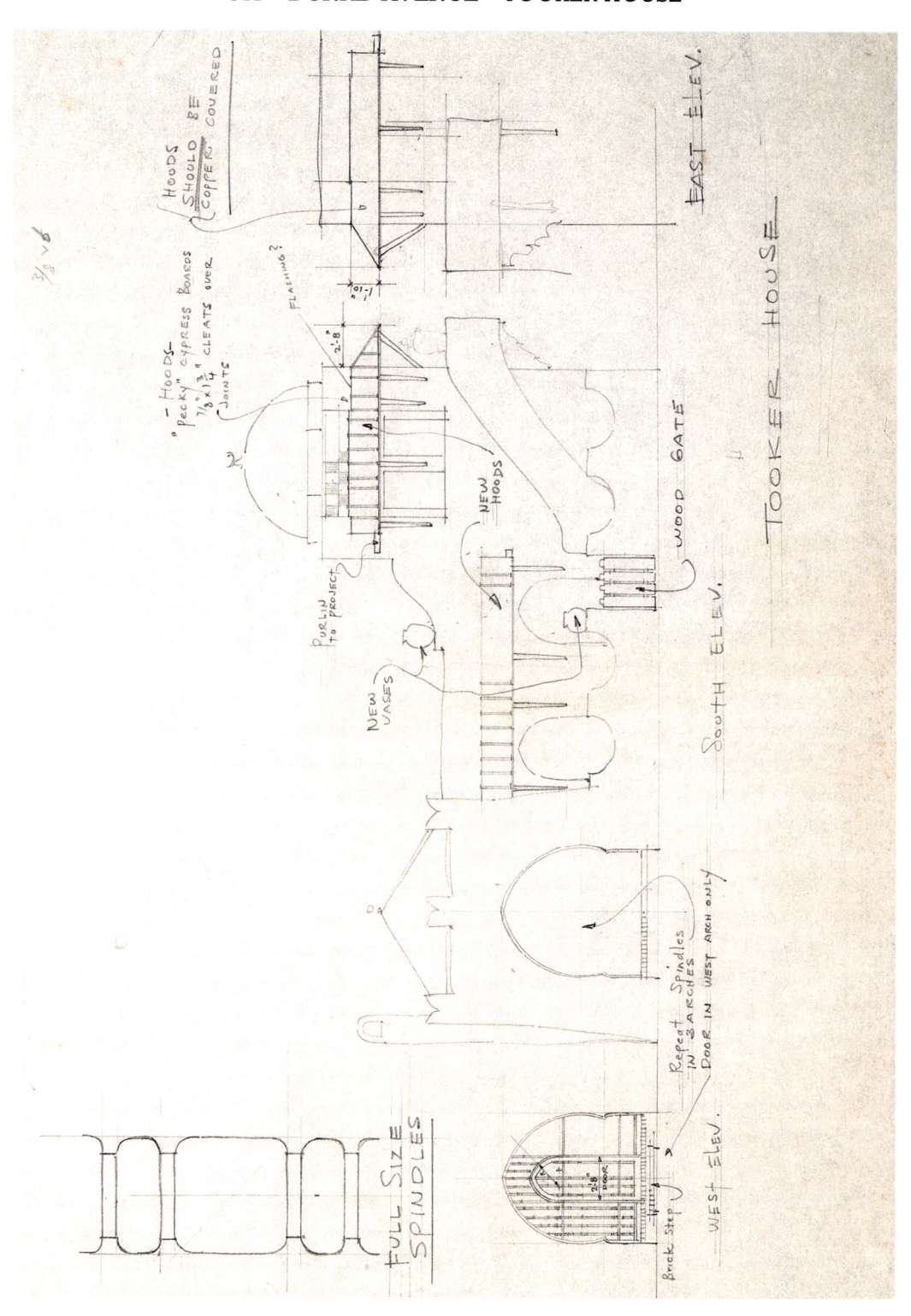

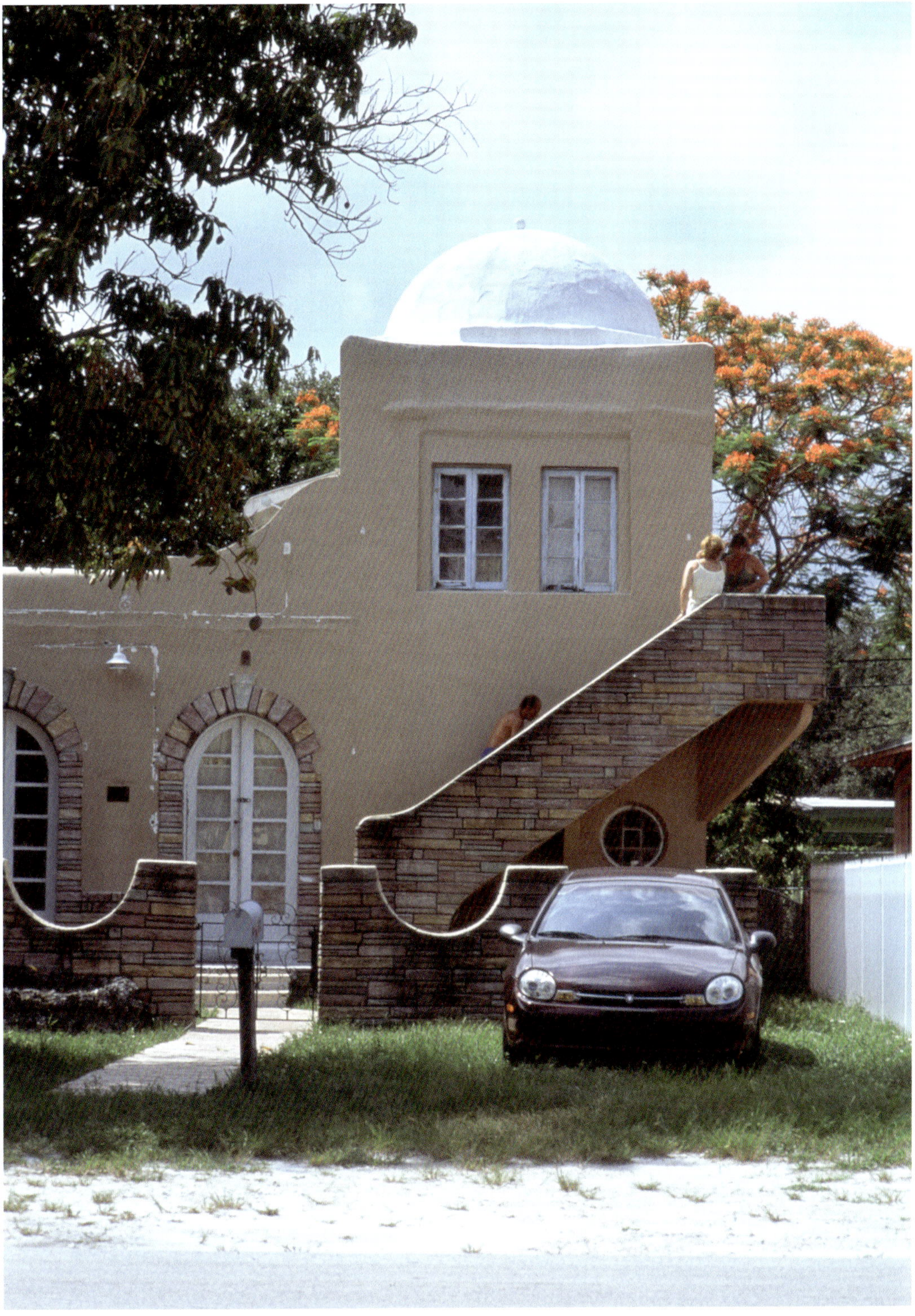

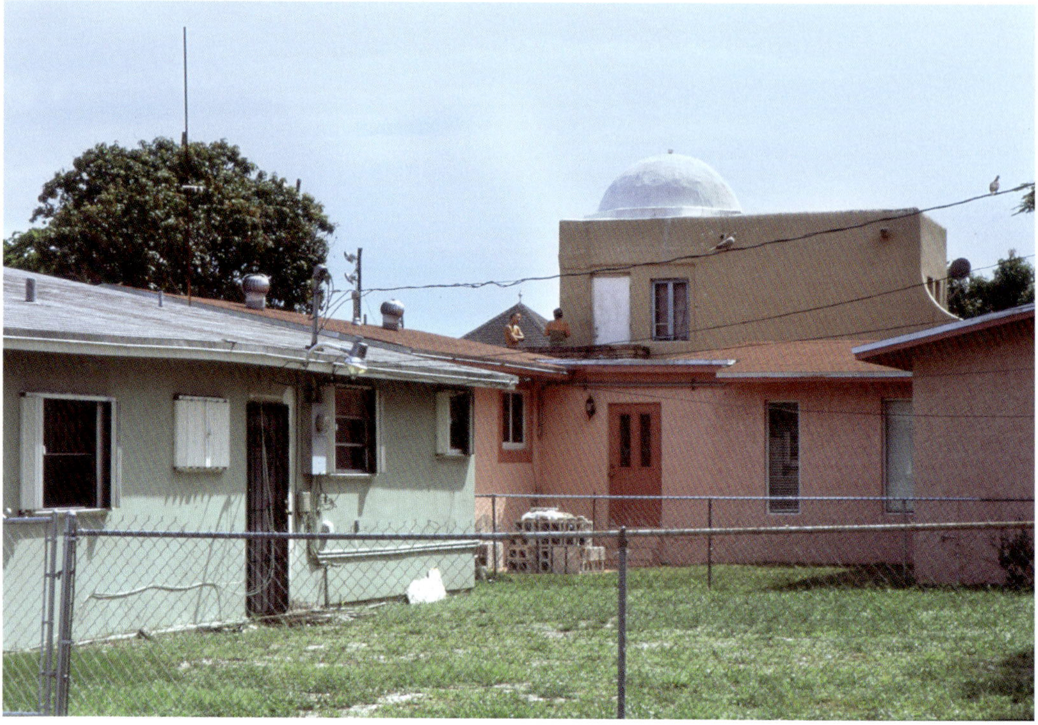

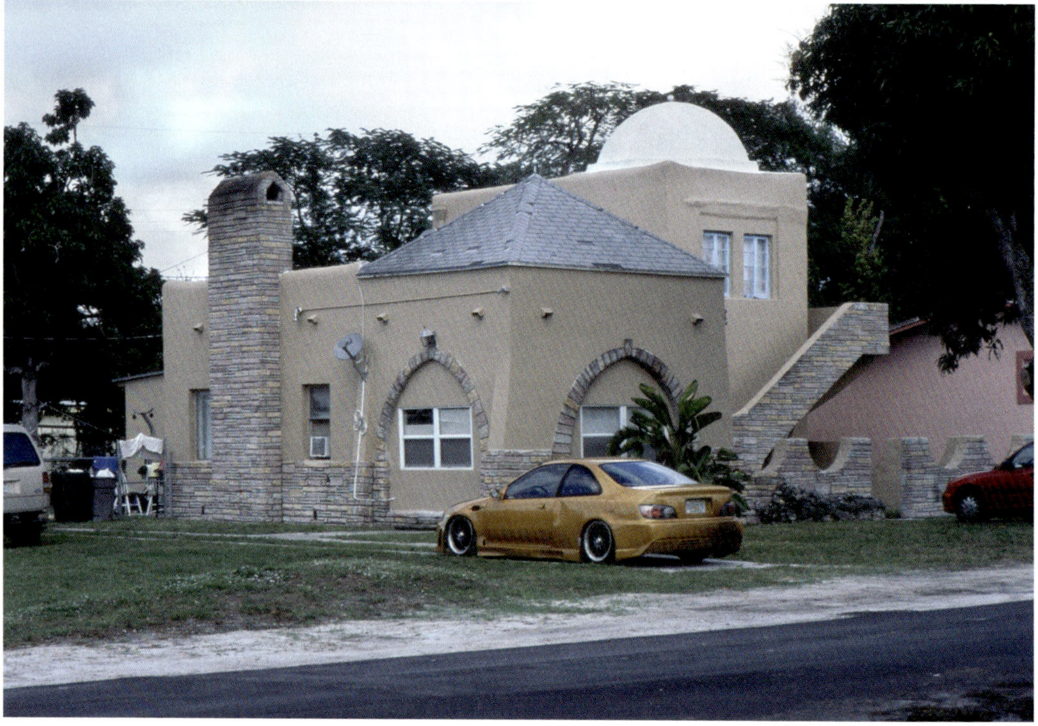

1035 DUNAD AVENUE *WHEELER HOUSE*

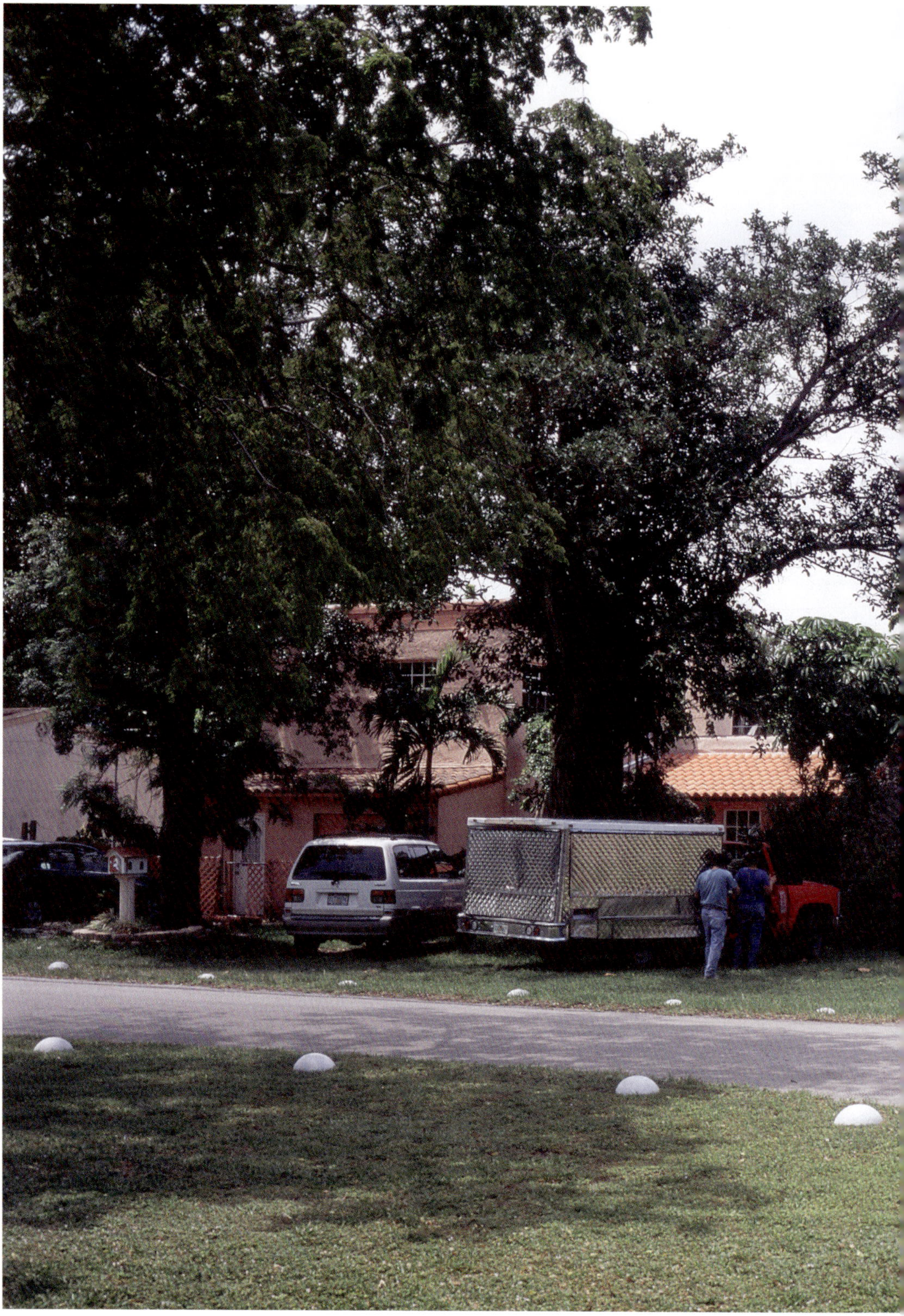

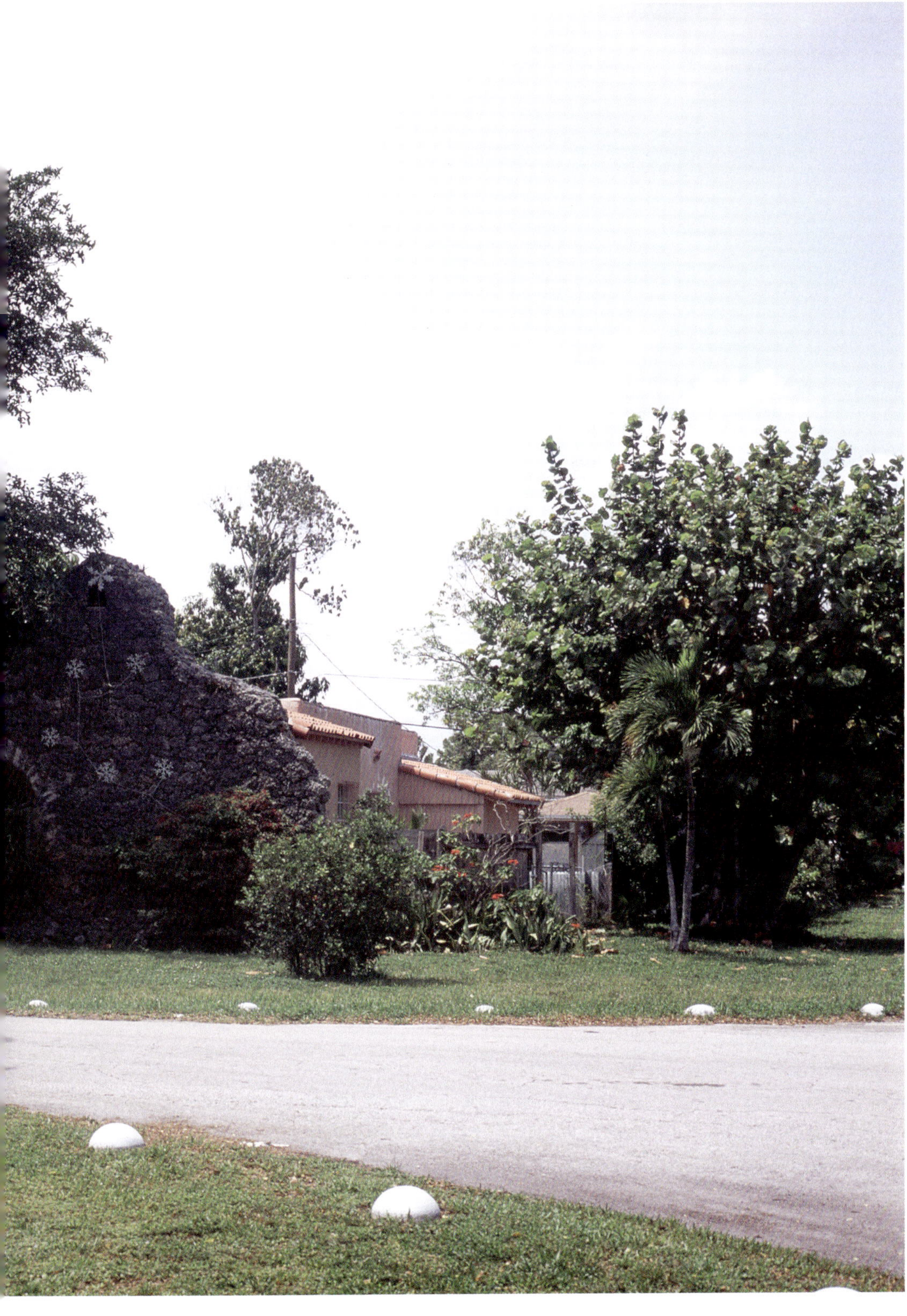

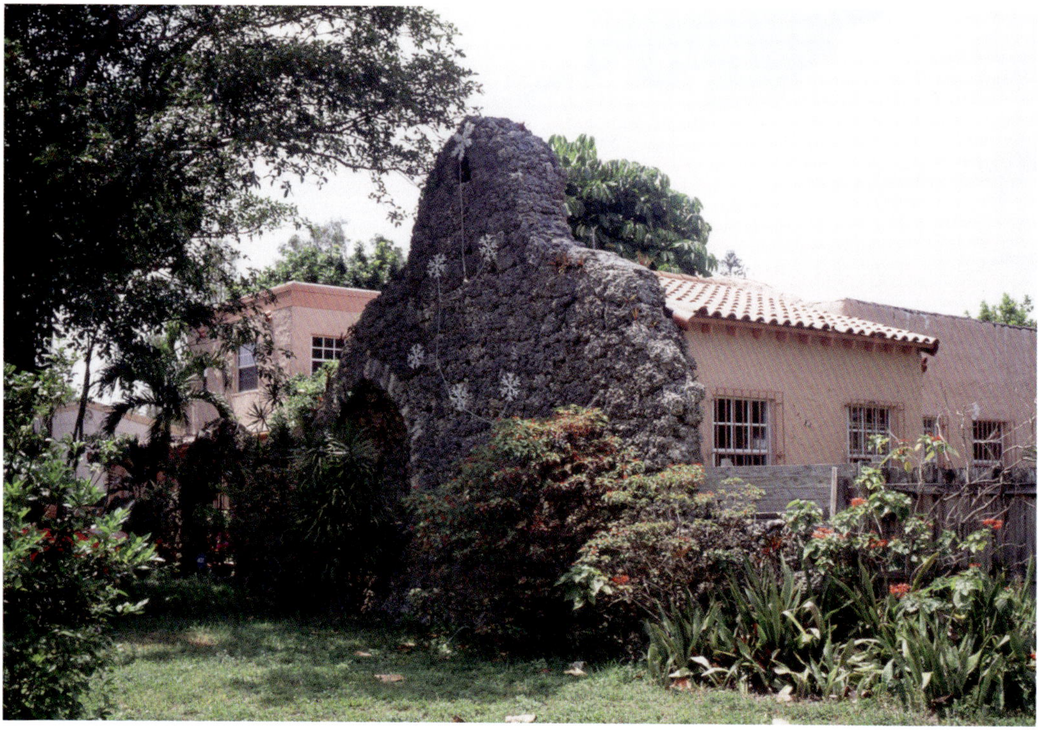

1036 DUNAD AVENUE *GRIFFITHS HOUSE*

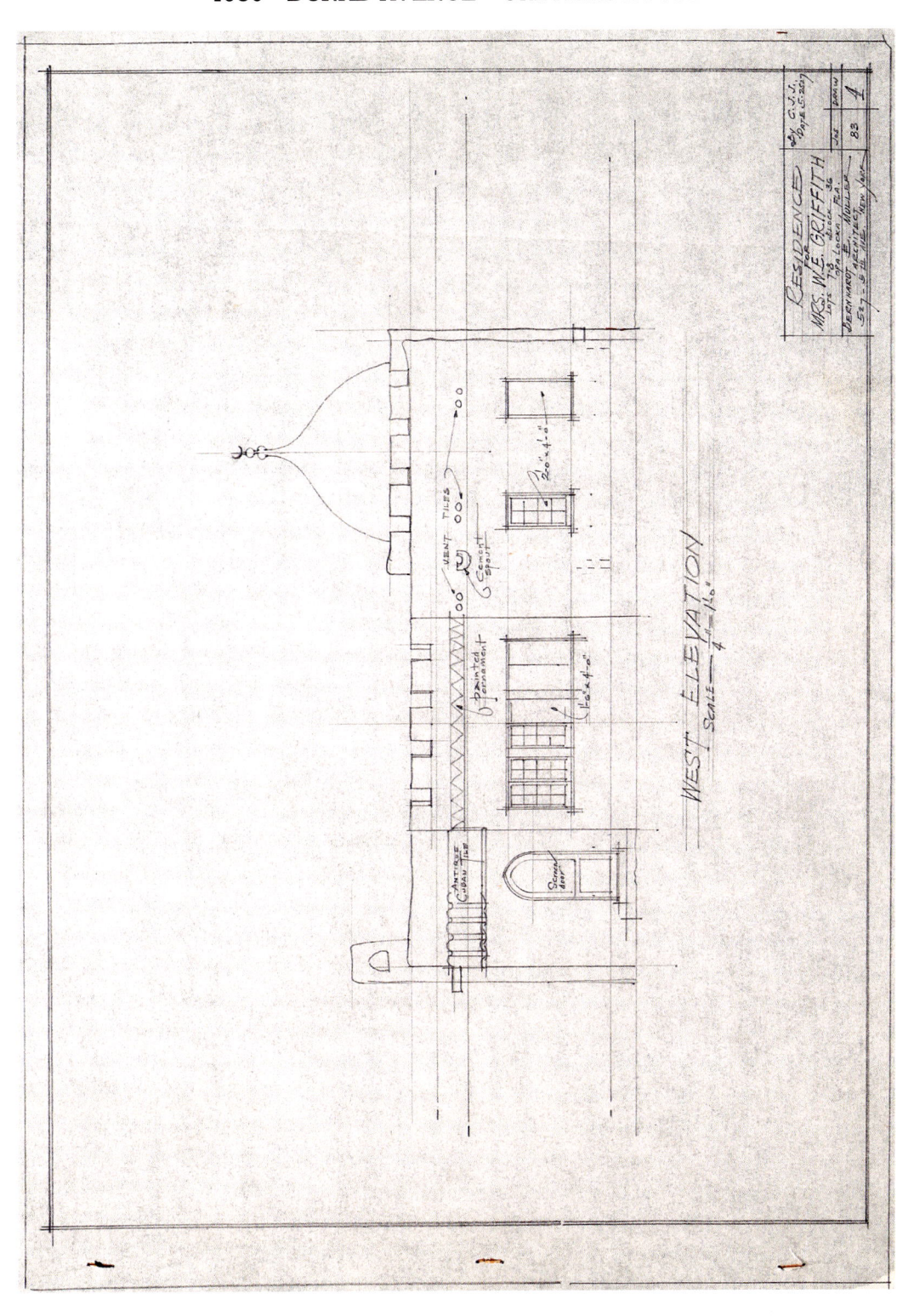

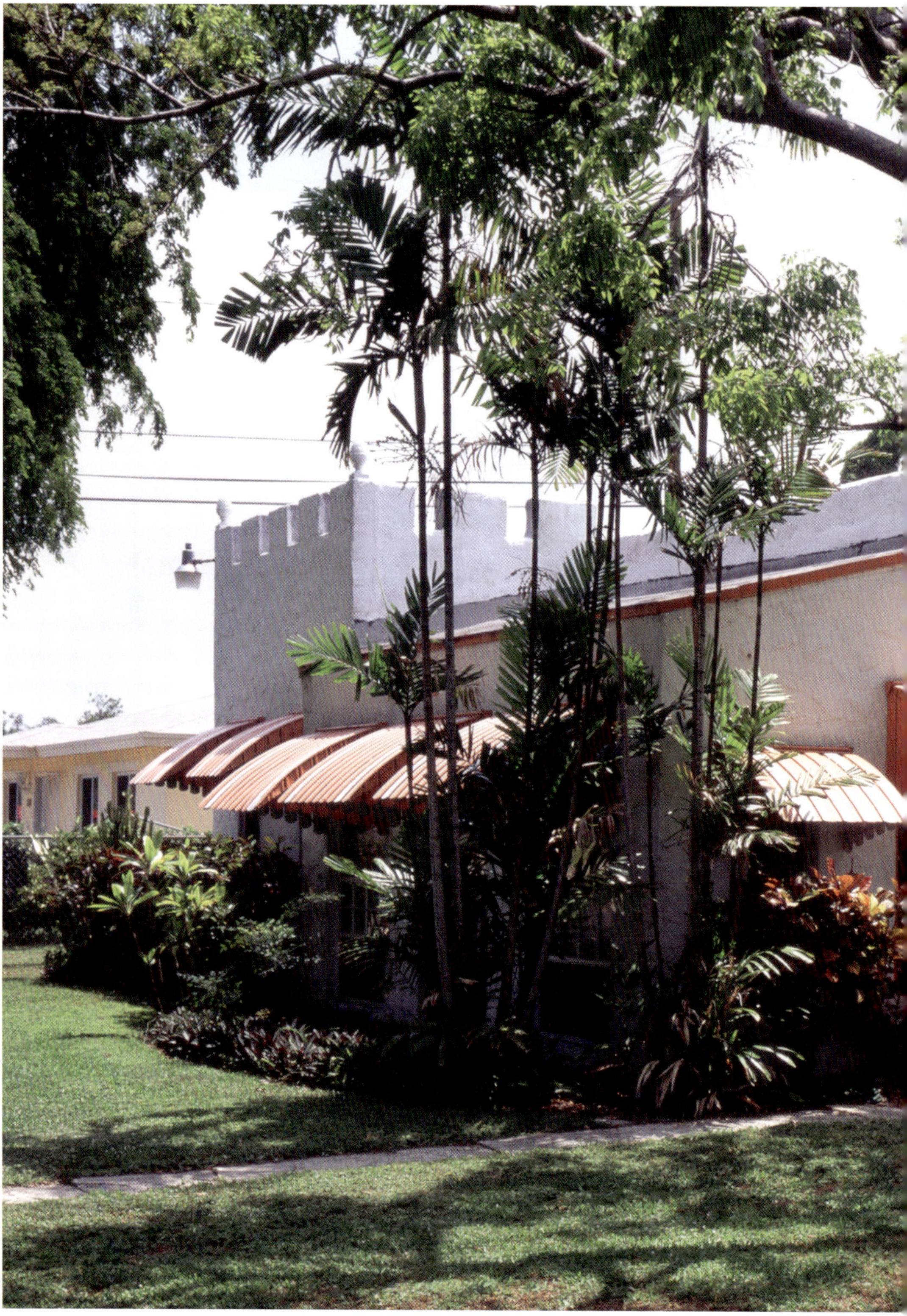

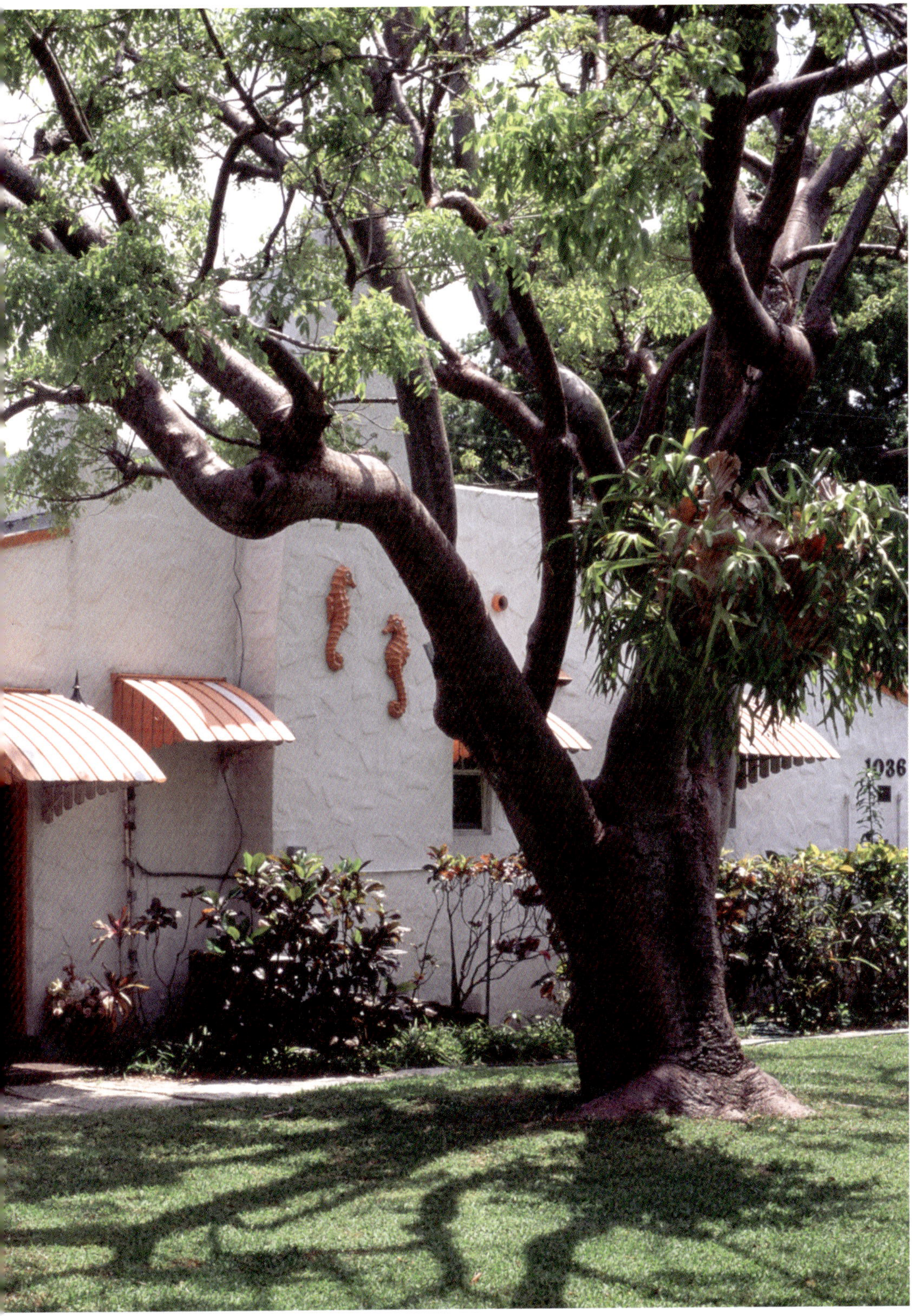
1036

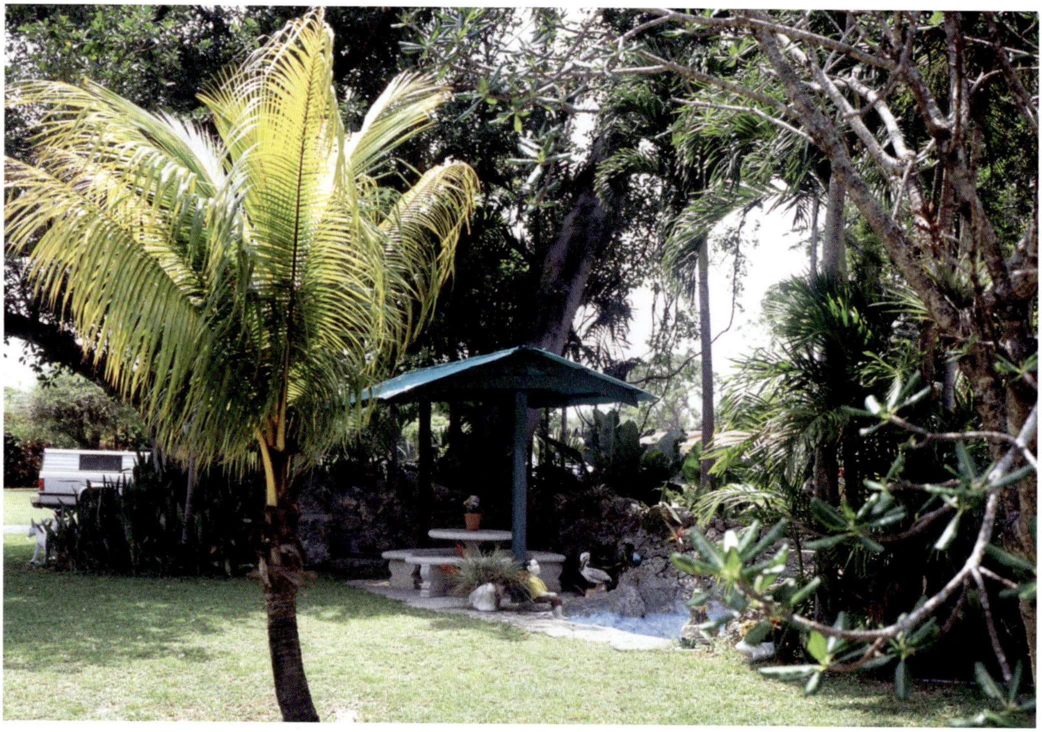

940   CALIPH STREET   *BANK BUILDING*

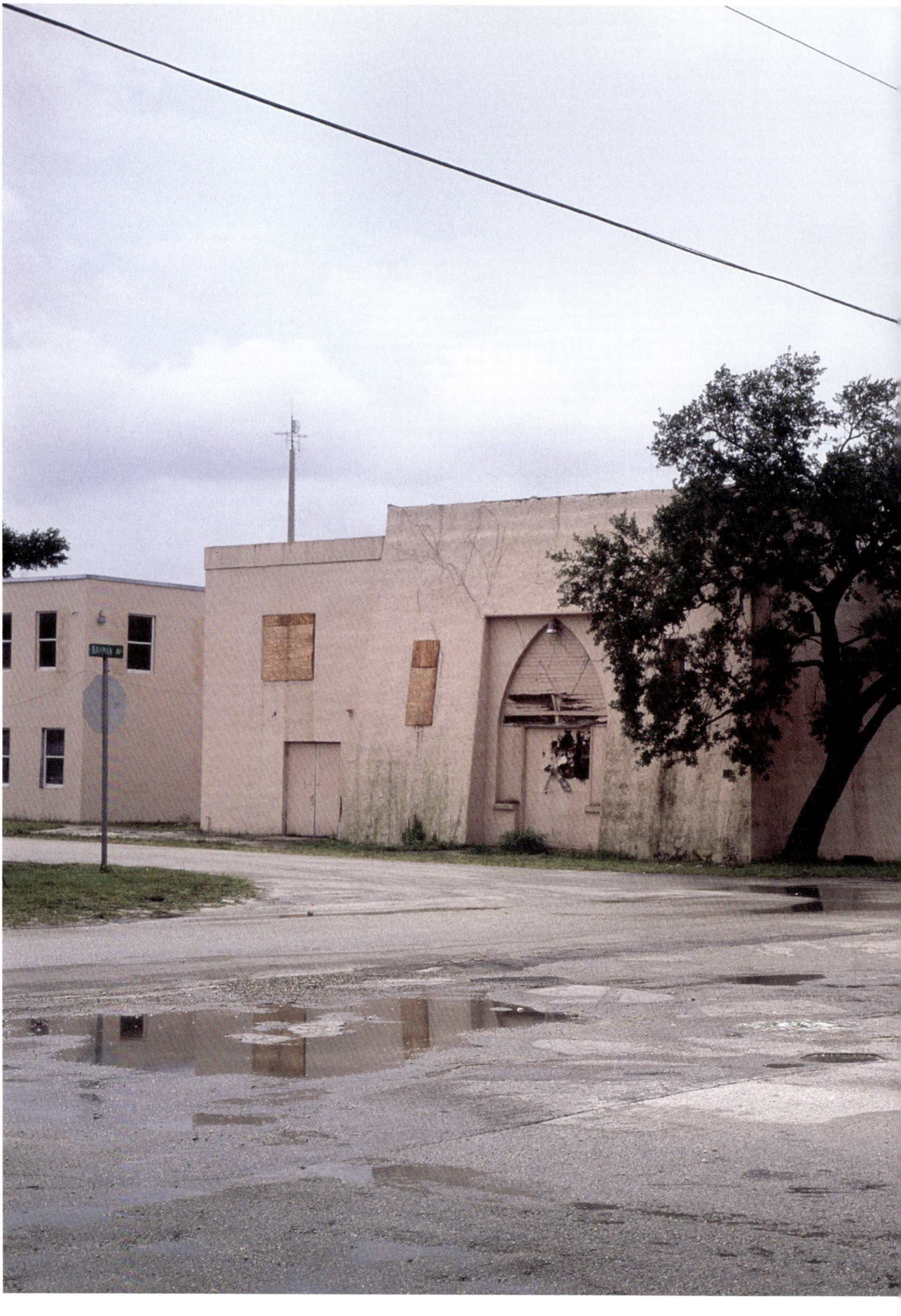

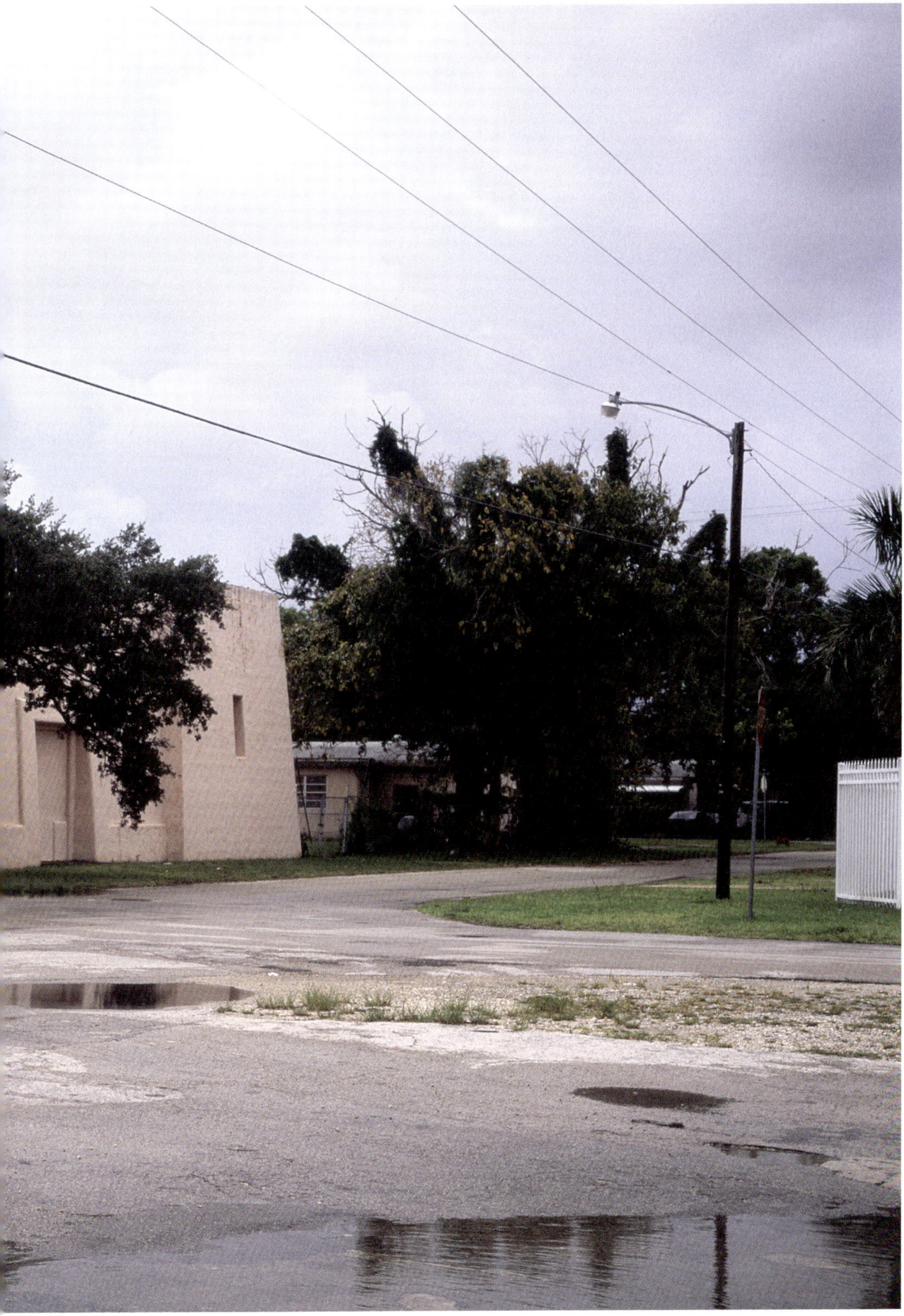

826 SUPERIOR STREET *GRIFFITHS HOUSE*

851 SUPERIOR STREET *KING TRUNK FACTORY*

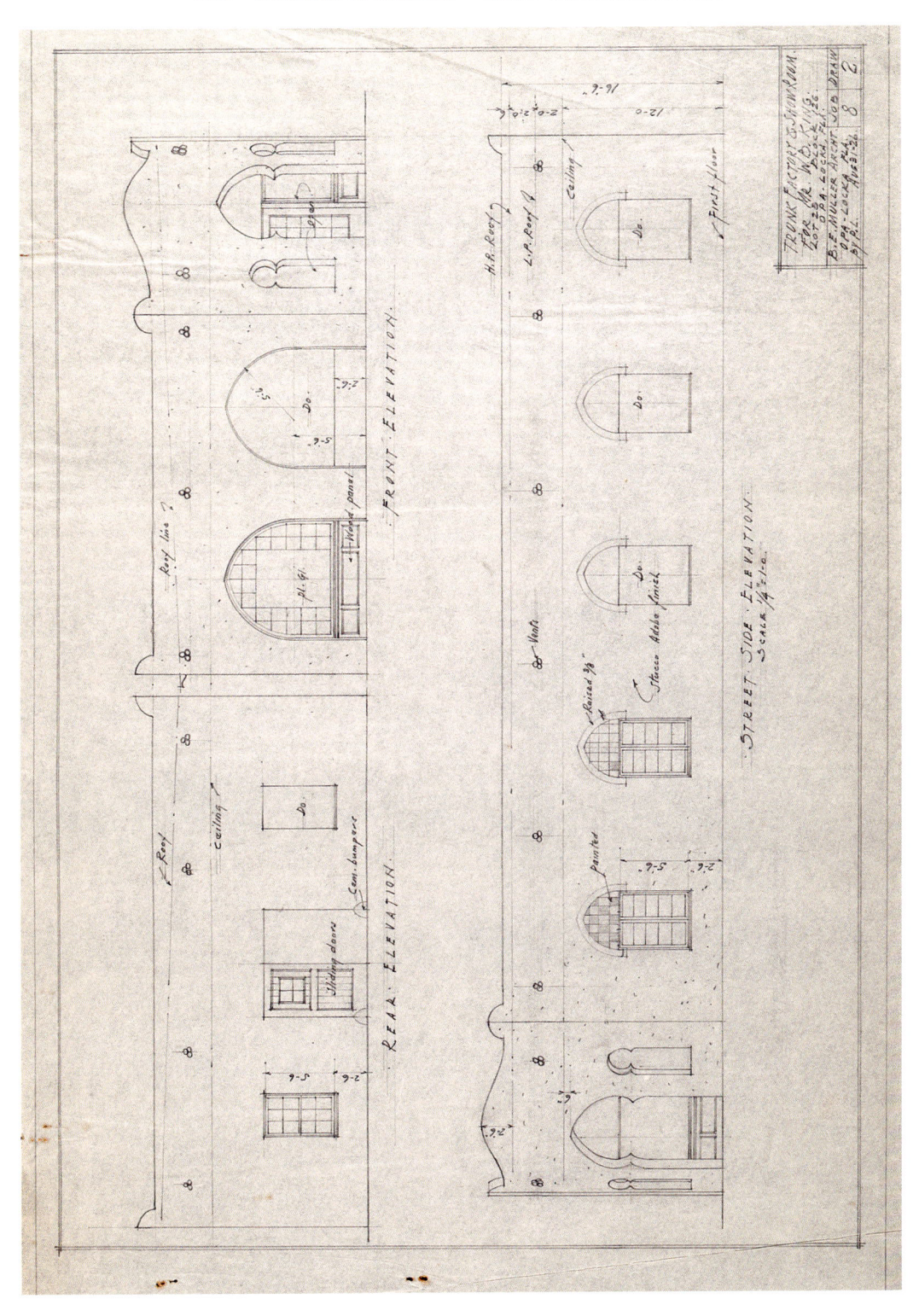

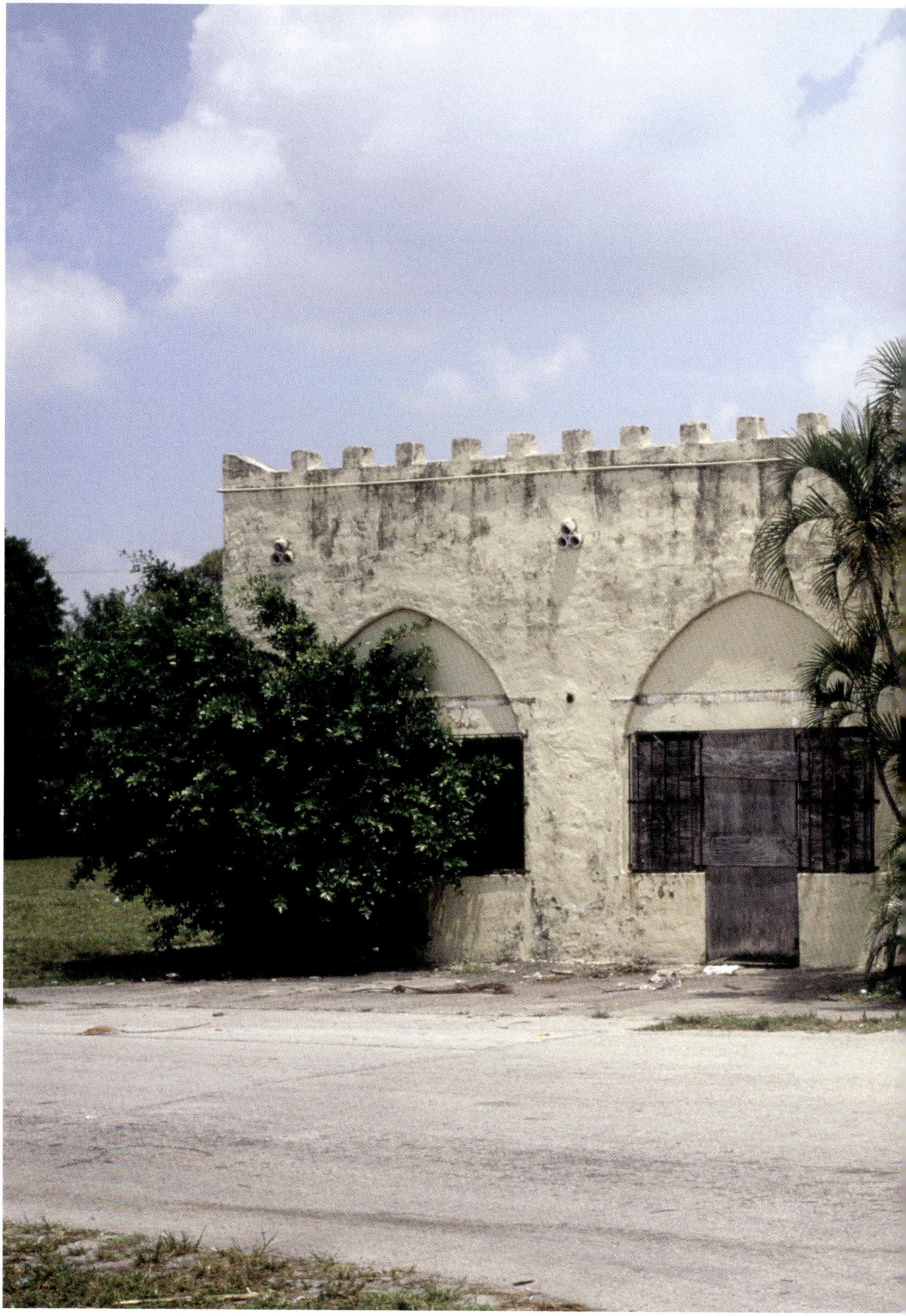

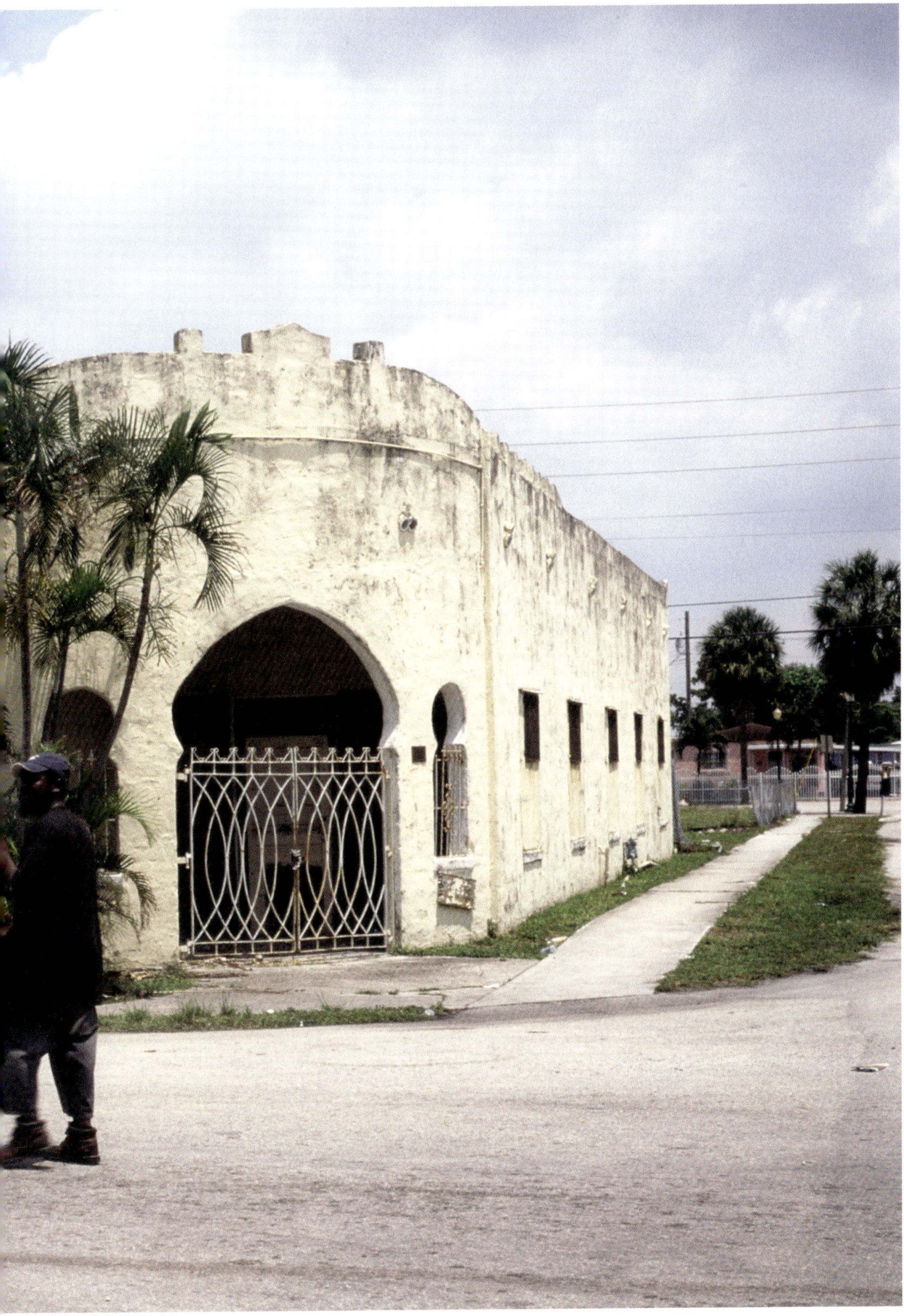

1111 SESAME STREET *(NAME UNKNOWN)*

1210–1212 SESAME STREET *HIGGINS DUPLEX*

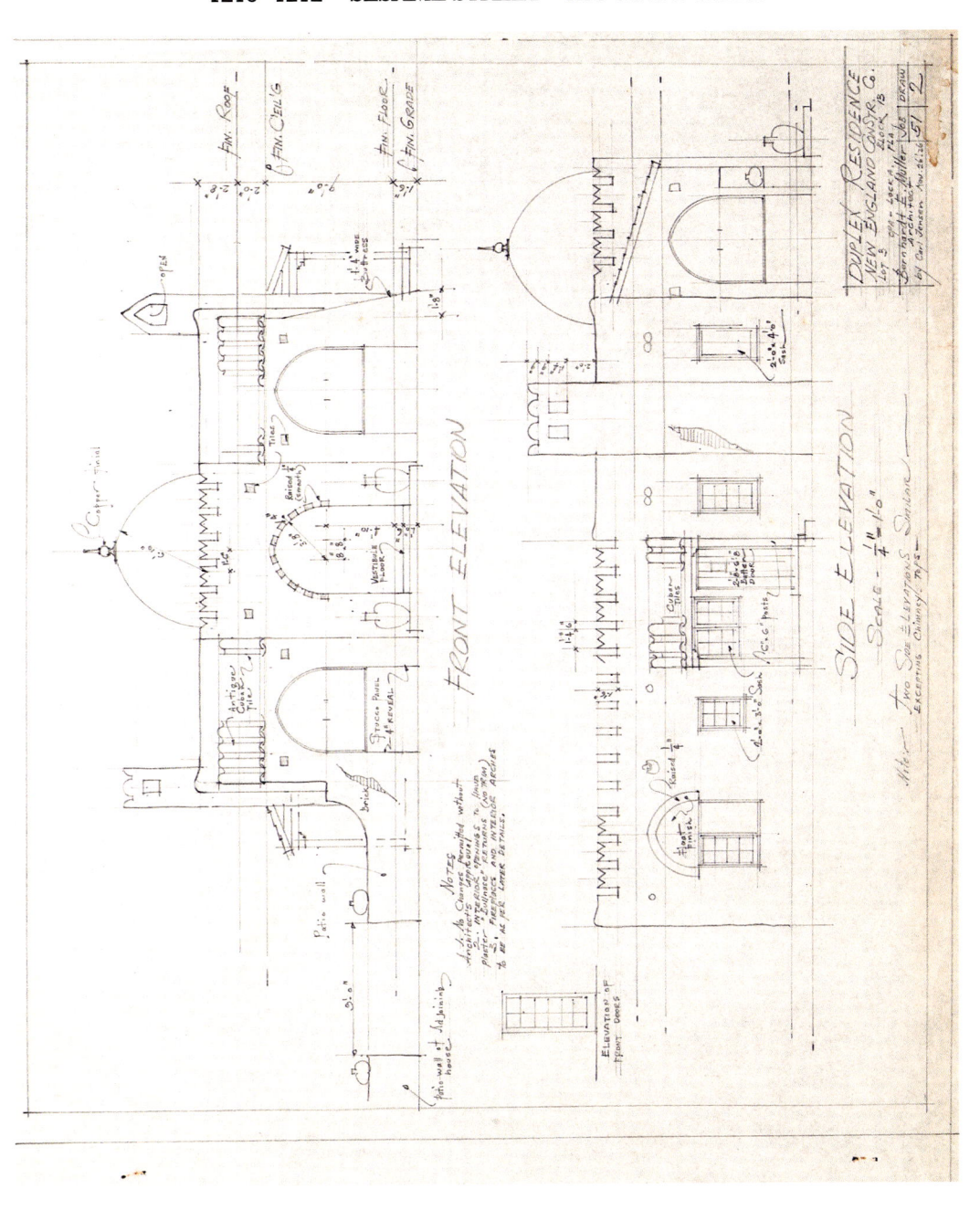

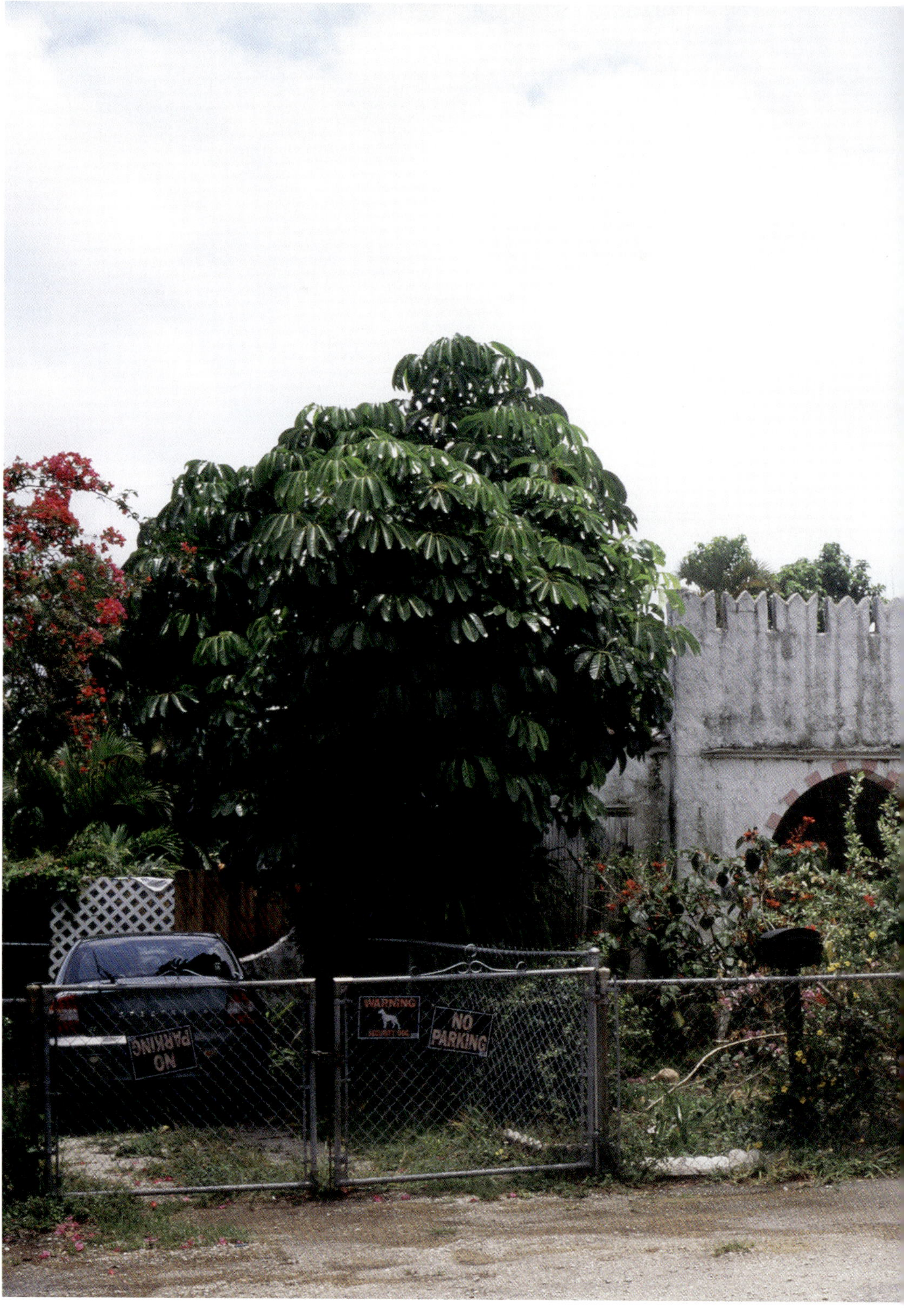
WARNING
NO PARKING
NO PARKING

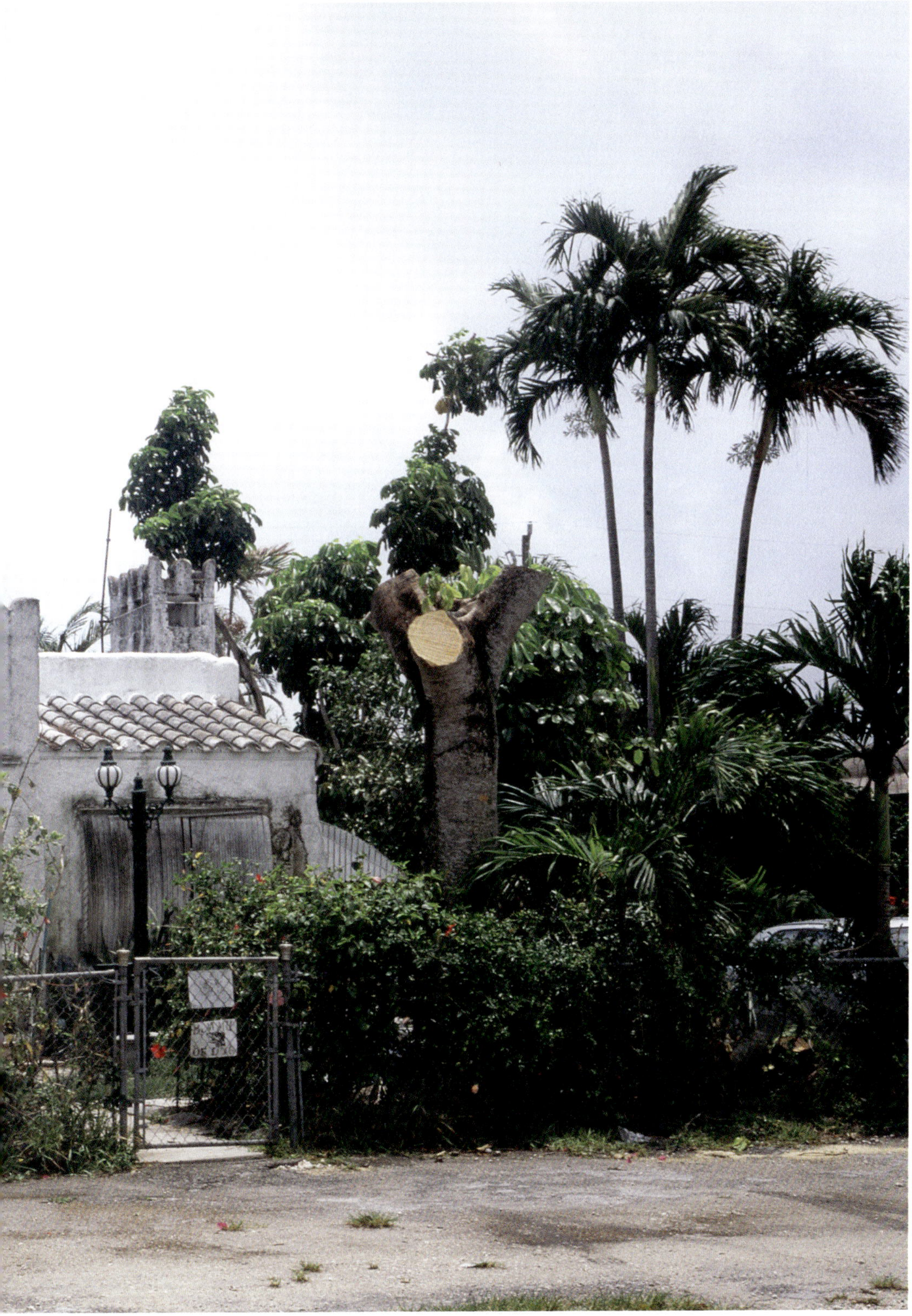

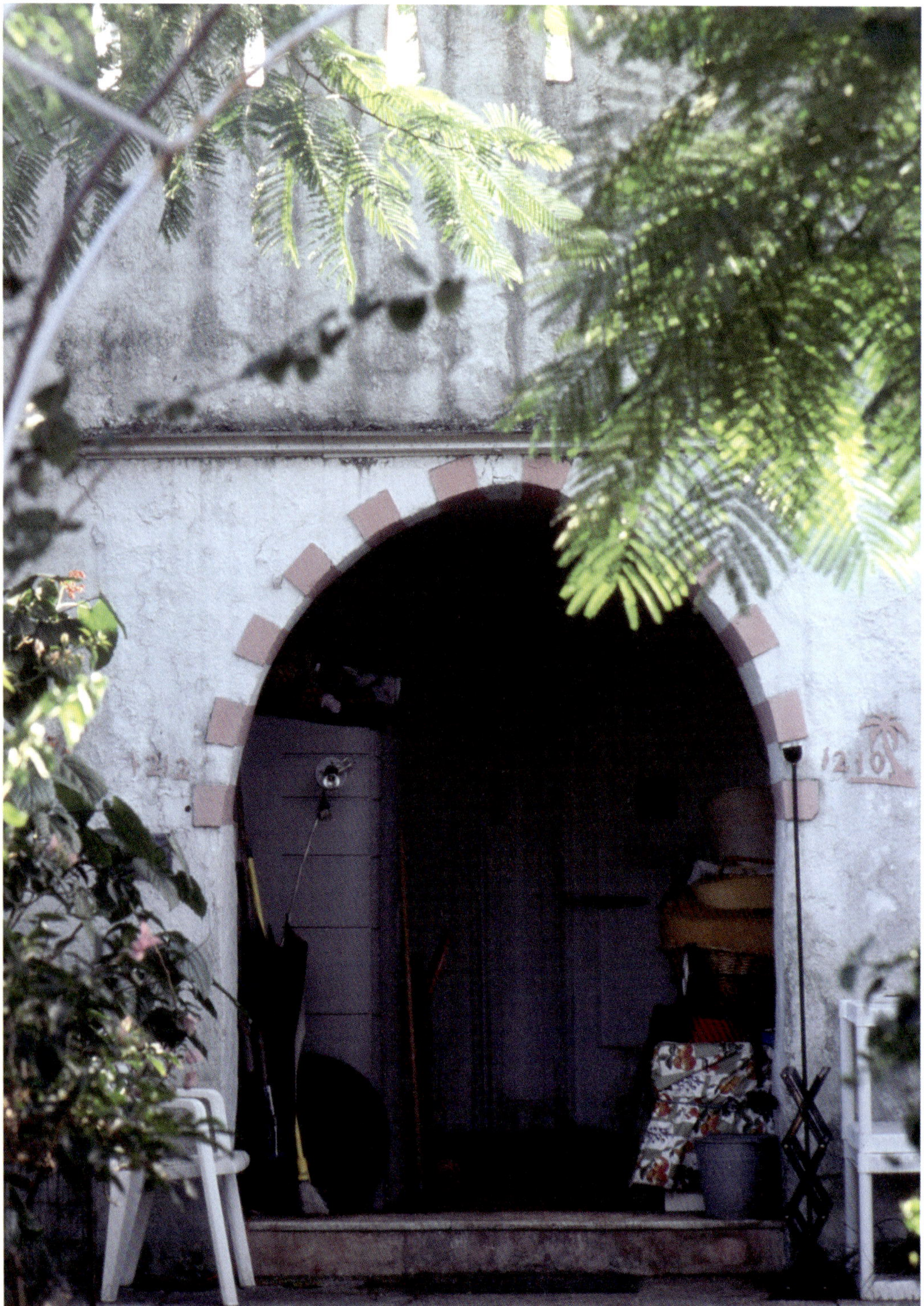

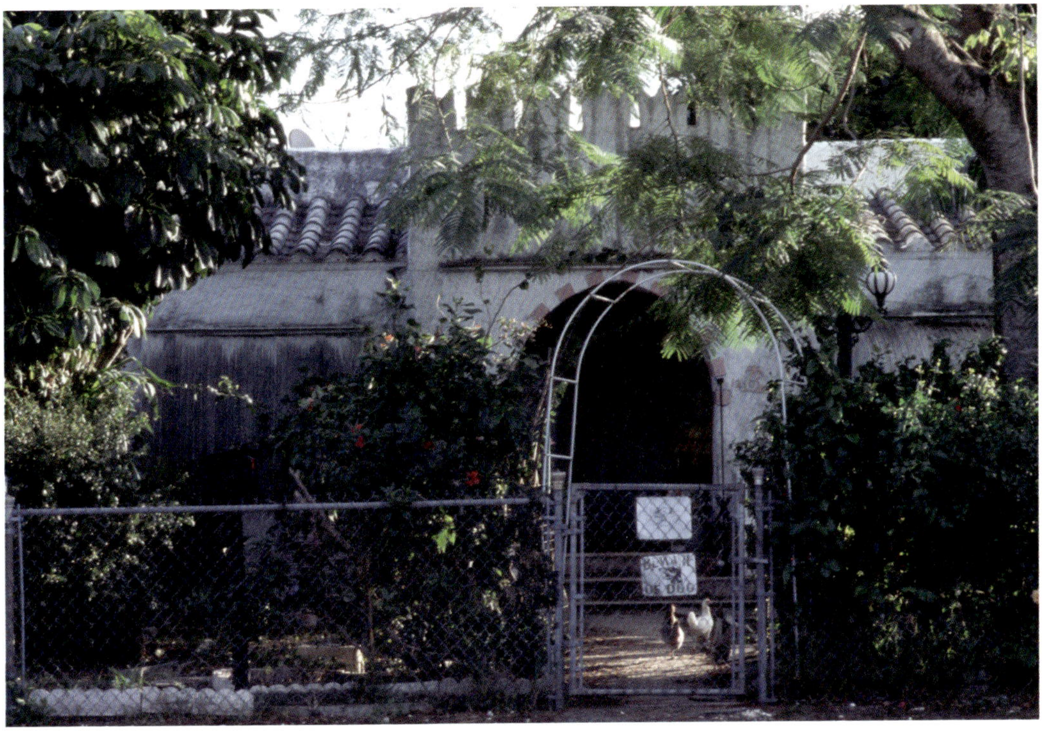

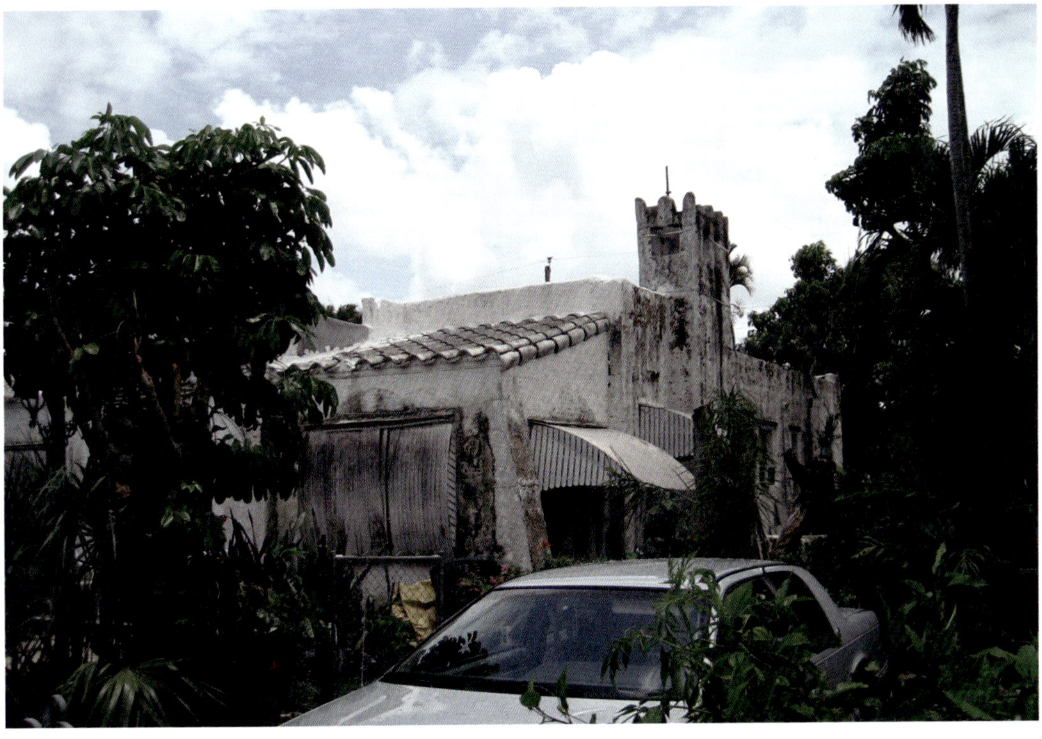

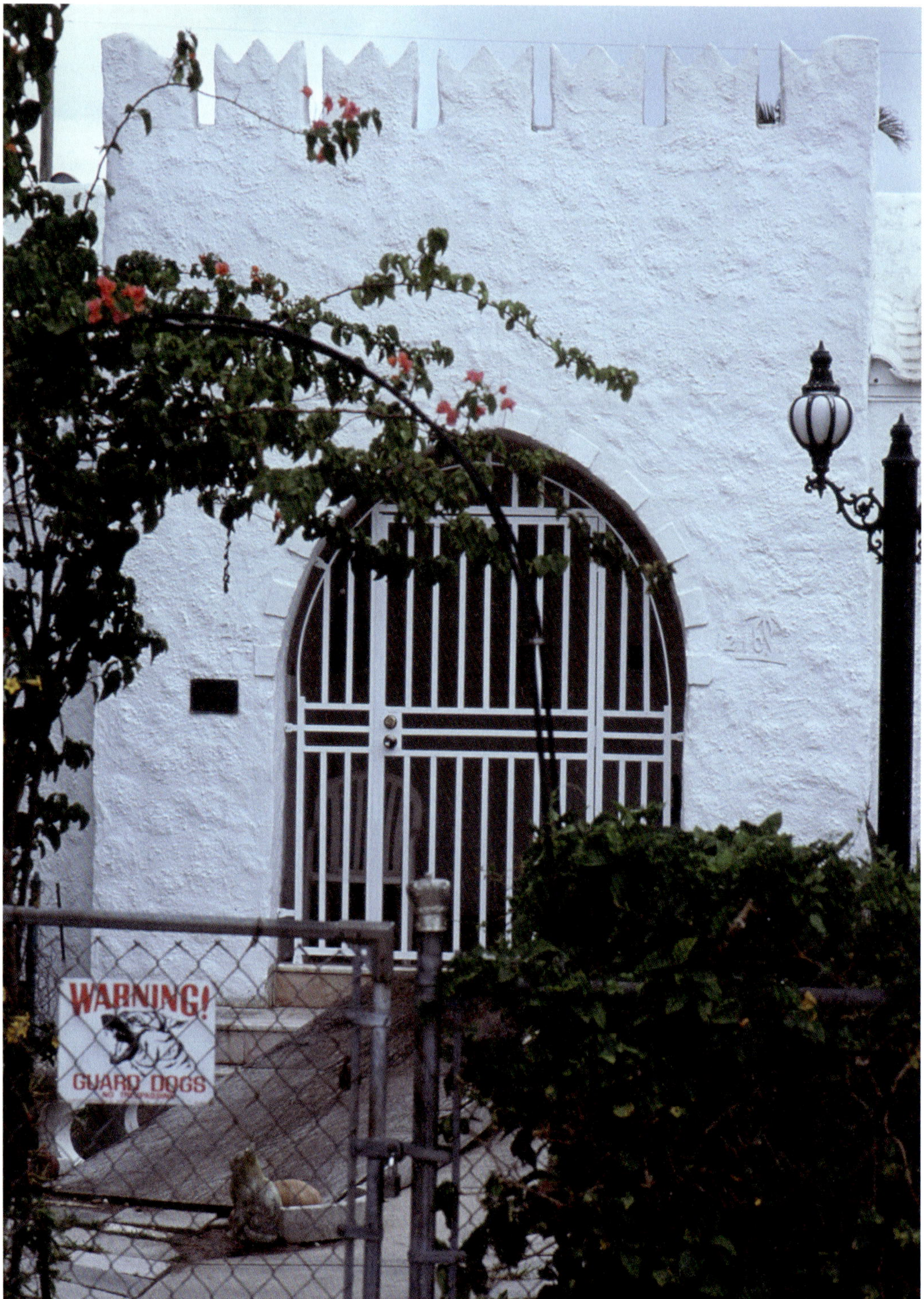
WARNING!
GUARD DOGS

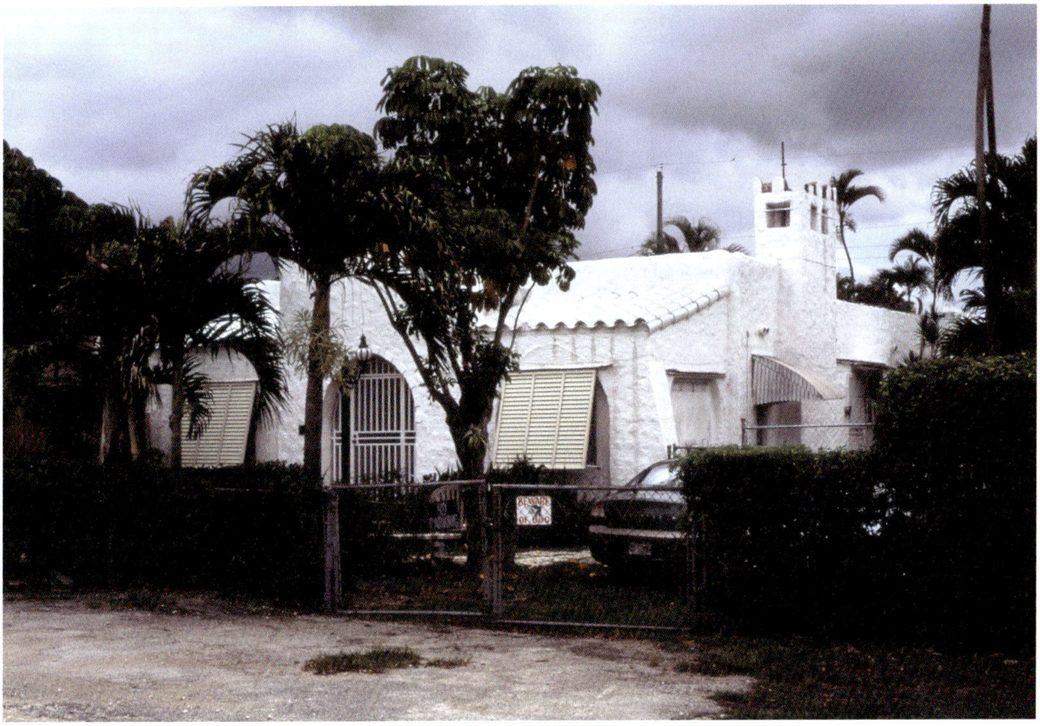

1214–1216 SESAME STREET *TABER DUPLEX*

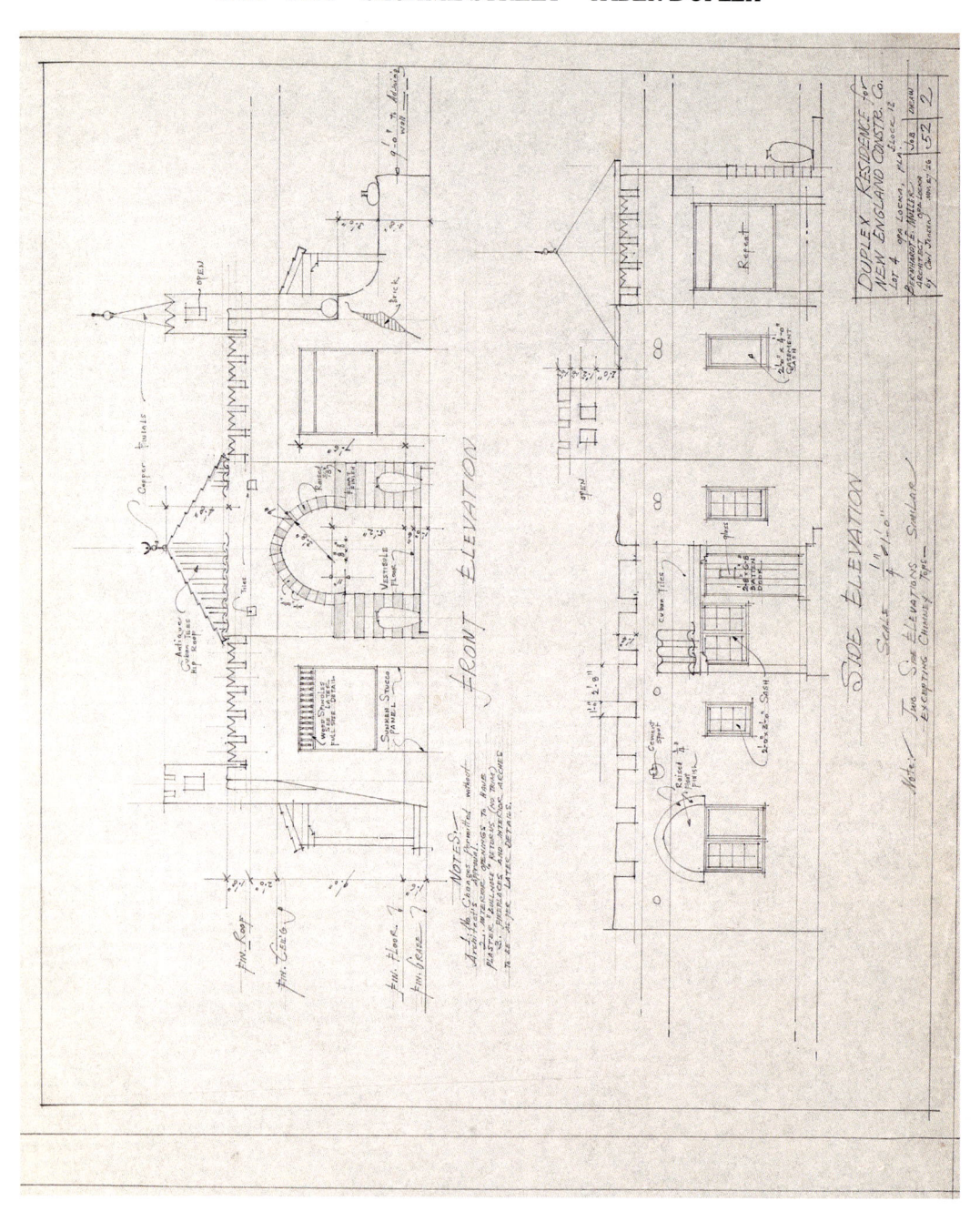

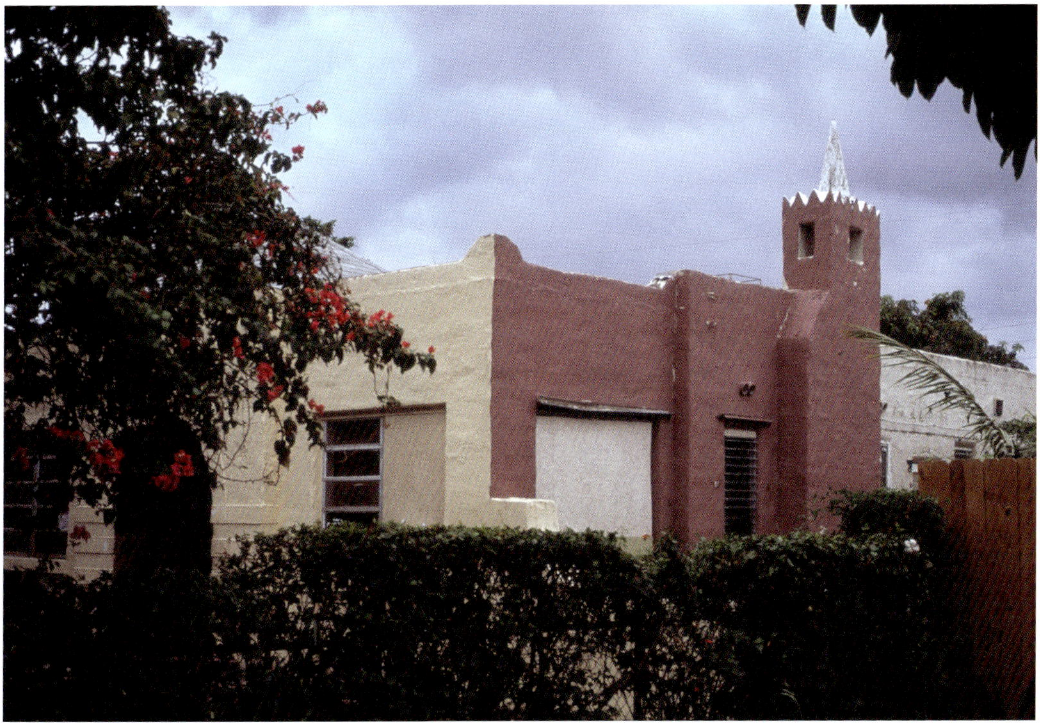

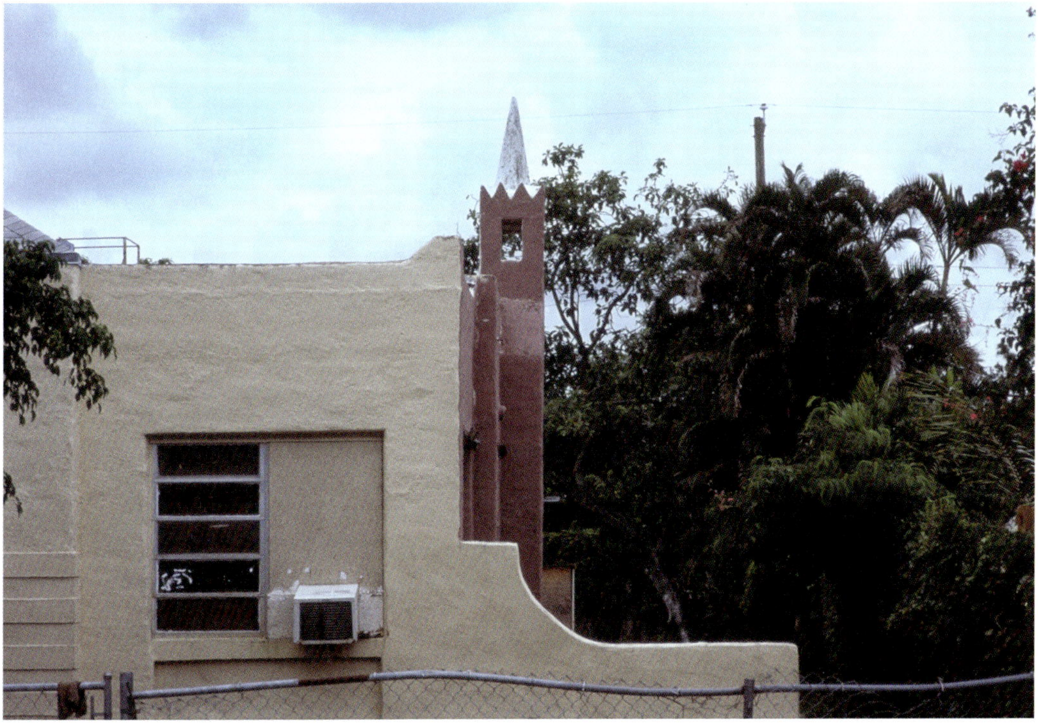

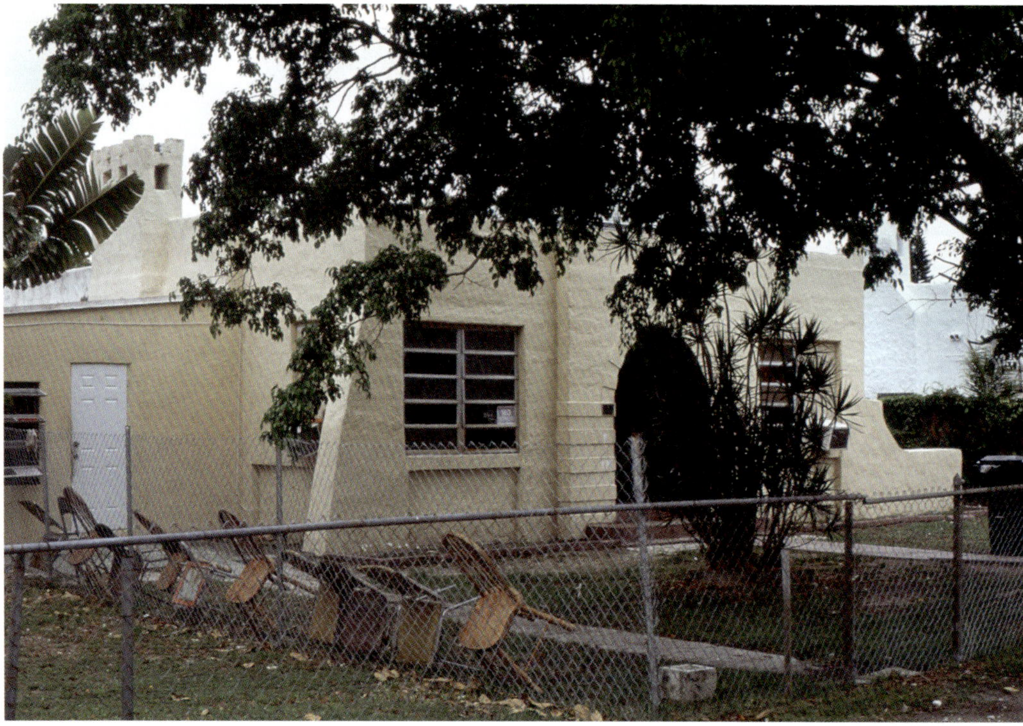

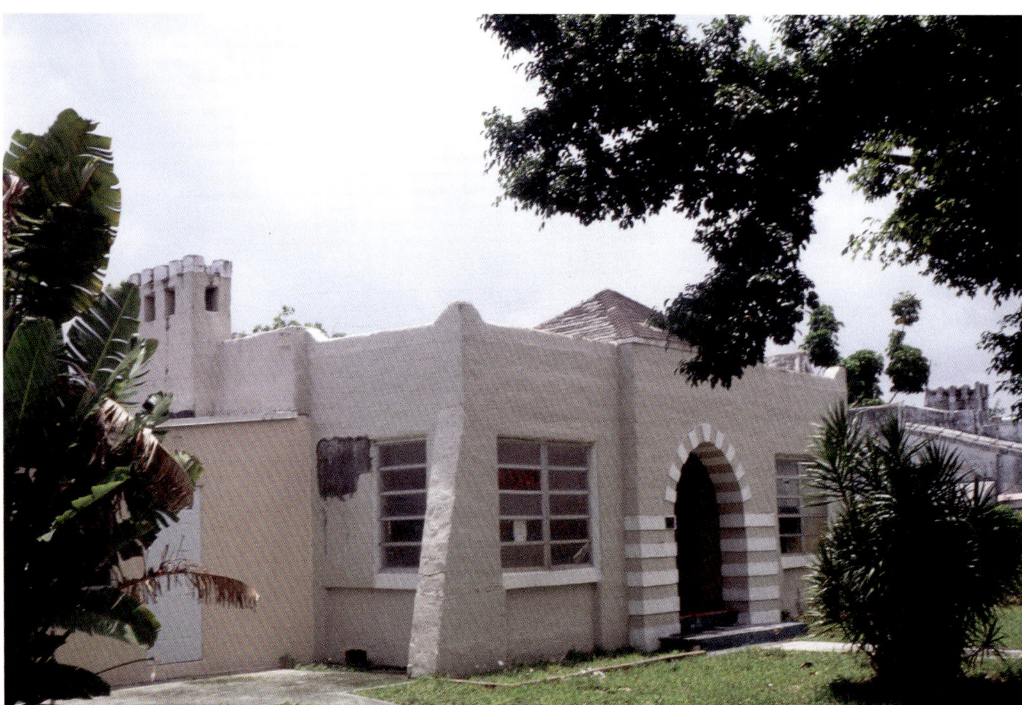

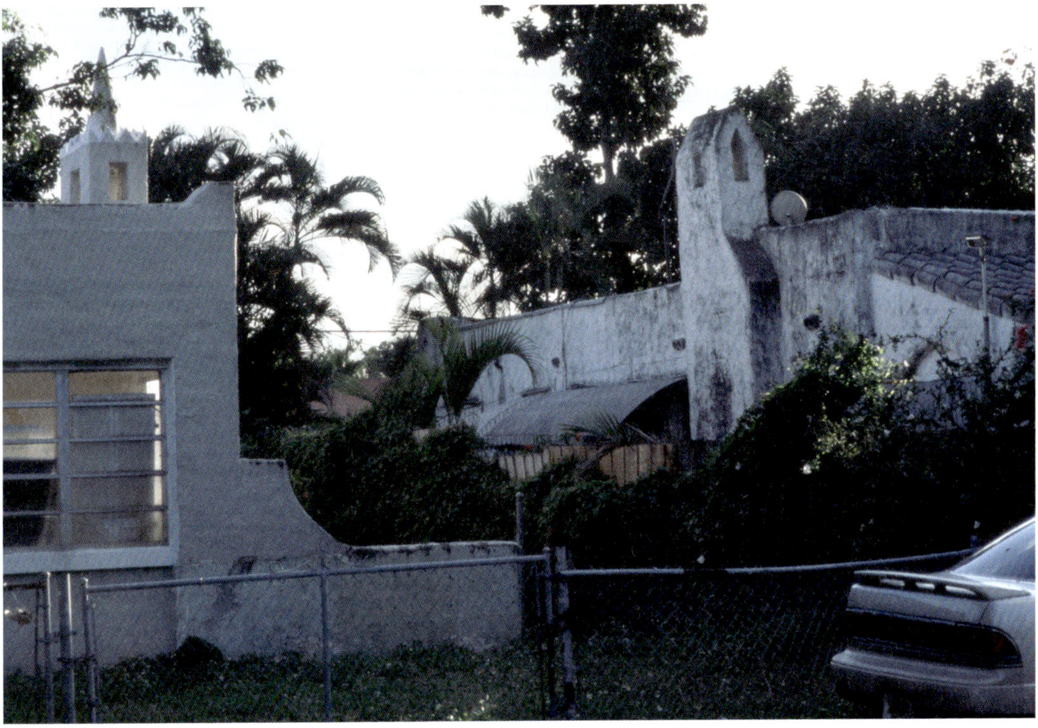

1240 SESAME STREET *BUSH APARTMENTS*

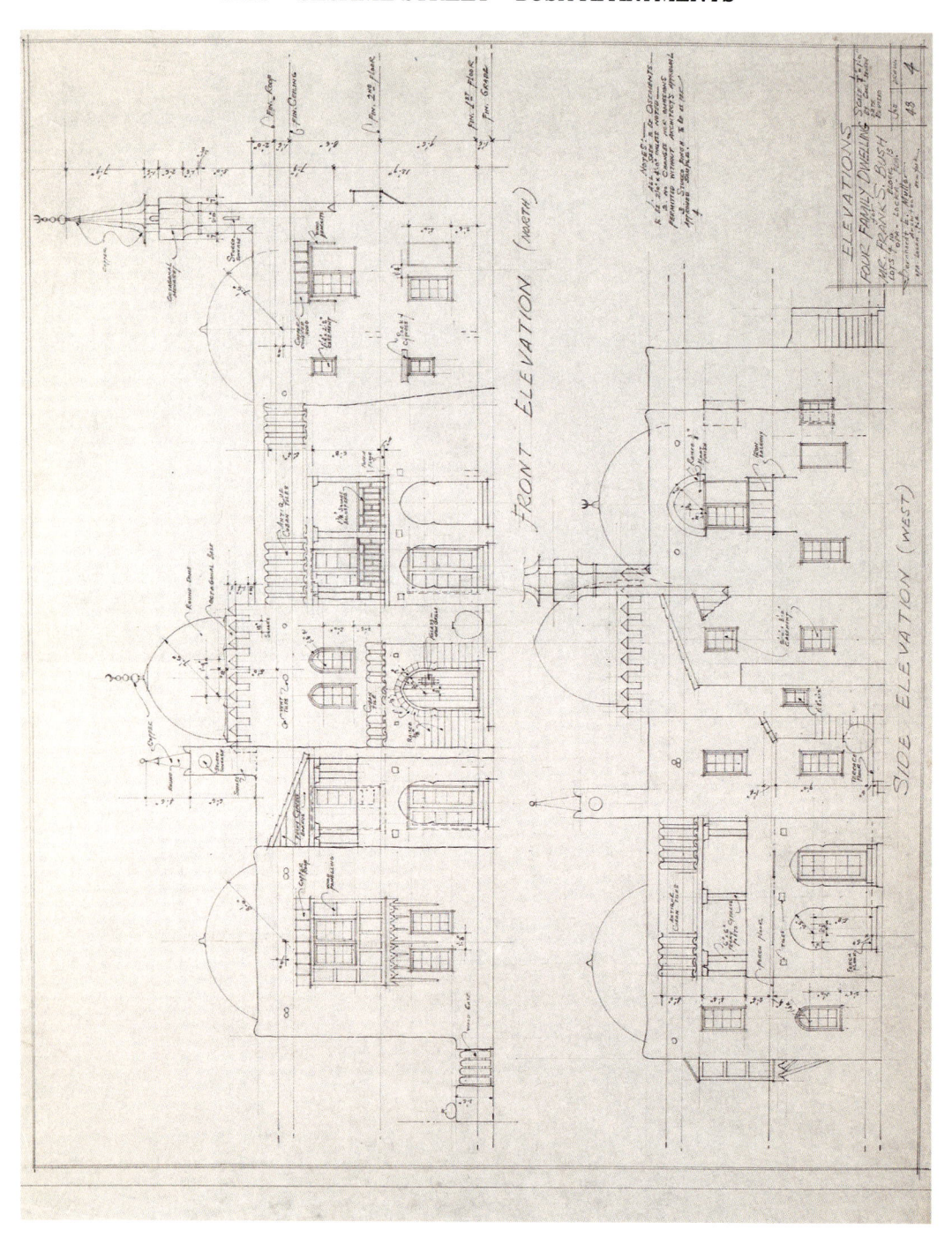

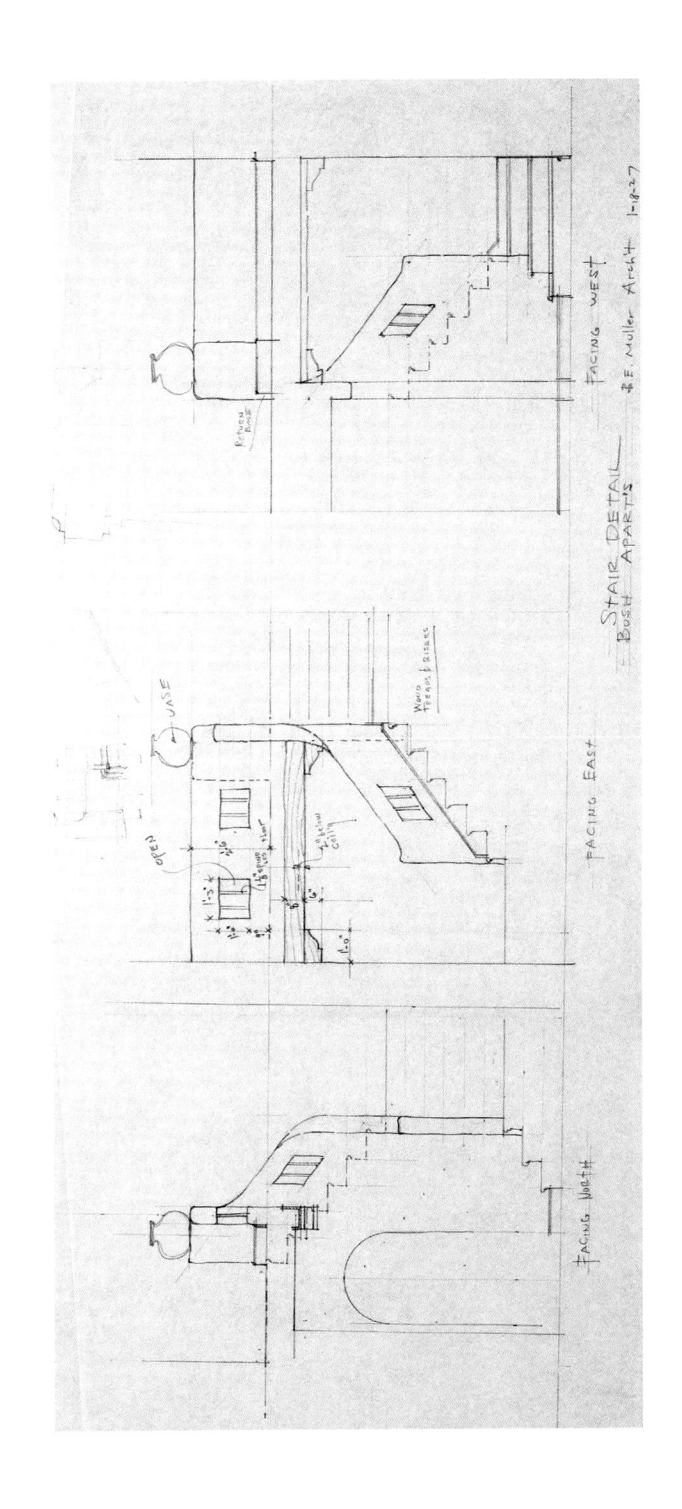

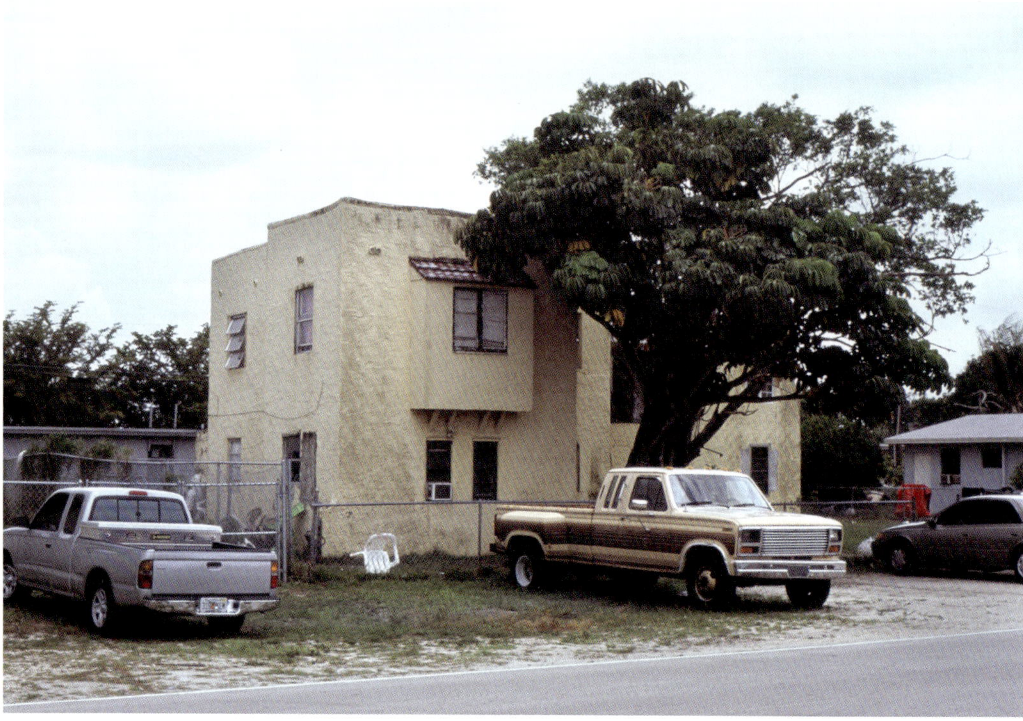

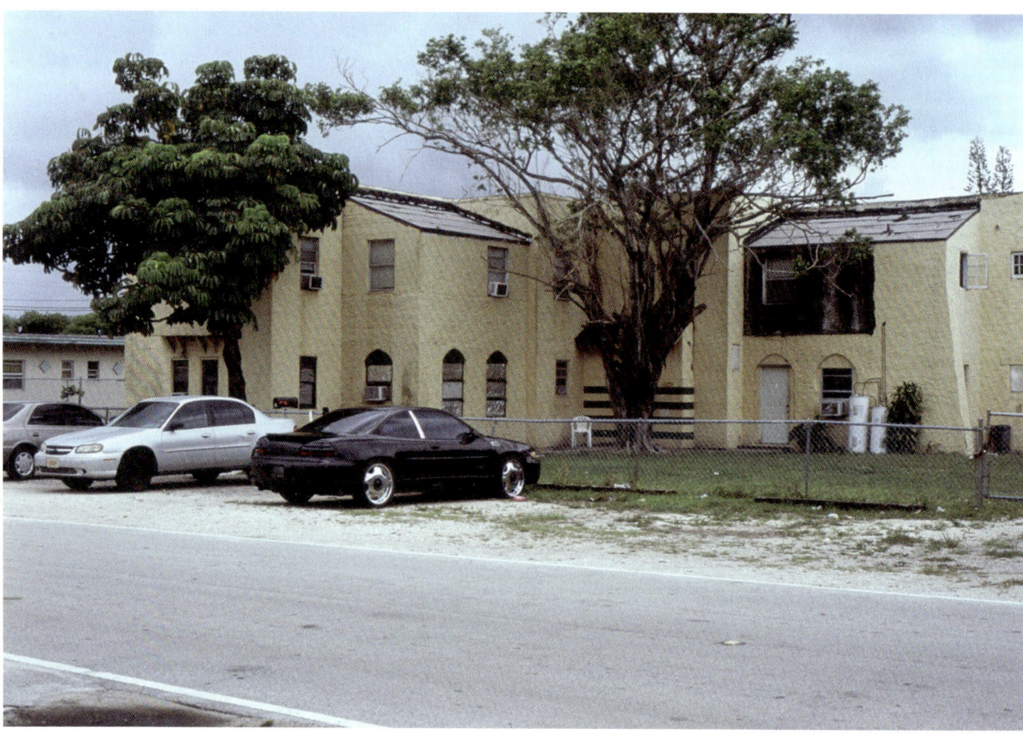

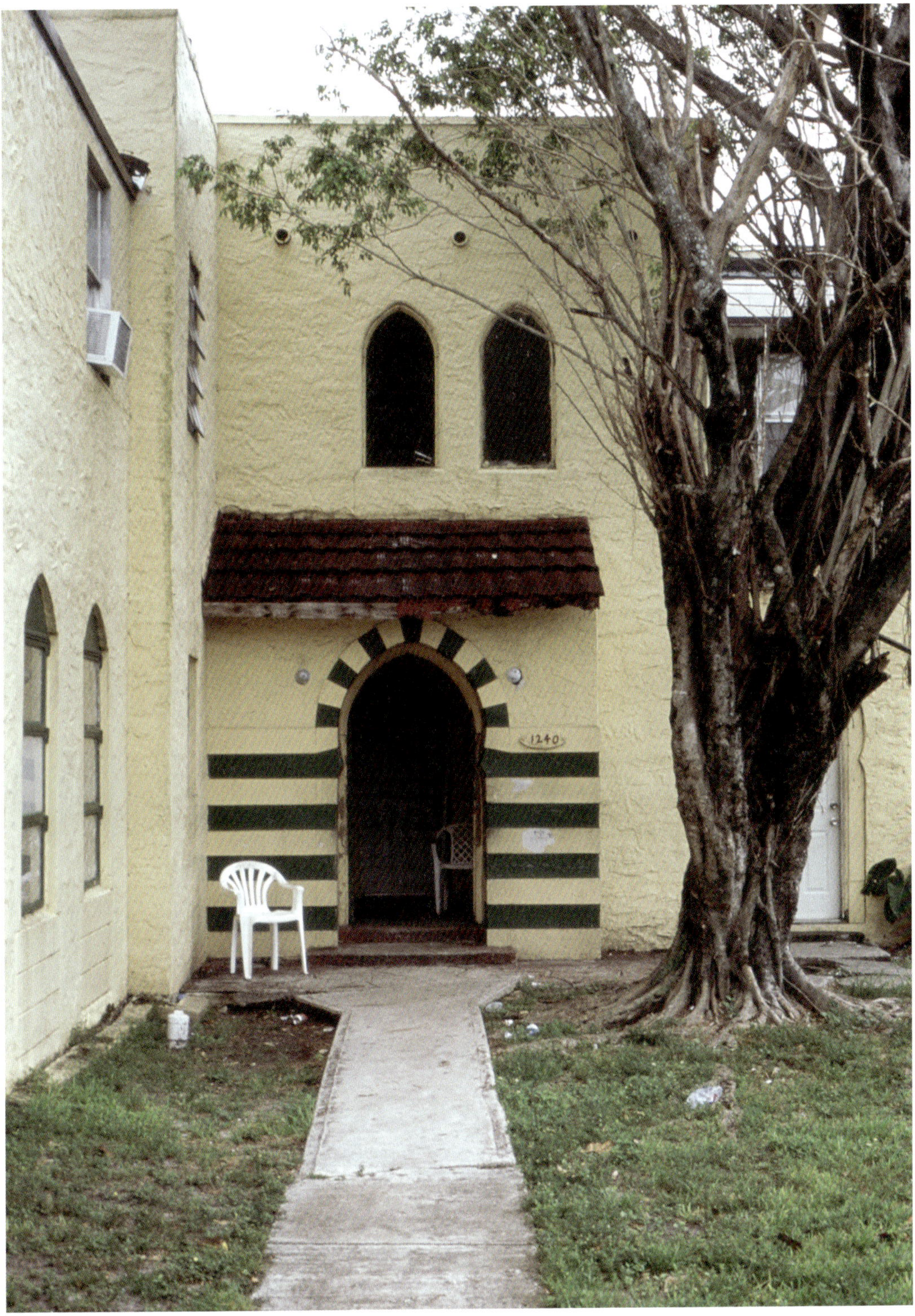
1240

916 JANN AVENUE *ETHEREDGE HOUSE*

1141 JANN AVENUE *HAISLIP HOUSE*

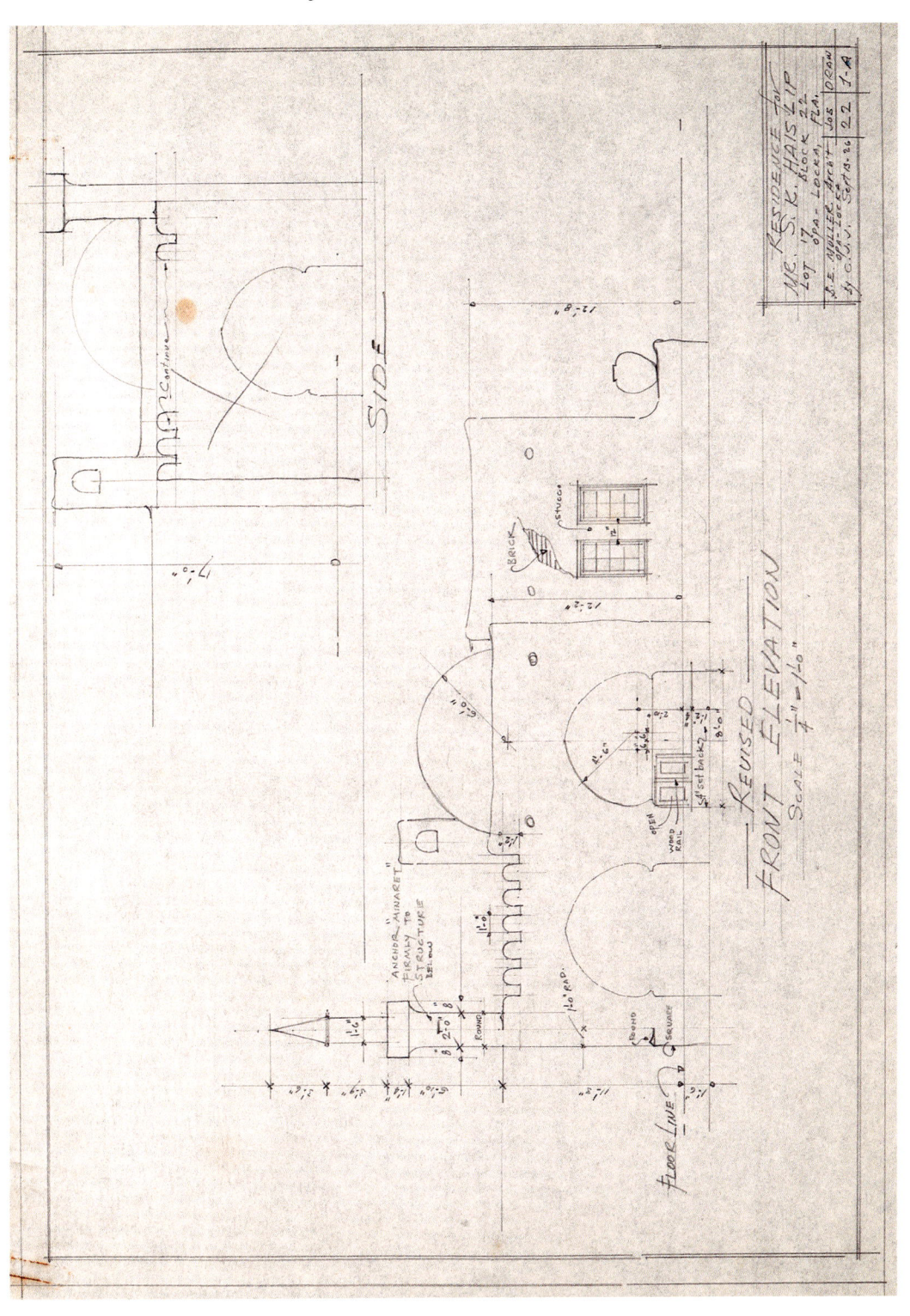

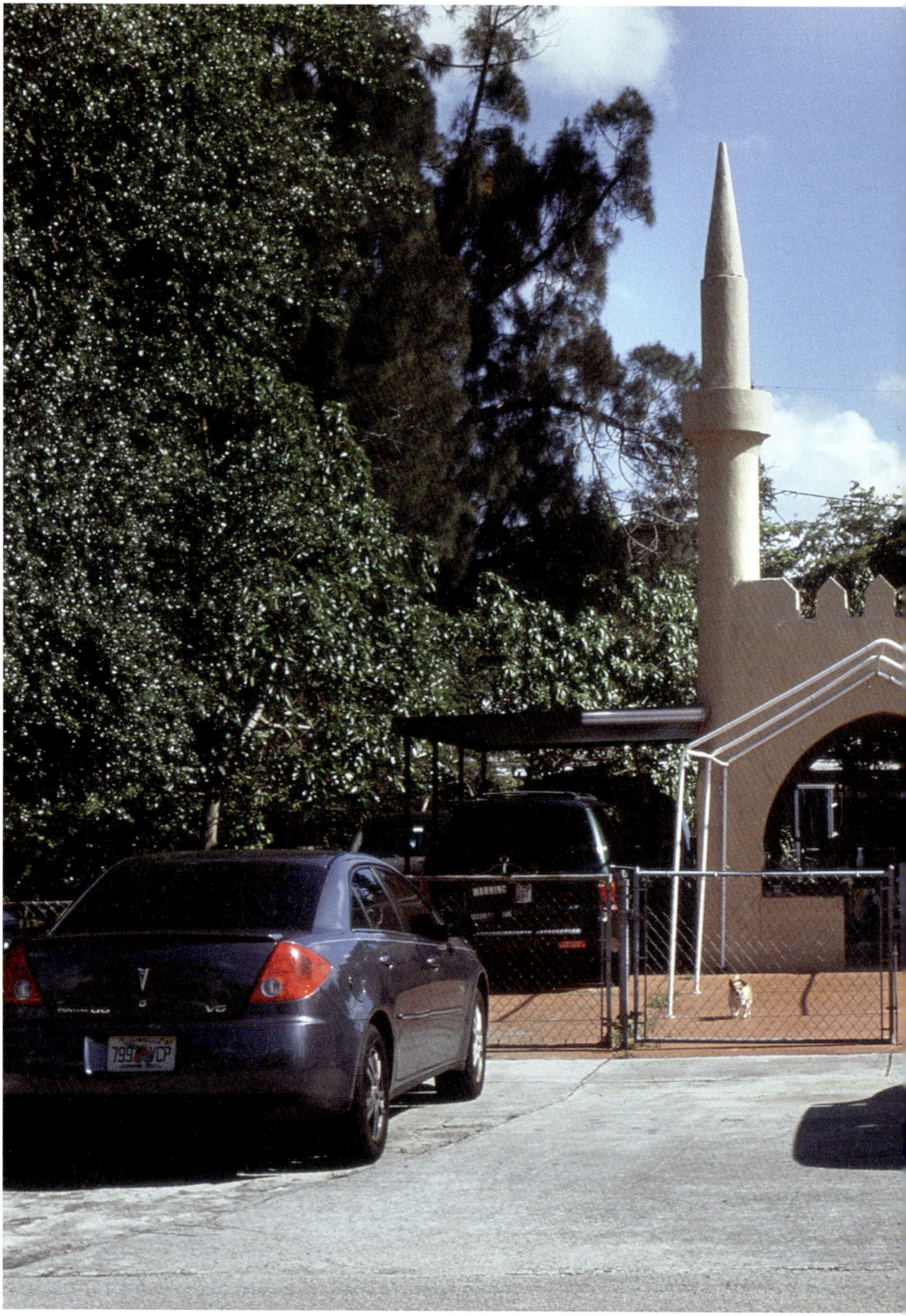

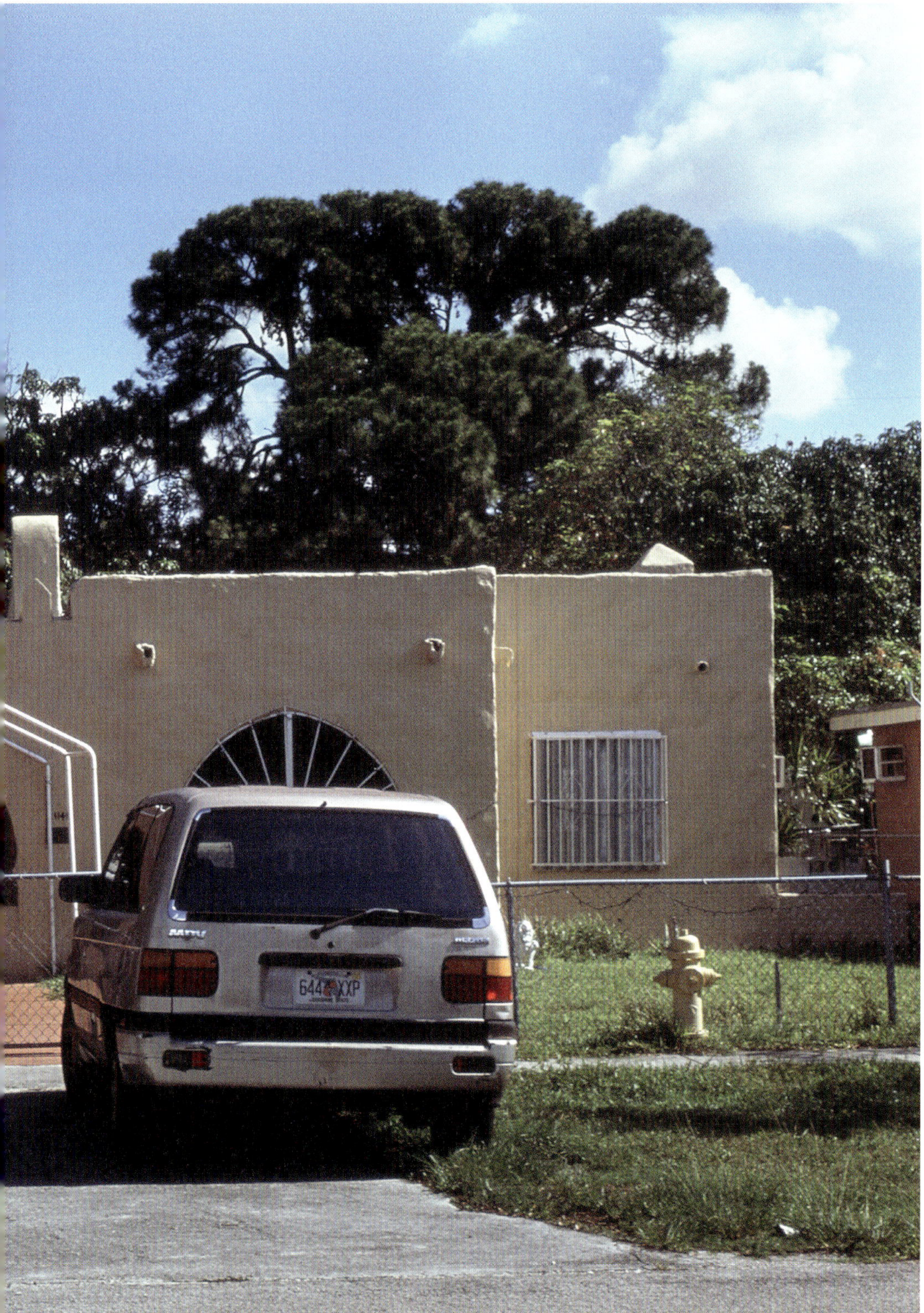

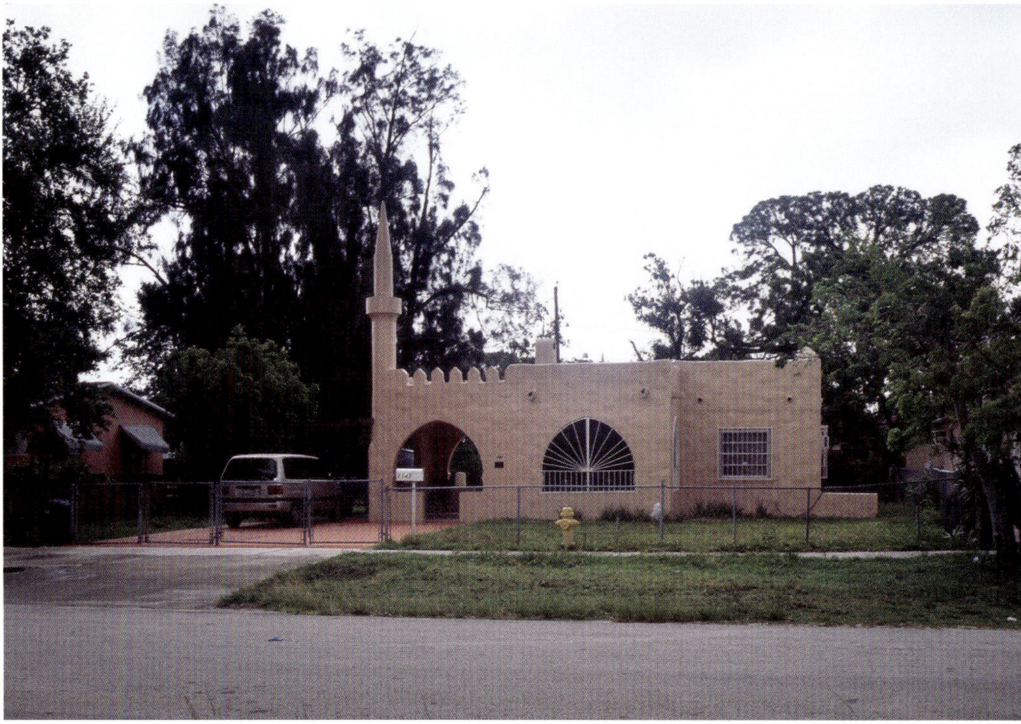

ANTHOLOGY

From autumn 1849 till 1852 Flaubert traveled to the Orient with his friend Maxime du Camp. The journey starts in Egypt where they stay till the summer of 1850 detailing his travel notes and letters, which would later be edited by Francis Steegmuller and published by Academy Chicago Publishers, USA, 1979. The following text is an excerpt from his journey followed by a text he wrote four years earlier, out of his romantic fantasy.

FROM FLAUBERT'S TRAVEL NOTES

Sunday, 24 March 1850. Palm Sunday. [Second excursion to Gebel Abusir.] Left at six in the morning in our dinghy for the Cataract, with Raïs Hasan and three other Nubians from the First Cataract. I had with me a little raïs of about fourteen, Mohammed; he is yellow-skinned, a silver earring in his left ear. He rowed strongly and gracefully, shouted, and as we rode the currents he led everybody singing; his arms were charmingly modeled, with firm young biceps. He had slipped his left arm out of its sleeve, so that on his entire right side he was as though draped, with his left side and part of his belly uncovered. Slender waist. Folds on his belly that rose and fell as he leaned forward on his oar. His voice was vibrant as he sang: "*El naby, el naby*" ["The Prophet, the Prophet"]. He was a child of the water, of the tropical sun, of the free life, full of distinction and nobility. And full of childish courtesy—gave me dates and lifted the end of my blanket that was trailing in the water.

Several vultures were perched on the rocks; and washed up at the foot of one rock was an old crocodile. That evening we saw the same vultures again, and nearby a jackal, which ran off as we approached.

I reach the foot of Gebel Abusir at nine, and fire a few rifle shots to call Maxime. From the distance of black rock, shining in the sun, gives the effect of a Nubian in a white shirt on lookout, or of a white cloth hung out to dry. How can something black come to look white in this way? It happens when the sun strikes the edge of an angle. I have frequently observed the same effect, and Gibert tells me that he too has noticed it, in Rome.

I lunch under the tent, in full sun. I had stretched out on the ground in search of a little shade, but the shade wasn't long in disappearing.

Walk around the two adjacent rocky hills. The tent was in front of them, before the Cataract (that is to say, *beside* the Cataract). As we rounded the first hill, we came to a great rolling stretch of sand on the desert side. From here (with one's back to the desert, of course) one sees the Cataract in the distance. From the top of the second hill you see the desert—first rolling, then stretching away in great flat lines. I return to the tent alone, via the desert and behind the hills. Silence. Silence. Silence. The sunlight beats down—it is of a black transparency. I walk over small stones, my head bent, the sun searing my skull.

Return to Wadi Halfa in the dinghy, with Maxime. Little Mohammed is as he was this morning. We are rocked by the wind and the waves; night falls; the waves slap the bow of our dinghy, and it pitches, the moon rises. In the position in which I was sitting, it was shining on my right leg and the portion of my white sock that was between my trouser and my shoe.

Francis Steegmüller, ed., *Flaubert in Egypt* (New York: Penguin Books, 1979), 133–135.

IV   THE PYRAMIDS AND SAKKARA

It has sometimes been suggested by scholars that the very act of keeping a travel diary played a rôle in carrying the Romantic Flaubert towards Realism. Before accompanying him on the expedition to the Pyramids, readers might enjoy seeing how, as a young Romantic, he had written about the view from the top of the Great Pyramid only four years before, out of his imagination and his reading. So far as I know, this passage has never before been put into English: it is fairly typical of Flaubert's writings on the 'Orient' before his journey:

"When the traveler has reached the top of the Pyramid, his hands are torn and his knees are bleeding; he is surrounded by the desert and devoured by the light, and the harsh air burns his lungs; utterly exhausted, and

dazzled by the brilliance, he sinks down half dead on the stone, amidst the carcasses of birds come there to die. But lift your head! Look! Look! And you will see cities with domes of gold and minarets of porcelain, palaces of lava built on plinths of alabaster, marble-rimmed pools where sultanas come to bathe their bodies at the hour when the moon makes bluer the shadow of the groves and more limpid the silvery water of the fountains. Open your eyes! Open your eyes! Those arid mountains hide green valleys in their flanks, there are love songs in those bamboo huts, and in those old tombs sleep the still-crowned kings of olden times. You can hear the eagle scream in the clouds; far off ring monastery bells; see the caravans setting out, the shells floating downriver; the forests grow vaster, the sea wider, the horizon more distant, touching the sky and becoming one with it. Look! Lend an ear, listen and look, O traveler! O thinker! And your thirst will be appeased, and all your life will have passed like a dream, for you will feel your soul go out toward the light and soar in the infinite." (From the first Education Sentimentale.)

Francis Steegmüller, ed., *Flaubert in Egypt* (New York: Penguin Books, 1979), 48–49.

Architectural historian and professor Catherine Lynn's article Dream and Substance: Araby and the Planning of Opa-Locka originally appears in *The Journal of Decorative and Propaganda Arts, Florida Theme Issue*, volume #23 published by The Wolfsonian–Florida International University and The Wolfson Foundation of Decorative and Propaganda Arts in 1998. An essential text on Opa-locka, which provides a detailed scholarly account of its origin and influence.

DREAM AND SUBSTANCE: ARABY AND THE PLANNING OF OPA-LOCKA

By Catherine Lynn

Opa-locka is a small city that attracts few of the tourists who speed past it on Interstate 95 just north of Miami. The signs point the way clearly enough to its center, inland a little west of the highway, where City Hall on Sharazad Boulevard is a fantastic concoction of a building that might have appeared on the pages of an *Arabian Nights* storybook. Part palace, part mosque, City Hall alone is well worth the visit. Its domes and towers terminate the busiest street in town, but business on Opa-locka Boulevard, even at the biggest store—the grocery—appears pretty slow, especially compared to the activity at South Florida's malls and beaches. Most people on the streets of Opa-locka are African American, as is their mayor.

The citizens are justly proud of their bizarre City Hall and of about one hundred other exotic structures build to fulfill a developer's dream of Araby: The most impressive and curious buildings went up in a few months, beginning in 1925 amid frenzied boosterism for this planned new town. Then the hurricane of 17 September 1926 struck. It was but the first of a series of misfortunes that were to distort the original plans for Opa-locka. Despite it all, domed, crenelated, and turreted houses of the 1920s are surprisingly numerous, and the layout and the names of the streets themselves recall Opa-locka's never-quite-realized glories. Still, only dedicated architecture buffs count the town among South Florida's tourist meccas.

From *The Arabian Nights Entertainments; or the book of the thousand nights and a night*,[1] Opa-locka's developer, the pioneer aviator Glenn Curtiss (1878–1930), plucked the theme for his real estate venture. For those who have read even the introductory chapters of that classic work of literature in its fullest and most authentic translations, a visit to Opa-locka can set off a string of meditations on irony, for the power of African Americans at city hall and their ownership of the little domed houses where tiny minarets hoist crescent moons above the telephone wires are unlikely elements in an epilogue to *The Arabian Nights*.

In the uncensored translations of "the great Arabic compendium of romantic fiction,"[2] fear of black power—especially of the sexual potency of male African slaves and its allure for the cloistered princesses of Araby—dominates much of the text's opening pages. That fear underlies the framing tale that ties together all the thousand and one, and figures repeatedly in those wondrous stories Sharazad began night after night, talking for her very life. Linking all the others, hers is the familiar story of how, through a thousand nights, she intrigued the misogynous King Shahryar, who had been so enraged by the multiple adulteries of his first wife with African slaves that for three years he had put to death each day his bride of the previous night. Every night Sharazad captivated him with a new tale, leaving it unfinished at dawn so that he would spare her to continue the following night. In Opa-locka, a thing unthinkable to King Shahryar has come to pass: the blacks have taken over the world of Araby—or at least this fanciful image of it. It would surprise Opa-locka's early residents as well. On 15 December 1926, special census takers reported a population of 251, but they failed to count twenty-nine black residents.[3] Few then could have foreseen an economically depressed Opa-locka enmeshed in the urban sprawl of Fort Lauderdale-Miami with a population that has held steady at just above 18,000 for the past decade.

Who first had the vision of a new town in Florida where every building would call up a particular scene from The Arabian Nights is a question that is itself enmeshed in a web of fanciful tales, varied by their tellers to suit the occasion. In publicity pieces of the 1920s the story goes this way: Soon after the New York architect Bernhardt Emil Muller (1878–1964) was hired to work on the project, he happened to read a new edition of the tales. That night, he literally dreamed up the scheme and early the next morning wired his client, Glenn Curtiss, proposing it. Curtiss promptly brought Muller to Florida, where the designer painted an enthralling word-picture of his dream of Araby on the verge of the Everglades:

I described to him how we would lay the city out on the basis of the stories, using a story for each of the most important buildings, naming the streets accordingly. In each building we would tell the story by means of mural decorations and wrought iron work carrying out the various features of the story. The style of the architecture would be governed by the country in which the story was supposed to have taken place. Mr. Curtiss was fascinated with my ideas and I made plans to actually create the phantom city of my mind.[4]

But there is another persistent account that credits the whole idea to Curtiss himself. In this version it was Curtiss who read a new edition of the tales, was inspired, and directed his architect to adopt the theme for Opa-locka. This story became part of the Curtiss biography retold in Miami newspapers on anniversaries of his daring flight of 1910 from Albany to New York City.[5]

Glenn Curtiss came to the Opa-locka project with previous experience in developing two other Miami suburbs. His first venture, launched early in the 1920s with a partner, James Bright, had been the city of Hialeah. There, unanticipated growth during the building boom had yielded chaotic sprawl, a disappointment to Curtiss. In their next venture, Country Club Estates, now Miami Springs, begun in 1924, Curtiss-Bright had tried to improve on that experience with careful initial planning that incorporated more rigid zoning controls and an architectural theme, the Spanish pueblo. A year later, Curtiss formed the Opa-locka Company to develop a whole new town bearing a name that was his shortened version of the Seminole name of the place, Opatishawockalocka [hammock].[6] He was clearly in the market for an inspiring theme. But it is equally clear that he was not bothered by questions of logical consistency between the place name and the theme itself.

And there is yet a third account of how Curtiss came up with his theme. In 1976 Frank S. FitzGerald-Bush, author of the only history of Opa-locka, credited his mother with giving Curtiss the Arabian Nights idea. Mrs. Bush was the wife of one of Opa-locka's first homebuilders, the electrical contractor for its development company. When Curtiss showed Mrs. Bush the town site with its unspoiled native hammock and talked of plans for building there she is supposed to have exclaimed: "Oh Glenn, it's like a dream for the Arabian Nights!"[7] FitzGerald-Bush also wrote that an English Tudor scheme had been Muller's first proposal for the new town in Florida, a proposal Curtiss dismissed in favor of the idea that Mrs. Bush inspired.

It seems most likely that the choice of the Arabian Nights theme for Opa-locka was in fact made in more mundane circumstances, in meetings and discussions among developers, architects, and planners who were competing with others of their kind during Florida's real estate boom. Curtiss seems to have known the work of his competition well and to have borrowed freely from it. Among the borrowings was the practice, already well established, of basing the architecture of a Florida real estate development on a theme. The advantages soon became obvious to everyone involved. Themes served to distinguish one flat tract of newly drained land from another. They were useful to writers of advertising copy: Festivals and other events could be keyed to them, attracting people—and free press coverage—to a site. But even more important, themes imposed architectural coherence when different designers and contractors were putting up large numbers of buildings all at once.

The dominant theme of the 1920s was Mediterranean, grandly exploited by the architect Addison Mizner (1872–1933) for Palm Beach and adapted by the developer George Merrick (1886–1942) for Coral Gables. Coral Gables had been under construction for four years when Curtiss, Muller and the town planner Clinton Mackenzie (1872–1940)—another New Yorker—began work on Opa-locka in the fall of 1925, and Coral Gables was clearly their most important model. In Merrick's work Curtiss found the seeds of ideas with which he was to experiment at Opa-locka: a theme linked to a specific work of literature with its own special architectural character, combined with careful town planning and elaborate landscaping.

The vernacular and classical traditions of southern Europe dominated the architecture of Coral Gables, but George Merrick also permitted a few more exotic details among the buildings he called Mediterranean. Under this rubric there was of course a perfectly logical basis for permitting Arabic architectural variations: they were appropriate to the Mediterranean Sea's African and Near Eastern shores, and to Spain. But Merrick chose to identify his exotic Eastern motifs exclusively with their Moorish incarnations in Spain itself, and quite emphatically with a particular literary work that enjoyed great popularity during the nineteenth and early twentieth centuries. This was Washington Irving's *Legends of the Alhambra*, first published in 1832. The numerous illustrations in its various editions inspired Moorish architectural embellishment such as crenellation, pointed arches, battered Egyptoid entrance pieces, and crescent motifs on little streets in Coral Gables like Obispo Avenue. Irving's work also furnished the names for the town's major thoroughfares—Alhambra and Granada—and for many of the smaller streets.

Like Irving's volumes, tales derived from *The Arabian Nights* enjoyed great popularity during the early twentieth century. That popularity was enhanced by musical works and ballets based on the tales, and it was extraordinarily broadened by the early movies they inspired. In hitting upon this particular motif, one so much more specific and fantastic than merely Mediterranean, Curtiss took the technique of theming much further than his real estate competitors yet had done. Indeed, he pre-Disneyed Disney by more than a quarter century. In building Arabian architectural forms he also placed himself squarely in the tradition of the nineteenth century's greatest showman and self-advertiser, P.T. Barnum. In 1848 Barnum moved into Iranistan, a minareted pleasure dome he built as his home in Bridgeport, Connecticut. It quickly became a wonder of New England, though a short-lived one, for it burned to the ground in 1857. Like Barnum, Curtiss needed publicity to sell his product, and he gave his own publicists good material to work with in *The Arabian Nights*. He also attracted free editorial coverage by turning out buildings that photographed sensationally, looked spectacularly unlike the competition, and came with ready-made stories that everybody loved.

Curtiss was drawing on tales with origins that have been traced to seventh-century Persia. Around the year 800, in Baghdad, on the court of haroun er Reshid, "Aaron the Orthodox" (786–809), the seamless whole of stories within stories that was to become *The Arabian Nights* probably began to coalesce. By the thirteenth century, with additions from Egypt, India, and Arabia, it was assuming the form that was to take an important place in world literature. The tale used to link all the others was by now Sharazad's.

By the seventeenth century a great compilation of the tales, including 264 romances, anecdotes, supernatural fictions, historical fictions, poems, inventions, fables—every kind of story gathered from the far ends of the Mohammedan empires—had taken its classic shape. Fragments of the work first reached Europe in French translations by Antoine Galland, published between 1704 and 1717. Between 1839 and 1841, E.W. Lane produced a multivolume edition of English translations "for the drawing-room table" expurgated of the eroticism that he thought too lurid for English readers. Not until 1881, when John Payne published his English translations in nine volumes from the Arabic, Persian, and Indian sources, was there any comprehensive edition of the work in a European language. In 1885 his friend Sir Richard Burton brought out another version in seventeen volumes that relied precisely on Payne's work, but added copious notes on Arab customs, especially the erotic.[8]

Victorian intellectuals deciphered the full texts replete with their dream-like, sometimes nightmarish, sequences of fantastic events; their representations of human sensuality, treachery, and violent dismemberments; their portrayals of greed, adultery, jealousy, trickery, and clever dodges of all kinds. In recurring accounts of the passion of faithless wives for black lovers, a modern reader

153

may sense thinly veiled explorations of obsessions and fears born of sexual and racial slavery. But such deep, dark, erotic, and exotic preoccupations were in large part left to scholarly contemplation when the great work was mined for wondrous fairy stories to be consumed by Anglo-American families.

Lady Burton's Edition of her Husband's Arabian Nights…prepared for Household Reading, which appeared in 1886, was but one among dozens of retellings of selected favorites in terms deemed appropriate for innocent Western sensibilities. In America as in Europe, Arabian tales were "arranged for familly reading," to quote from the title page of a Philadelphia edition of 1860. Harriet Beecher Stowe (1811–1896), who was much concerned with the propriety of wholesome literature for the Christian home, included selections from the tales among "nine standard masterpieces" when she edited *A Library of Famous Fiction*, published in 1873. Carrying this nineteenth-century tradition well past World War I, publishers filled American homes with nursery tale versions of "Aladdin and his Magical Lamp" and "Ali Baba and the Fourty Thieves." Any child who had not read the tales at home was sure to encounter them at school, in the primers where they had become standard fare.

Frank Lloyd Wright's (1867–1956) six children had an image of what he called the "allegory" of "The Fisherman and the Genii from the Arabian Nights" as a mural over the fireplace in the playroom he added to his home in Oak Park, Illinois, during the 1890s.[9] The great architect mentioned the painting only cursorily in his autobiography, commenting that a "lesson was to be drawn from the subject matter by the children. I forgot what it was. Perhaps never be too sentimental, or curious, or meddlesome, or there would be consequences."[10] No wonder Wright had lost track of the point, so convoluted is the fisherman's tale, or rather the series of tales that begins with a fisherman netting a brazen vessel with a leaden seal that, when removed, releases a genie or Afrit who promptly vows to kill the fisherman. Their duel of wit and power takes the form of swapping stories about kindness repaid by treachery—or alternatively by great reward—and in the end leaves the fisherman the richest man of his day—a status to which he had been led by the genie. In the surviving Oak Park mural the fisherman is realistically rendered sitting to one side of the great half-round scene dominated by the central figure of the enormous, abstractly rendered figure of "the Genii… done in straight line pattern," as Wright described it.

During these years, while school children and their parents everywhere where reading the tales, *The Arabian Nights* was also inspiring major works of performance art elaborately produced in the cultural capitals of Europe and the United States. Nikolai Rimsky-Korsakov based his symphonic suite, *Scheherazade*, on the theme and in 1910 his music inspired Sergei Diaghilev, the great Russian shaper of the modern ballet, to mount his production of the same name.

But without doubt it was the movies that tales from *The Arabian Nights* made their most vivid impression on the generation to whom Curtiss hoped to sell lots in Opa-locka. The magical new medium itself seemed to rival a flying carpet in its ability to take moviegoers anywhere on earth. Genie-like, it conjured up every conceivable image and showered sudden riches on moviemakers and fame on actors. Listings of the earliest known movies reveal titles that include *Allabad, The Arabian Wizzard* in 1901. *A Princess of Bagdad* was a silent film of 1916 advertised as "an original Arabian Night's story." It was followed in 1917 by *Aladdin and the Wonderful Lamp*, and in 1918 by *Ali Baba and the Forty Thieves*. Even more numerous were silent movies that put magical objects, familiar from the stories, into modern hands. Among the first of this type were *The Carpet from Bagdad*, a film of 1915 with a New York setting, and *Aladdin's Other Lamp*, which brought a genie to the America of 1917. When Terry Ramsaye wrote one of the earliest histories of the movies in 1926, the title, *A Million and One Nights: A History of the Motion Picture*, further suggested the new industry's fix on the theme.

In the movies the aura of eroticism that had been all but deleted from the storybook versions of *The Arabian Nights* was spectacularly rehabilitated. Though the plot was not based on one of the tales, Rudolph Valentino, in *The Sheik* (1921), made it practically impossible for his swooning fans to separate their notions of Araby from the very image of the romantic sex idol.

In 1924 when Douglas Fairbanks produced and starred in *The Thief of Bagdad: An Arabian Nights Fantasy*, he definitively glamorized the theme for a whole generation.[11] *The Thief of Bagdad* set new Hollywood standards. Technically, the magic and the flying-carpet special effects surpassed anything the industry had produced to date.

The magnificence and splendor of the movie's costumes and sets, created by the art director William Cameron Menzies, also established a new standard. To make the movie, Fairbanks build a city that covered six acres of movie lots. It's palaces, gates and public squares were architectural hybrids, dream images of Baghdad, stylized—sometimes blank and abstract, sometimes dense with geometric patterns. Often, great expanses of plain walls fill most of the screen, focusing attention on a few rickety balconies, on pointed and horseshoe shaped arches, and most of all leaving the eye to seek gleaming domes of many shapes atop nearly every structure. Mammoth jars are always in sight; Fairbanks seemed to find constant cause to leap in and out of them, or to hide evildoers within them. Menzies interjected touches of Art Deco, especially in interiors with pierced and filigreed screens. And he created visions of China as well, of the Mongol empire and its swarming armies. It was dazzling.

A full-page advertisement for Opa-locka that appeared in Miami newspapers during May 1926 suggests that Glenn Curtiss counted on those movie sets to have impressed just about everybody in the United States. In presenting Opa-locka as a "City of Parts"—the parts including plan, landscaping, public utilities, recreation, and transportation—the architecture part needed little description. The advertising copy ran: "Of course you have seen Douglas Fairbanks' 'Thief of Bagdad,' with its wealth of Oriental picturesqueness reminding one, indeed, of the famous illustrations to the Arabian Nights."

At Opa-locka the architecture 'part', or the Arabic part of the architecture, was much like a movie set: all facade, all for the camera, which here was a still camera for publicity shots. While Opa-locka's publicists were reaping the benefits of associating their project with the famous movie, they clearly sensed a danger in identifying it too closely with Hollywood. "No 'flats' of Arabian scenes built for moving picture 'sets,' but solid massive structures designed to live for generations to come," they stressed in an advertisement of 5 February 1926, published in the *Miami Daily News and Metropolis*. Beneath the exotic trappings, Opa-locka's houses were as solidly built as most of the others springing up across Florida during the 1920s. These Arabian Nights structures were in fact much like the others except for their novel system of exterior decoration.

Bernhardt Muller was not perhaps so 'famous' as the Opa-locka Company was to bill him. He was forty-seven when Curtiss hired him in 1925, and had covered a lot of territory since 1878, the year of his birth in Fremont, Nebraska. He based his architectural career on studies in Paris at the École des Beaux-Arts between 1903 and 1905, and in Italy, France, Austria, and Germany during an additional year. He settled in New York in 1906 and worked for a succession of firms, including Trowbridge and Livingston, Robert J. Reiley, and D. Everett Waid, until 1914, when he opened his own office. In the two years before coming to the Opa-locka job, he had designed several Mediterranean and Spanish-style houses in and near Miami.[12]

Like the moviemakers, Muller dealt in pictorial, painterly, and narrative terms with buildings appropriate to the *Arabian Nights* theme. He wanted his buildings to call up the narratives visually, an intension expressed in the statement, quoted above, that he "would tell the story by means of mural decorations and wrought iron work carrying out the various features of the story."

Muller's drawings for Opa-locka have been well preserved. In the 1960s the Archives and Special Collections of the Otto G. Richter Library at the University of Miami acquired a large number of Muller's drawings for Opa-locka as part of a collection of more than nine hundred architectural drawings and related materials. The materials have provided documentation for subsequent preservation efforts in the town.

Ephemera in the library's Bernhardt E. Muller Collection includes a publicity piece of February 1926 that describes the "famous New York architect" as having "extensive experience with the technique of the ancient architects of Persia, Arabia, and South Central Europe." But in 1959 Bernhardt Muller himself told Janet Bolender, an interviewer whose article about Muller was published in the *North Dade Hub*, that his wife had become his instant expert on exotic styles once the theme was set: "Muller proclaimed that his wife deserved much of the credit for the Arabian-Persian architecture. His wife fell heir to the huge job of delving into books, doing research, categorizing, providing her husband with all the background material he needed as a prelude and guide to designing the buildings."[13]

What Muller pulled from these sources were the facades, the outside effects. He and the developers required only exterior conformity to a look deemed appropriate to the geographical setting of a story selected from *The Arabian Nights*. To ensure that they would get a degree of stylistic conformity throughout the town, Muller was to review and approve drawings for any proposed building that he himself did not design. His basis for judgment was a very generalized and eclectic understanding of the styles appropriate to the settings of the far-flung tales of Arabia, Egypt, Persia, China, India, and their neighbors.

The most ambitious example of the image that Muller and the developers were after is the Opa-locka Company's Administration Building, now City Hall. It was the first major structure they built and it remains the grandest emblem of their *Arabian Nights* theme. By August of 1926, less than a year after initial plans for the town were seriously discussed, the building was ready for occupancy. That striking exterior served its owner far better than a billboard could have done to announce that a grandiose—to many a ridiculously fantastic—real estate scheme was becoming actuality.

It looks enormous in all the photographs and drawings, and the Opa-locka Company published pictures of it right through its hasty construction process and afterward at every possible opportunity. A gorgeous five-domed, many-colored, and multi-balconied structure, crowned by crenellations, and surrounded by minarets and walled courtyard-gardens, it is impressive as it rises today in restored splendor above Opa-locka's low-lying buildings. But in fact it is not a large public building. Its interior scale seems nearly domestic, a surprise considering the impact of its silhouette seen from afar.

About fifty of Muller's drawings for the Administration Building survive in the collection at the University of Miami, more than for any other single building in the town. The design was his most elaborately detailed effort for Opa-locka.

The presentation rendering of 1925 would have made a fine illustration for yet another edition of *The Arabian Nights*, as the watercolor drawing has that storybook quality. In it the building looks vaguely like a mosque but was entitled the Palace of King Kosroushah (or Khusrau Shah), from the tale of "The Two Sisters Who Envied Their Cadette." *Cadette* is a Persian word meaning "City-queen," according to Sir Richard Burton. The Story is a long and convoluted account of how the Persian king was united with his two sons and daughter, Princess Periezade, whose births had been kept secret from him by his queen's wicked sisters. In large part the tale recounts successive quests for the Singing Tree, the Golden Water, and the Speaking Bird. The young men fail arduous tests en route to these peculiar prizes, and it is their sister who finally faces down the perils, stopping her ears against the frightful sounds along the way.

Opa-locka's publicists pointed out that Muller had used Moorish and Arabian architecture to concoct a palace associated with a Persian king. From the beginning, then, it would seem that the reviewers were pretty lax about deciding which architectural style was appropriate to the geography of a given tale. As architectural specificity faded, a generally Eastern air could be suggested by propping large terra-cotta jars against a wall, and the jars were always handy for leaning on when celebrants of early Arabian Nights Festivals posed for photographs.

Muller, however, stayed close to the specifics of the story in designing and naming details within the Administration Building. Drawings for the Fountain of the Princess Periezade are signed "E.S." and bear the most distinctive stamp of Art Deco stylization of any illustrated here. Publicity pieces of the 1920s enumerate other features of the courtyard-garden, such as the Singing Tree, the Golden Water, the Talking Bird, and a man-shaped black rock like those into which the brothers were transformed when they failed in their quest for the three rare objects. "Mural decorations giving the splendid banquet scene where the identity of his children was revealed to the king by the dish of green cucumbers stuffed with pearls," are recorded in a feature article on Opa-locka in the English magazine, *Country Life*, of November 1928. Muller was at pains to design and to have designed other elaborate, if nonnarrative, details for this building, such as the banding of colorful tiles gleaming around the base of the principal dome. The tiles were made by the Batchelder-Wilson Company of New York. The domes were "blue or soft browns, the colors graduating upward to white or cream," according to an article in the *American Institute of Architects Journal* published in April of 1928 and signed by Opa-locka's mayor, H. Sayre Wheeler.[14]

The domes of the Administration Building cast a large shadow over the foreground of Muller's sketch for Opa-locka's marketplace. In fact, Muller was cheating, as the shadow would not have been so grand, nor fallen just that way, but with this device he pictorially interlocked the dominating structure with the commercial center. In a series of drawings of 1926, Muller gives us closer looks at simple little stands, like stalls in an Eastern bazaar, that would have brought bustle to the marketplace. One group of them is captioned "Stone City Shops" an ironic name for the proposed site of lively commerce. The Stone City is described in the "Tale of the Ensorcelled Prince," a tale within the "Tale of the Fisherman and the Jinn." Here, a truth-searching king found that every inhabitant had been turned to stone by the enraged and faithless wife of the prince, and that she had conceived even more excruciating tortures for her husband. She had turned him to stone too, at least from the waist down, after he had mortally wounded her black lover, whom she then nursed and comforted within her husband's hearing. But the visiting king punished her and her lover with death and restored all the good people and the prince to life and health once more.

Among the commercial necessities of a new town of the 1920s was, of course the gas station, and Muller seems to have enjoyed designing one as an Arabian whimsy. He gave it a dome, splaced tiny minarets where they seem to dignify and protect the pumps, which he drew rather like little sentinels. A negative print, white on black, makes it all look like a night scene, glowing in the dark. His perspective drawing is dated 1927 and captioned "Super Gas Station, Opa-locka, Florida." This gas station, however, was probably never built.

In one of the most romantic of his renderings, Muller envisioned a ruinous Egyptian temple to serve as Opa-locka's bank. Here he seems to have conflated images of two of the most familiar temples that still have their double pylons—the temple of Horus at Edfu and that of Amon at Luxor. Muller's central portal is like the one at Edfu, topped by a cavetto cornice ornamented with the royal symbol of the winged sun. He placed an obelisk in front, just to the left of the portal, where an obelisk stands at Luxor. This essay in Egyptian architecture was sanctioned by identifying it with the "Tale of Zayn al Asnam" which relates the adventures of the young inheritor of the Sultanate of Bassorah, who lost his father's riches in profligate living during the first years of his rule, and regained them only after two dream-directed journeys to Cairo.

The drawing shown here is dated 1928, a date of some significance because construction had begun two years earlier on the "Egyptian Bank." Opa-locka's developers rushed to begin it, but despite reports in the *Hialeah Press* of 6 August 1926 that the "Bank building also is nearing completion," it never was finished and never opened as a bank. At some point, Muller drew another version of it, more lavishly detailed with a cavetto cornice crowning every wall. Perhaps that was the design on which construction was originally based. The drawing eliminates the cornice detail, which would have reduced building costs, and presents a dreamier and a more abstract image, in which the temple looks decayed. Could this rendering have been part of a proposal for a less expensive revision, a pretty picture painted to induce a baker to complete the standing shell? If so, it failed. The shell was soon adapted to serve as the First Baptist Church. Today it is home to another congregation, and the imprint of Muller's intention can still be seen in its battered walls and its massing.

Muller's scheme of December 1925 for an observation tower more than fifty feet high was fully and promptly realized, for it had an important role in the chief activity of the Opa-locka Company, which was selling lots. It provided a platform high above the native trees of the hammock from which prospective buyers, brought out from Miami in busloads, could get the best view of the town-in-the-making. Given his theme, when the chief requirement was height, it is surprising that Muller did not create an overgrown minaret or a crenelated watchtower. He may have been recalling and heightening the low, rounded forms of North African villages built of mud, or perhaps images from Fairbanks' *The Thief of Bagdad* took over here: Menzies' dream visions of the towering, domed "abode of the flying steed" in the film may have lodged in Muller's mind.

Like many of the sets in the movie, the observation tower was all balconies and exterior stairs. Whatever Muller was after, he surely achieved an exotic effect in the building. It was demolished during World War II when a nearby Navy base, for which Glenn Curtiss had given the original land, ruthlessly expanded, destroying everything of Opa-locka in its path. It wreaked havoc on Muller's buildings, about 100 of which had been built during the 1920s. In 1943 five domes were removed from the Administration Building.[15] Indeed, the Navy did Opa-locka far greater damage than any it had suffered in the hurricane of 1926. It was neither the forces of nature, nor neglect when money ran out, that ruined Opa-locka's beautiful natural setting. The Navy bulldozed the hammock that Curtiss had preserved as a park.

In a few cases the Navy kept Muller's buildings at the core of the structures it altered and enlarged beyond recognition. The old archery club was the most important of these. In 1941 the Navy expanded it for use as an officers' club, engulfing Muller's crenellations and arched openings. The archery club had been completed late in 1926, one of the major amenities that Curtiss continued to build after the hurricane in September of that year. Among the others was a large bathing casino including a dance floor, volleyball courts, and a pool with grandstand seating for much-advertised performances by Johnny Weismuller and Jackie Ott, "The World's Perfect Boy." Muller's office also produced specifications and forty-five working drawings for the golf club of "Ali Baba and the Forty Thieves." Although they continued to work on the design, which began in June of 1926, it never was built.

A design that was executed was the tiny archery pro shop

built north of town, beyond the hammock. In his drawing for it Muller carefully detailed simple adornment—crenellation and a little turret holding a crescent aloft—that stamped this utilitarian structure "Arabic." Today there is a nondescript hot-dog stand in the middle of Opa-locka, very near City Hall, that looks suspiciously like the old archery pro shop. Perhaps it is, moved and shorn of decoration.

When Muller designed a hot-dog stand for Opa-locka, he crowned a small stucco-covered structure with a dome and gave it exterior stairs to a roof enclosed by a parapet whose edges are rounded and irregular. It looks like something shaped by long use in a dusty North African town, thought the front of the parapet is inscribed "DOGS." The drawing is dated 1929. During the previous year, Curtiss admitted the impossibility of continuing to build his dream for Opa-locka. However, it would seem that even with the Great Depression closing in, Muller was still designing buildings.

One of the grandest of his post-hurricane designs is for a "Hotel for Opa-locka" dominated by a tower that would have looked like an enormous Chinese pagoda. A sketchier rendering of the same design is inscribed "The Tale of Aladdin and His Lamp," one of the most familiar of the tales that few would have failed to know was set in "a city of the Cities of China." (The South Dade town of Aladdin was also inspired by this tale, but it was a very different project from Opa-locka. The Aladdin Company of Bay City, Michigan manufactured and shipped "redicut" houses to factory towns. "A New City" in South Dade was to bear the company name that played on the wonder, worthy of Aladdin's own genie and his lamp, of the nearly instantaneous erection of houses that arrived as kits-of-parts on railway cars. The South Dade project had just started when the hurricane of 1926 was followed by Florida's real estate crash. The place name Aladdin survives just east of the intersection of Southwest 216th Street and Southwest 167th Avenue). Dates in 1927 and 1928 appear on several of the twelve unrealized plans, elevations and perspectives for this building. They give evidence that long after the hurricane had precipitated an early depression in Florida, Curtiss continued to support Muller's work on extravagant attractions that he still hoped to build in Opa-locka.

As late as 10 April 1930, just a few months before Glenn Curtiss died, one of Muller's drawings for this "Hotel Aladdin" was published in Boston's *Christian Science Monitor*. It appeared in an article inflated with the expectation of future construction in Opa-locka and with the boosterism so typical of earlier publicity.

One remarkably late drawing for a public building for Opa-locka is that for the First Church of Christ, Scientist, dated 1930. A Christian Science connection is supposed to have won the Opa-locka job for Muller in the first place. According to Frank S. FitzGerald-Bush, an aunt of Glenn Curtiss belonged to a Christian Science Church in New Jersey that Muller designed, and she recommended him.

Among Muller's proposals for Opa-locka, this drawing seems unusually sober and blank. The simple frontal-gabled facade is distinguished only by a stark arched central opening under a relatively small window and by corner piers topped by finials made up of two little globes. At the time it was designed, there had been no funding of design or construction work in Opa-locka for about two years. With this drawing of 1930 could Muller have been proposing a memorial to Curtiss, who died in July of that year? Whatever the case, it was not built.

Even though Muller and the publicists for Opa-locka lavished a great deal of attention on the town's institutional and commercial buildings, it was the residential buildings that were at the core of the real estate venture. Success depended upon their sales and Muller's designs for them were key sales tools. By providing many kinds of housing—among them single-family and multi-family houses, mixed commercial and residential buildings, and apartment buildings—Opa-locka's planners hoped to attract many kinds of people to their new town.

Drawings for more than sixty houses survive. Sixteen bear no dates, but the vast majority, forty-seven, were designed in 1926. During August and early September, just before the hurricane hit on 17 September, Muller's office seems to have been especially busy with them. Drawings for fifteen clients who are named bear dates for the remaining days of 1926, and three more houses were drawn up for other clients in 1927. No later dates appear on residential designs in the collection. During the post-hurricane period, Muller's office also produced drawings for one four-family building, three duplexes, and one residence with a shop.

Most of the house designs are labeled as Muller's, though a few are clearly credited to his assistant, Carl Jensen, who, with Paul Lieske, also executed many of the plans and elevations in the collection. The assistants almost certainly contributed to house designs that became fairly formulaic. Some houses were commissioned by the Opa-locka Company, some by investors who bought lots and put up several houses for resale, but most by individuals. Surprisingly, fewer than five sets of drawings seem to have been dreamed up simply as models when no client was at hand. One of these was the undated "Residence of Ali-Baba on Sharazad Boulevard, Opa-locka."

Drawings for the diminutive "Thatched Roof Residence" and for the "Oriental House" suggest a wide variety of architectural styles in Opa-locka houses, which is perhaps misleading. Although there were still other variations, including Egyptian designs with lotus capitals, battered walls, and cavetto cornices, Muller's brand of "Arabic" is more representative of the houses that were built. To create it, he shuffled a repertoire of forms and ornaments around the elevations, including crenellation, balconies, pointed and horseshoe arches, and awnings supported by spears (a feature in Coral Gables houses as well). Domes crown houses of every estate, and roofs sport diminutive turrets with crescents for finials. The "Proposed Residence for Opa-locka, Suitable for 50'-0" Lot" may stand for a great many of the smaller essays in this genre. Carl Jensen executed the rendering two months after the hurricane, and it virtually sums up much of the firm's residential design for Opa-locka during the previous year. Even the inevitable terra-cotta jar is in view beside the entrance arch.

The elevation and plan for "The Hurricane-Proof House" is a more modest presentation of many of the same elements, with a jazzier checkerboard paint scheme, and a heavier grille barring the windows. The drawings were executed in November and December of 1926 specifically for publication in the *Miami Daily News and Metropolis*. While Muller's name is the one that appears prominently on the elevation, Jensen's signature is hidden in the grass of the lower left.

Among more substantial designs for larger houses, the Muller Collection includes a perspective dated 1926 for the residence of Opa-locka's mayor, H. Sayre Wheeler, a house that survives in a fine state of repair. Its construction between March and July of 1926 is amply documented in photographs.

Neither in plan, nor volume, nor material were Muller's buildings true to their various Eastern sources, as his drawings for Opa-locka make clear. Scrutinizing the plans, one might stretch a point and cite his use of enclosed gardens—especially the walled courtyards of the Administration Building—as a planning element taken from Eastern models. But Muller's plans overwhelmingly conformed to American standards of his day. His house plans were much like those in other Curtiss-Bright developments and like the smaller houses of Coral Gables. Many were modest arrangements of rectangular rooms on a single floor—two bedrooms, one bath, kitchen, living room, dining room, perhaps an entrance hall, and often a porte-cochere to shelter a car.

In section as well, the houses were a great deal more ordinary than their elevations might lead one to expect. Although domes topped many of them, they were merely exterior decorations that were not expressed in interior volume. No great vaulted rooms greeted visitors, whether they entered a private residence with a single small dome, a commercial building like the Hurt Building where a larger central dome was flanked by two others, or the architect's most ambitious essay in domes—the Administration Building, which was originally topped by six of them. To get the exterior effect he wanted, Muller simply set hollow half-spheres on the flat roofs of his buildings. Their placement bore no relationship to the interior plans, nor was their presence visible from rooms immediately under the domes. In fact, domes often spanned the partitions between two rooms on an upper floor.

Muller's drawings reveal no concern for using authentic materials appropriate to his Eastern models. He used reinforced masonry block finished with stucco for the major public and commercial buildings. For the Administration Building he specified hollow tile blocks, brand-named "Natco," manufactured by the National Fireproofing Company, steel reinforcement, and brick spanning for arches, as well as a stucco finish with pseudo-aging. In drawings for his showplace, the Administration Building, Muller carefully detailed just where the stucco was to be interrupted so it would look as if it were cracked, revealing a fake structure of "ancient" bricks that had to be inserted into the real structure at the proper places.

Opa-locka's publicists boasted that all the houses were made of reinforced concrete block. However, details for wood-frame structures supporting a stucco finish show up in some of Muller's working drawings, including those for Mayor Wheeler's house. The construction photographs clearly confirm that the structure was built as Muller drew it, with broad horizontal boards filling a wooden frame and supporting veneers of stucco and native coral rock.

Whatever they were made of, Opa-locka's buildings survived the infamous hurricane of 1926 better than did construction in other Miami suburbs. Mayor Wheeler assured readers of the

159

American Institute of Architects Journal in April 1928 that "the domes obviously caused less wind resistance than the flat surfaces while the thin minarets and towers successfully withstood the blow." Opa-locka's publicists failed to mention that the eye of the storm avoided the city. But after that date there was a shift in their emphasis. They wrote a great deal about substantial construction, as their promotion of the hurricane-proof house directly after the hurricane attests.

"Substantial" is a word that had figured prominently in the advertisements for Opa-locka from the first, and the copywriters seem to have delighted in the shock value of juxtaposing it with pictures of the most improbable fantasy architecture. But they nearly always associated the word with the town plan as a whole. "The City Substantial" headlined full-page newspaper advertisements that carried long columns detailing the superiority of Opa-locka's planning and singing the praises of its planner, Clinton Mackenzie.

Glenn Curtiss put his faith in planning after he saw what a lack of preplanned, regulated growth had yielded in his earlier venture Hialeah. In his advertisements for Opa-locka he emphasized the plan as the special feature from which a homebuyer would benefit: "Beauty in Building—Permanence in Plan" began an advertisement in the *Miami Daily News and Metropolis* of 5 February 1926.

On these subjects, one of the most explicit advertisements appeared in the same newspaper on 3 May 1926, which read in part:

Nothing is haphazard—nothing guessed at—nothing left to chance… First of all, Opa-locka was born… in the trained mind of Mr. Clinton Mackenzie. In his New York Studio he made "study" after "study" of the city that was to be. In his vision—at once artistic and practical—he "saw" Opa-locka…and it was only when he had thus "seen" that pencil was put to paper… Everything was thought out in advance…the locating of Civic Centers, Parks, Public Buildings, Golf Course, Residences, Commercial and Industrial Sections, Seaboard Air Line Passenger Station was completely and fully planned…

When Mackenzie got the Opa-locka job in 1925, he was in his mid-fifties and in his stride as a planner whose practice, based in New York, was beginning to have a national impact. He was a director of the National Planning Association and Tenement House Commissioner for the State of New Jersey. During World War I, he planned Amatol, New Jersey, for the United States Ordinance Department, and designed the massive office, dormitory, and munitions factories there. He also provided planning and architectural services for the U.S. Housing Corporation at Milton, Pennsylvania; for the National Cash Register Company in Dayton, Ohio; and for the International Coal Products Corporation at South Clinchfield, Virginia.

Mackenzie's most important work—a railroad station, hotel, apartment buildings, streets full of houses—had been executed in Kingsport, Tennessee, a planned industrial town, and the largest project of John Nolen (1869–1937), dean of U.S. planners. Just before the war, Kingsport was launched as a business venture and by 1920 it was being hailed as a model of profitable, rather than charitable or social, planning and housing.

In 1920 Mackenzie published a small volume called *Industrial Housing*. The town plan for Kingsport appears in that book, bearing the names of "Clinton Mackenzie, Architect, NY City," and "John Nolen, Town Planner, Cambridge, Mass." The geometry of that plan for a town in the mountains is clearly the model for the layout of the streets of Opa-locka on the flat lands abutting the Everglades. As at Opa-locka, railroad tracks form the base of a rectangular grid that is confined to an asymmetrical triangular area. Above and around it curves an arc of parallel streets connected by cross streets that fan out like spokes.

Mackenzie's planning was impressive, so impressive that Opa-locka, like Coral Gables from which Curtiss borrowed so heavily, might even have pulled out of the Great Depression and resumed development along the lines he laid down in the 1920s. But everything in Opa-locka was haphazard from the Depression on. The Navy's expansion decimated the land and the landmarks, and swarms of naval personnel and their families swamped and then deserted the area. The Navy agreed to lease vacant facilities for private, industrial, and commercial development, reneged on the deal, and later decided it would lease some buildings. But by then tenants had lost confidence in ventures subject to the Navy's whim. The local economy has yet to recover fully from the dizzying pendulum swings.

"Streets will be always wide and wherever possible gently winding; every section of the city will be readily accessible by direct highways," promised and early brochure for Opa-locka. That promise, if few others of the mid-1920s, has been kept. From the heart of Miami, you can zoom very quickly up Interstate 95 to the economically depressed community that is Opa-locka today. Its native oak hammock is long gone. Donald Lawrence, "one of the most experienced landscape gardeners in south Florida," was never able to plant all the royal poinciana, bamboo, pithicolobium, eucalyptus, and some 2,500 coconut palms that, he believed in 1926, "would make Opa-locka without question the most beautiful city on the East Coast."[16] But street signs still mark Sharazad Boulevard, Ali Baba Avenue, Aladdin Street, and dozens of others that have Arabic names and follow the geometry Mackenzie laid down on the land.

The Administrations Building was restored in 1987 and, as City Hall, it is the pride of the community. Muller's drawings were vital to that restoration and to the more recent work of rehabilitating the Hurt Building, completed in 1991 by Grafton Architects, Inc. For the burned-out train station—the only major Arabic landmark that Muller did not design—the future is still in doubt.

Since preservationists have identified over one hundred of the original buildings, more people are taking an interest in them. A well-stocked shelf of *Arabian Nights* storybooks at the public library makes it easy for children who live on Sesame Street to learn that it got its name not from a program on television but from Ali Baba saying "Open Sesame" to the magic door that guarded the treasure of the forty thieves. Aladdin has become a household word to them, as to most American children, since Disney brought out its film that takes the mischievous boy a long way from his fabled origins. But few of the African-American children who constitute the majority in the local classrooms of the town will ever encounter the erotic tales that reveal the ancient Arabian world's obsessive fear and hatred of the sexual power and allure of black slaves. Nor will their parents, who annually celebrate at the Arabian Nights Festival, donning costumes just as outlandish as those in which Opa-locka's residents of the 1920s posed for the sepia-toned photographs, smiling as broadly as their successors of the 1990s, who still lean, Fairbanks-like, on jars ever-handy for these now traditional occasions.

Catherine Lynn, "Dream and Substance: Araby and the planning of Opa-locka," originally published in *The Journal of Decorative and Propaganda Arts*, vol. 23 of Florida Theme Issue (Miami, Florida: The Wolfsonian—Florida International University and The Wolfson Foundation of Decorative and Propaganda Arts, 1998), 162–189.

NOTES

1. The title given here is as rendered by Richard F. Burton in his edition published in London in 1885. Burton's translation seems to have been the one most widely used by subsequent generations of popularizers who wrote in English. There are many alternate versions of the title.
2. This is the description offered in 1882 by John Payne, in his preface: "The present [which] is, I believe, the first complete translation of the great Arabic compendium of romantic fiction that has been attempted in any European language." John Payne, *The Book of the Thousand Nights and one night* (London: printed for the Villon Society by Private Subscription, 1882), 1:vii.
3. Esperanza B. Varona, *The Bernhardt E. Muller Collection: 1923–1960, Register*. A typescript document in the Archives and Special Collections of the Otto G. Richter Library, University of Miami, dated 30 December 1986, revised 21 January 1987, accession number 65–2, 11.
4. Bernhardt E. Muller, "Bernhardt Muller's Dream of Arabian City in Florida is Reality," *Opa-locka Times*, 23 February 1927, 1.
5. Several Miami newspaper articles celebrating Curtiss' flight are preserved as clippings in the Bernhardt E. Muller Collection of the Archives and Special Collections of the Otto G. Richter Library at the University of Miami (hereafter referred to as the Muller Collection).
6. Frank S. FitzGerald-Bush, *A dream of Araby: Glenn H. Curtiss and the founding of Opa-locka* (Opa-locka, Fla.: South Florida Archaeological Museum, 1976); and Muller Collection, clippings.
7. Ibid., 4.
8. This summary of the history of the tales is based on Bennett A. Cerf's introduction to *The Arabian Nights' Entertainments or the Book of a Thousand Nights and a Night* (New York: Modern Library/Random House, 1932), vii-xiv, 1, and on Joseph Campbell's introduction to *The Portable Arabian Nights* (New York: Viking, 1952), 1–35. Cerf's edition is based on Burton's translation; Campbell's on Payne's.
9. Neil Levine, *The Architecture of Frank Lloyd Wright* (Princeton: Princeton University Press, 1996), 25. According to Levine, the mural was designed by Wright and painted by Orlando Giannini, an attribition he based on Ann Abernathy with John G.Thorpe, ed., *The Oak Park Home and Studio of Frank Lloyd Wright* (Oak Park, Ill.: Frank Lloyd Wright Home and Studio Foundation, 1988), 26.
10. Frank Lloyd Wright, *An Autobiography* (New York: Duell, Sloan and Pearce, 1943), 112.
11. *The Thief of Bagdad* is available on video. My descriptions of the sets are based on viewings of the film itself.
12. The Muller Collection includes clippings, zobituary, and typescript biographical information on Muller.
13. Janet Bolender, "Architect Believes in City: 'It Can Still Be Done' Muller Tells Opa-locka," *North Date Hub*, 9 July 1959, 3.

14. H. Sayre Wheeler, "Opa-locka, Created from the Arabian Nights," *American Institute of Architects Journal* (April 1928): 157–8.
15. In addition to clippings in the Muller Collection, FitzGerald-Bush's *A dream of Araby* is the source for some of this later history of Opa-locka, as are the National Register Nomination for Opa-locka, Esperanza B. Varona's register of the Muller Collection (cf. note 3), and Clarke Ash, "Opa-locka: A Page from Arabian Nights," *Florida Living Magazine of the Miami News*, 5 April 1059, 6–7.
16. "Beautification Work is Progressing Nicely at Opa-locka," *Hialeah Press*, 13 August 1926, 1.

Poet and local historian, Frank S. FitzGerald-Bush (1925–1998) authored *A Dream of Araby: Glenn H. Curtiss and the founding of Opa-locka* which was first published and printed in Opa-locka in 1976 by the South Florida Archeological Museum whose headquarters were once in Opa-locka's historic city hall. FitzGerald-Bush was born in Opa-locka to the Opa-locka's electrical contractor and good friend of Glenn Curtiss. We attach the preface off his book, which is at once both deeply personal and the only published account of its kind. The book is now out of print.

PREFACE TO A DREAM OF ARABY: GLENN H. CURTISS AND THE FOUNDING OF OPA-LOCKA

By Frank S. FitzGerald-Bush

Opa-locka is—and always has been—much more than a city to me; my thought of it is a tapestry interwoven of the dreams of my parents, of my father's kinsman friends Glenn H. Curtiss, and of Bernhardt E. Muller, mutual friend of all three and architect of most of the city's earliest buildings. Dreams do not often come true. The dream of Opa-locka did so only in part. 1976 marks the fiftieth anniversary of Opa-locka, as well as our nation's bicentennial year. It seems appropriate that the first attempt at a thorough history of the founding of Opa-locka should be published at this time.

There is another, more deeply personal reason, which has impelled me to write this book. When I pass down any street in Opa-locka, observing well-kept homes in neatly-groomed gardens, I feel a strangely personal satisfaction. This is the Opa-locka Mr. Curtiss and Mr. Muller dreamed of and worked for. Conversely, when I encounter neglected buildings or unkempt yards, my resentment is similarly a personal one. When confronted by written or oral accounts of the city's history which depart from or distort the facts, each error (and there have been many) seems also an affront to Opa-locka's founder, and hence painful to me.

During the years of my family's absences from Florida (and always they seemed like exile) Opa-locka was for us a constant beacon, and our return to it our ultimate goal. During our many travels my sisters and I—and later our brother Jason, born after our departure from Opa-locka—often joined our parents in singing what were to become family anthems: "Carry me back to Opa-locka," and "The sun shines bright on our Opa-locka home." When I discovered that the states of Virginia and Kentucky respectively had purloined for their state songs our beloved melodies, I reported this theft to my father with great indignation. I still recall his amusement, and my chagrin, when he enlightened me as to who had been the actual borrowers. Still either melody summons up for me a vision of Opa-locka—not a vision of the city that is; perhaps not even of the city that was. My vision of Opa-locka is one which may not—perhaps could not—ever have been a reality, so beautiful and so perfect it is to me.

In preparing this account I am deeply indebted to all who shared with me their memories and their treasured photographs or newspaper clippings. These individuals and organizations I have listed elsewhere in this book, with my profound thanks. My greatest debt is to the unpublished manuscript entitled "Memories of the Founding of Opa-locka," written by my father, the late Frank S. Bush. Wherever possible I have checked his account against public records or contemporary published accounts and found him to have been correct in his recollection.

In rare instances where contemporary verification was nowhere to be found, I have depended upon my father's version, even in the several cases where later writers, using secondary sources, differ from him. Those who knew my father will, I feel confident, agree with this decision.

As an historian, I do not put forth this as the definitive history of Opa-locka. Many records, documents, and photographs I know to have once existed could not be found. What is here presented is a deeply personal narrative in which my own involvement may have rendered cold objectivity impossible. Nonetheless, in so far as it was within my power, I have told only the truth—not the truth entire (no man can claim to possess that). What I have left out was whatever might give pain to anyone. These few deletions were not of essential matters. I hope that there is nothing in this book which is false, and nothing that would cause injury to anyone. What I offer is—or so I have strived to make it—a poetic evocation of the past, with all its beauty and some of its tragedy. Perhaps it will help those who have always worked to retain something of the original dream of Opa-locka, and cause others to join with them in that task. If this should prove to be so, I shall be content.

Originally published in Frank S. FitzGerald-Bush, *A dream of Araby: Glenn H. Curtiss and the founding of Opa-locka* (Florida: South Florida Archaeological Museum, 1976), 1.

Journalist, Calvin Godfrey's article *Baghdad West: In Opa-locka, gang warfare, drug dealing, and decay are a way of life* was first published in *Miami New Times* in 2007. His article examines and reveals the complexities of law-enforcement within Opa-locka. Here he re-introduces the text with his current thoughts on Opa-locka.

WELCOME TO OPA-LOCKA!

By Calvin Godfrey

I spent about three months hanging out in the town and writing about it back when I was 23 years old. I rode around wearing a bulletproof with Officer Pedro Rojas—a man who seemed trapped in the Opa-locka Police Department by a number of major mistakes, including a failed attempt to impersonate his father, Deputy Pedro Rojas Sr. during his mandatory fitness test at the Miami-Dade County Sheriff's Department. Despite the bleakness of his professional future, Rojas was funny and eager for exposure. I clearly suffered from what *Rolling Stone* Editor Matt Taibbi called "access drift—when you really, really love the drama of the story you're hearing [and] you start leaning in the direction of your sources even if the truth doesn't quite cooperate."

I still stand by much of what I said in this story, which was published in the *Miami New Times* on 26 April 2007. But there is much that I did not say. I did not mention the breakfasts Rojas had, every morning, with his closest friend on the force: Officer German Bosque, a man that reporters as far away as London have dubbed the "worst cop in America." Bosque's personnel file contains a mountain of complaints and disciplinary actions for crimes and infractions that included, among so many things, brutalizing suspects in handcuffs. Last October, Bosque was fired for the sixth time—in this case, for giving his body armor and department-issued AR-15 to his girlfriend's dad. Bosque's first short-lived termination (which Rojas went down for as well) came about after the pair called in sick together to take a trip to Cancun. They were both re-hired and have been tight ever since.

Naturally, I was shocked when Rojas landed a job in a small, safe municipality known as South Miami. From that point on, I was left to ride along with Bosque—an awful character, even on his best behavior. At one point, after spending an afternoon of writing out traffic tickets for him ("Just fill in all the boxes," he'd say after tossing me a license and registration), Bosque told me he believed that everyone in the city of Opa-locka was using drugs. To illustrate his point, he pushed a mentally challenged pedestrian up against a chain link fence and went through his pockets. Bosque produced a charred wad of steel wool (crack paraphernalia, he said) and then sent the man on his way.

I spent two months riding around with arguably the most corrupt and incompetent police in the United States and that fact is hardly reflected in the story you're about to read because it didn't fit within the drama that I'd fallen in love with. As a white rich kid, my only insights into a place like Opa-locka had come from rap videos and the early episodes of The Wire, in which a bunch of earnest police officers do their best to dismantle a drug syndicate in spite of the shortsightedness of their higher-ups. I wanted to tell a similar story about the Opa-locka Police Department—framed as an underfunded, outmanned frontier force, struggling to clean up the mean streets. But the reality of what was going on in Opa-locka was quite different.

During my time touring the infamous Back Blue apartment complex, I was placed in the care of an officer, Balom, who recently pleaded guilty to federal charges of selling bulletproof vests and information to the violent drug gang that operated the federally funded complex as a kind of fortress from which to sell crack. I would later expose Chief James Wright (written about in the pages to follow as a kind of tough new sheriff) as a Napoleonic pervert—a man whose bizarre sexual ego compelled him to bully and harass seemingly all of his female subordinates, including those who had been given plum jobs in his department by relatives in city hall.

At the time, I felt it would be cheap to expose the failures of the people who had become trapped in the worst law enforcement job in the country. I didn't really consider how much worse it would be to be a person trapped under their authority. I didn't understand the longer narrative of The Wire, which illustrates how the War on Drugs destroys both the lives of the people prosecuting it and the communities it purports to serve and protect.

In these places, the proverbial American dream seems almost as darkly absurd as the notion of an Arab-themed American ghetto.

The United States is in love with the notion that tough cops can 'clean up' 'bad neighborhoods'—that the whole country can simply go to war with abstract concepts and, against all evidence, make the world a better place through violence. Opa-locka is enduring proof that it cannot.

BAGHDAD WEST: IN OPA-LOCKA, GANG WARFARE, DRUG DEALING, AND DECAY ARE A WAY OF LIFE

Eleven 40-caliber shell casings lay just beyond the front lawn of the little white house on Service Road. Blood ran like latticework from the street, up the driveway, and pooled in the doorway, where 23-year-old Major Johnson lay dying. His aunt stood back in the darkness of her house, her hands clasped over her mouth. Major's girlfriend wandered the front yard with eyes that seemed to see through everything—the sprig of dry black hair that dangled over her face, the shouting police officers, the growing mass of sad and angry people—as if the world had become suddenly transparent.

Miami-Dade Fire Rescue arrived. Eight burly firemen began snipping away at Johnson's clothes. Three Opa-locka cops struggled to clear the crowd of about fourty neighbors, passersby, and friends. The scene had cut off traffic entirely on Service Road, a poor residential loop sandwiched between a dirty canal and a set of Tri-Rail tracks.

Ofcr. Pete Rojas arrived at the scene with a swagger, his hair slicked back in a kind of lothario pompadour. Waving his short, thick arms, the Cuban-American cop sliced through the horror with terms of familiar endearment.

"Pumpkin, I'm gonna need you to step back."

"Mama, you need to get back inside the house. How's that other girl? Still crazy?"

"Lemme see that baby good, she doesn't look like me."

Behind him paramedics strapped Johnson to a backboard. A single gunshot had severed the bone in his left arm and made small holes in his chest and neck. Blood trickled from his wounds. His eyes had become glazed slits, as though he were watching a movie he didn't quite care for.

Rojas got into his cruiser and reversed up the street to clear a path for the ambulance. He stopped next to a heavily tattooed girl holding an infant.

"Mama," he called, waving herover. She smiled gold. "Did you hear the shots?"

"Yeah," she said.

"Was he in the dirty business?" She shook her head no.

"Who's the best, baby?"

"Rojas," she answered, smiling.

Arriving at the hospital with the ambulance, Rojas followed the gurney into the trauma ward and watched as a team of frenetic, green-scrubbed doctors set upon Johnson's naked body. Machines bleated with the beating of his heart while the doctors took him apart piece by piece, removing dead organs to a nearby tray.

Rojas walked back to the waiting room. He took a seat near Major's girlfriend. (She declined to provide her name to *New Times*.) She kept her eyes fixed on the linoleum floor and answered each of his questions in a low, flat voice.

The shooting had been the work of a short fifteen-year-old known as Pee Wee, she said, who had eyed her and Johnson at the grocery store from the back seat of a Grand Prix. The car had stopped, reversed, and followed closely, boxing them in a few blocks later.

Pee Wee emptied a black boxy pistol into Johnson as he tried to make a dash for his aunt's front door, she recalled. While her boyfriend slumped against a gold Pontiac parked in the driveway, she pursued the shooters—through the neighborhood streets and back alleys—to get a tag number. She remembered just the first three letters: TAA.

Rojas returned to the operating room just in time to see Major die, the digital squawk silenced like a felled bird. The doctors snapped off their gloves and tossed them onto the bloody sheets, sterile wrappers, and tubing that surrounded Major's corpse. His toes had turned a jaundiced yellow.

"6:32," a voice rang out. "6:32!" several voices echoed.

Two orderlies set to work filling a trash can with the gory detritus while a surgeon began stuffing Major's remains back into his demolished torso, sewing it up for the medical examiner.

Rojas entered the family room flanked by a Miami-Dade detective. A few women chatted; a handful of men muttered, through clenched teeth, about revenge. Major's father, a tall man with long, ropy dreads and a natty beard, paced outside, distractedly snapping a short white towel he held in his hand.

The hospital's grief counselor led him in, by the arm. "The man needs to talk to you," he said softly.

"My son dead?" Major's father muttered, making a wobbly advance toward Rojas. The homicide detective's knee twitched slightly with the weight of his task. "My son dead?" he cried and collapsed—first onto his knees, then his face—into a crescent formed by friends and family. *"My baby," he wailed, pounding the floor with his fists.*

Rojas turned and left the room. Major Johnson was the first homicide victim in Opa-locka this year. Two more would follow the next week. By the end of April there were six. "You've got to build up a shield," Rojas said flatly in the hallway of the emergency room. "The things we see every day you just can't take them home."

Walking down the street after sundown in Opa-locka is widely regarded as either foolish or deviant; there are places in town where the same is true even in daylight.

Amid the decaying liquor stores in Middle Eastern-style buildings, illicit auto body joints, and cinder-block ant-farm apartments, a preponderance of idlers can make Opa-locka appear as though it's trapped in a kind of morbid summer vacation. People can be found, at all hours, hanging out in every nook and cranny, bored by the passage of each car and person.

Though there has been a relative dip in the city crime in recent years, there were eleven homicides in 2006, compared with a record fourteen in 1988. As of the 2000 census the city's per capita income was less than $10,000 a year, and more than a third of its 15,000 residents lived below the poverty line, 17 percent of the population was unemployed, and 72 percent had incomes below $35,000.

City Clerk Deborah Sheffield Irby says Opa-locka's unemployment rate is 4.7 percent, compared to a regional average of 3.1 percent; the U.S. Labor Department, which tracks unemployment nationally, does not keep data at the level of small cities like Opa-locka. (Asked where Opa-locka ranks among Florida cities in terms of citizens living below the poverty line, Irby is flabbergasted. "Who says we're living in poverty?" she asked. "I don't know anyone in poverty here.")

When quitting time rolls around for the city's employed, the streets flood with ATVs, dirt bikes, and go-carts. They're illegal, but the police can't do a thing about them. The likelihood of instigating a deadly accident, in pursuit, is simply too high. Rojas nearly wrecked his cruiser in 1999 when a pack of ten ATVs swarmed him at high speed.

"This is Iraq in America," he mutters as he makes his way into "the Triangle": nine infamous blocks that make up the town's northwest corner.

It's a neighborhood where piles of rotting furniture and garbage are left to mount; where apartments are rented with shot-out windows; where the only tenable form of commerce appears to be trade in drugs, cheap alcohol, and fried food. Aside from four bunkerlike convenience stores and four restaurants, the Triangle is little more than vacant lots, churches, and sub-standard housing.

All of Opa-locka's high-crime areas have the look and feel of occupied zones, but the Triangle looks more like a blast site. Two clusters of multi-unit public housing have been shut down entirely—bricked up, only to be burrowed into by crack heads.

"I always get nervous right here," says Rojas, turning up Duval Street and into the bullet-pocked intersection known as 21 Jump Street. "You never know when you'll come up on a shooting. I'm telling you—it's Baghdad."

Since 1986, low wood and metal barricades (similar to guardrails situated along freeways) have restricted traffic into the Triangle. Last year three entrances along 22nd Avenue were opened up. The barricades limited escapes, but they also trapped crime inside the neighborhood. Like bandages applied to a dirty wound, drugs and violence seem merely to have festered behind the low metal structures. And the busts keep coming.

In February Opa-locka teamed up with the DEA to haul a drug-trafficking ring of forty-five people out of the Triangle. Fourteen of them face ten-to-fifteen-year sentences on federal drug charges, if convicted. If released, they will likely wage war on those who have taken up business in their absence.

The commerce along the Triangle's exposed western edge offers the last vestige of the economy wrought by Rickey Brownlee's notorious narcotics operation. The kingpin attained a kind of Robin Hood status, opening a pair of restaurants and a grocery store, paying rents and comping food for the needy. In 1989 the DEA noted his operation was worth about $26 million annually, shortly before they sent him to prison. He is now serving a life sentence.

But Brownlee's incarceration seems to be something of a dubious achievement, like the toppling of Saddam. There is no longer a central authority in the Triangle; instead, warring factions vie for control.

Seven Cent Hole (the nickname for a bar and motel functioning as a known heroin and prostitution locale) forms the filthy southwestern tip of the Triangle. On his way out of the neighborhood, Rojas notices a weathered, middle-age man whose teeth are missing along one side of his mouth. He wears a blue baseball cap, a plaid shirt, and pants flecked with paint. In his right hand he holds a bag of chips; tucked under his other arm is a copy of the New York Times.

"*Cornbread!*" hollers Rojas. The man looks up and wanders over to the window of his cruiser, bashfully. It's Ronnie Brownlee, the only one of the six Brownlee brothers not currently serving time. (Most recently DeLeon Brownlee, 33, a felon on probation, was charged with murder in last month's shooting of 19-year-old Leonard Mells.) Ronnie did his time for drugs and racketeering in the late 1990s, but now makes a living painting houses.

He's straightened himself out, Rojas whispers. "I got kids to feed," Ronnie explains dutifully. Though pleasant and soft-spoken, Ronnie loses his cool at the mention of his brother's name.

"Rick showed love," he says. "He did everything he could. Rick looked out for this place for real. He helped people from inside prison; he'd bury your mamma and your daddy. Our father and mother passed away—they didn't even let him come to the funeral."

Things have gotten safer, he says, but worse.

"It's going crazy," he says. "When I grew up they want a real fight; they ain't even fight no more, they just grab a gun. It's safer in a sense, but it gets bad. One day it's good, one day it's bad; the next day, it's really, really bad."

Police pressure on the Triangle has pushed drug commerce into a HUD apartment complex known as "the Back Blues," one of several such buildings staked out by rival drug gangs in neighborhoods southwest of the Triangle. The buildings have all been slapped with fresh coats of dull brown paint, but they continue to be known by their original colors: "the Pinks," "the Browns," "the Front Blues."

The "Back Blues," officially the Alexandria Garden Apartments, achieved notoriety this past October when a shootout erupted between local dealers and police. Opa-locka's only narcotics detective, Miguel Galvez, and Miami-Dade Det. Raymond Robertson had received a tip that a vacant apartment there had been stockpiled with guns and drugs. One of the dealers approached their cop car holding a pistol. All hell broke loose. Robertson was shot seven times by three different suspects. He returned fire with gunshot wounds in both arms. The pair took refuge in a Kwik Stop one block north—the same place where Opa-locka Police officer Ephraim Brown was gunned down in 1986.

Since then County Tactical Narcotics teams have been hopping out of pickup trucks in bulletproof vests, tackling suspects in broad daylight, searching cars, and setting up radio lookouts throughout the besieged projects.

But pressure on the Blues will inevitably push activity back into the Triangle. "It's like rats and roaches," said one officer, wishing to remain anonymous. "You burn out one nest and they just scurry into another."

Kevin, a 33-year-old drug dealer working the Back Blues, regards Rickey Brownlee's incarceration without sentimentality. "More spots opened up," he says, "and prices went down."

He doubts that the local police will ever be able to root their operations out of the federally funded apartments. "We never go to jail," he said, while a trio of visiting Opa-locka cops conducted interviews just out of earshot. "To put us away they'd need informants and stuff. And that's never gonna happen." Kevin and his colleagues provide every child in the building with subsidies of up to $7000 per year, he said, a strong incentive in a town where 42 percent of children under 18 live in poverty.

In his thirteen years as a cop, Pete Rojas has been everything from a dispatcher to a domestic violence detective. He's received twenty-five commendations (including six so far this year), primarily for drug arrests. An ex-partner nicknamed him "K-9."

He is, by all accounts, a good cop who enjoys a kind of celebrity status in town. Last year he was featured in the lyrics and video for "Get Yo Money," a thug ode sung by up-and-coming Opa-locka rappers Brisco and Henessi:

"Rojas got me calculatin' every move / Ask about the Bris they'll say that boy is hella smooth."

In the video, the camera quickly cuts to Rojas leaning against his cruiser, arms folded sternly over his expansive chest, his eyes shielded by a pair of wrap-around sunglasses.

He appears to be having the time of his life.

Well-known around town, Rojas leaves his body armor in the trunk most days. You get the feeling he doesn't need it.

He is swarthy and oversexed, cool and clever. After a few hours on patrol with him, he seems the only kind of person who could possibly stomach the Herculean task of being an Opa-locka cop.

In 1968, the year before he was born, Rojas's father took a job as a patrolman in Opa-locka. (He left in 1972 to work for the Broward County Sheriff's Office.) Rojas Jr. didn't know much about the town as a child. When he enrolled at Hialeah/Miami Lakes Senior High, he came to know Opa-locka as the place people went to buy weed.

Since joining the department in 1994, he has witnessed the comings and goings of nine Opa-locka Police chiefs. He has been fired three times: once for taking a weekend in Cancun without leave; once without nominal cause (Rojas cites his testimony on behalf of two fellow officers during an arbitration); and again during a layoff.

He managed to get rehired every time, thanks to his impressive record and shrewd politicking. But like most cops in Opa-locka, Rojas seems more at ease amid the constant automatic weapon fire of the city's mean streets than within the police station walls.

In 2002 the Florida Department of Law Enforcement nearly shut the ailing department down for being noncompliant in 80 percent of FDLE's professional standards. State investigators found the department lacking in (among other things) basic equipment, manpower, and fundamental organization.

Most cops were working without body armor, sirens, or vehicle radios, according to the report. While per capita crime rates were nearing the highest in the United States, officers took home the lowest pay in the county.

Commendations and criminal investigations were equally scarce. Many cops nominally in charge of subdepartments (i.e. traffic) were not aware of their titles—to say nothing of their responsibilities.

A former indoor shooting range had been turned into the evidence depot and piled, willy-nilly, with aging drugs, guns, and weapons with no ostensible order or system for keeping track. In 2003 two senior cops were prosecuted for selling the stuff back to criminals.

At times, according to the report, as many as eight calls for service were put on hold due to a lack of officers: thirty four patrolled a city of more than 15,000 people, down from fifty four in 1996. The report cited one particularly troubling evening, 18 May 2002, when one cop and his supervisor were left to handle "a homicide and barricaded hostage situation"—alone.

A 2004 followup found little improvement. A pair of grant-funded detectives struggled to tackle sixty cases a week; they had almost no investigative training. Officers were burning out. The five reserve cops Opa-locka hired failed to pass their probationary period. "The recruitment function is still nonexistent," the report stated.

In 2005 James Wright, an ambitious lieutenant from the Miami-Dade Police department, took over as Opa-locka's Police chief. Wright's was the first police chief contract to promise such a high degree of job security: a five-year guaranteed payout (whether the town dumps him or not). Detractors outraged by his juicy contract photocopied and distributed it throughout the city as a kind of effigy: his $98,500-a-year salary, take-home SUV, and Blackberry did not go over well with entrenched officers, many of whom regard him as an occupying force.

In a sense, he is. Wright is the first chief in the city's history to be brought in from outside the department.

Since his arrival he has tackled the department from the top down. After Wright took over, three administrative officers retired and a former chief, one lieutenant, and five officers resigned. He has demoted four lieutenants to beat cops and is openly waging war with the city manager, Jannie Beverly, who hired him.

He regards his mission of professionalizing OLPD with a humorless severity.

"*I envision Opa-locka as a jewel in the crown of Miami-Dade County,*" he said, dressed in an immaculately pressed uniform and patent leather shoes. To the chagrin of Opa-locka's veteran cops, that vision did not include many of them. He has staffed vacant positions with people from outside the agency. His most recent officer hire, a female lieutenant, was brought down from Connecticut.

"I'm still not done," Wright said of his housecleaning, as he sat behind the desk in his white-carpeted office. A matching white Greek Revival couch sits against the far wall. Flanked by busts of Roman soldiers, copies of *The 48 Laws of Power* and Sun Tzu's *Art of War* are at arm's length.

At the geographical heart of Opa-locka—not one block away from city hall—a concrete monstrosity known as "the water tower" juts out of the skyline as a glaring symbol of the town's central dysfunction.

The derelict industrial facility is Rojas's white whale. He has railed about it being a city-owned haven for junkies and fugitives for the duration of his career, he says. Nothing has ever been done about it.

The tower was abandoned in 1985. Since then Opa-locka has paid Miami-Dade County Water and Sewer roughly $2 million a year for services. The 38,000-square-foot treatment facility sits empty, with vague plans to get it up and running. In the meantime the structure has filled with all kinds of biohazardous slime.

Last fall an exhaustive feasibility study by Florida International University's Department of Civil and Environmental Engineering brought the tower's sad state to the attention of city commissioners.

"Due to twenty years of idling, the water treatment plant had been trespassed by homeless people," wrote Dr. Walter Tang. "It became a major hazard for the city due to illegal dumping, illegal residence, and drug trafficking."

It could be saved, Tang explained. The state had already offered $5 million to turn it into a miraculous plant capable of turning out ten million gallons of reclaimed water a day. But the county is holding tight to the $6 million in matching funds needed to go ahead with the project.

"This is environmental injustice," Tang said by phone. "The county thinks the safety of those people is the city's problem. It is all of our problem. They need to re-invest in Opa-locka and they won't. Could it be because the town is 80 percent African-American? I can't think of any other reason."

(*New Times* attempted to contact City Manager Jannie Beverly, who was presented with the study in October. She has not returned multiple phone calls and was unavailable for comment at city hall on three separate occasions.)

On his way to the tower, Rojas swings by the S & D Wash House, a coin laundry at 621 Opa-locka Blvd.

"Hey, Hadley!" Rojas calls from the driver's seat. A man emerges from behind the counter, dressed like a television detective: blue-checked button-down shirt, tan pants, Timberland boots. His hair is maintained in a microscopic fade. His eyes dart to the corner across the street, where a pair of fat, scantily clad women are negotiating with a hairy drunk.

"*Hey!*" Hadley barks, yanking a thumb over his shoulder. The three drop their eyes in shame and scatter. Hadley sneers, turns to Rojas, and shakes his hand vigorously.

Steven Hadley describes his residence in Opa-locka with fatalistic stoicism, like an Orthodox Jewish settler in the West Bank.

"*I live here; I have a vested interest here,*" he says, scanning the street for challengers. "*I'm gonna be here until it's gone.*"

He was born in Overtown and moved to the outskirts of Opa-locka in the sixth grade. He can remember walking past the Brownlee house on his way to middle school.

Hadley enlisted in ROTC during his senior year of high school and left for the Army soon after graduation. "*Opa-locka was always my reason for staying in the service,*" he said. "*Every time I came back, I'd hear someone died, or went to jail, or caught AIDS.*"

In 1999, after retiring from the Army and taking a job as a Miami-Dade Schools detective, he and his wife purchased a home and moved to Opa-locka with their three children. Every other night, Hadley says, he can hear gunfire from his front porch.

Six months ago he purchased the S & D Wash House. He allows no drinking, no loitering, no dope smoking. He keeps watch over the place from his laptop computer, which is networked to nine closed circuit security cameras on the premises.

When Rojas mentions a trip up the block to the water tower, Hadley taps his pistol beneath his shirt, almost mechanically. "I'll come and back you up."

Rojas arrives at the torn chainlink fence marking the entrance to the tower a few minutes after Hadley, whom he hears shouting from inside the tower: "*Stop, police!*" Rojas darts in to find Hadley counseling a ragged veteran on where he might spend the night.

The three-story concrete mass looms behind him like the setting for a film noir shoot-out finale. It connects to a series of industrial substations by a precarious iron catwalk. To the north an entire section of fence has been torn out, providing access to the railroad tracks, which, on this particular afternoon, lay littered with sacrificial chickens and a trash bag full of goat bones.

"Too many damned veterans out here," Hadley says as the tattered man disappears along the tracks. Hadley looks around in disgust at the patchy grass. He is surrounded by piles of stolen luggage, rags, bottles, needles, crack pipes, and a carpet of empty dime bags—Batman bags, ganja leaf bags, yellow ones, red ones—a moldering plastic log of every hit taken in the crumbling degenerate haven.

Inside the tower, a thick, festering layer of human waste coats the second floor. The stench is indescribable. "Careful where you step," Hadley says, pointing to hypodermic needles jutting up through the muck.

"I've seen as many as fifty people living in here," Rojas says, surveying a burned-out box spring. "A lot of them are dope boys just out of jail. They spend all day slinging crack on the streets and come back here at night."

Hadley and Rojas continue up the stairs, away from the stench. They navigate the sloping tar paper and brittle iron rebar that make up the roof, tiptoeing toward the building's concrete edges. Rojas shoots a disparaging gaze toward the spires of city hall. Officials fled the palatial government center this past March, citing a leaky roof and a relentless rat infestation.

"Look at this," Hadley says, pointing to the near distance, beyond the tower's eastern boundary. "That's an elementary school. We've got 500 registered sex offenders living in this four-mile town. I feel like no one's going to do anything about this until one of those guys drags a kid in here and rapes them."

Just then, as if on cue, Rojas hears a stirring from a small room to his right. "Police!" he barks, stepping onto a forklift pallet that provides a shaky bridge to the closed metal door. After a tense minute, a bleary-eyed 25-year-old named Dre shuffles reluctantly into the daylight, sporting a gold grill and baggy black clothing. "I'm homeless," he grumbles. "I'm a runaway. I can't find no work."

Rojas brushes him aside. Standing behind him, in high heels and tangerine "going out" clothes, is a pretty fourteen-year-old girl. While Rojas and Hadley question the girl, Dre bolts.

"I'm gonna get you help whether you like it or not," Hadley says. On the way back to the station, she smiles and jokes with Rojas about nightclubs and his fly car. "Please don't call my mother," she begs. Hadley spends his day off looking up her school records and contacting crisis counselors. Rojas buys her McDonald's and begins a mountain of paperwork.

Hours later her mother arrives at the station from work, wearing her Miami-Dade County bus driver's uniform. They live just a block away from the police station; she is familiar with the water tower. "All kinds of things go in and out of there every night," she says. Around 10:30 p.m. the girl drops her guard and begins to cry.

She says she snuck out on Friday night to see a boy in Miami and spent the night dancing. A friend had given her a lift back to her house. She was afraid to come in, she says, having skipped her afternoon classes, and instead roamed the streets alone. She met Dre in front of the Kwik Stop on Aswan Road, just north of the Back Blues. She was tired and needed a place to sleep. He knew one.

When they lay down on the filthy mattress in the tiny dark room, he pulled her clothes off and raped her. Rojas called some people he knew in the street and, within a few hours, Dre was in custody.

It is the second Tuesday in March: Chief's Night Out, a day some rank and file cops dread. Chief Wright has called in the entire force to canvas the town, asking residents if they have any complaints or concerns about policing in the area. Most people shake their heads and smile shyly (spooked, it seems, by the odd manifestation of cops), but every now and then someone asks how they plan to put a stop to the nightly gunfire.

Wright snaps his fingers and has an officer take down every name, address, and complaint. He then hands out a flyer (in English, Spanish, and Kreyol) featuring his smiling glamour shot and personal cell number, urging them to call about trouble. The flyers are supplemented by a sheet informing residents that anonymous phone tips may lead to $1000 rewards. Wright calls it "regaining the trust of the community." But it looks more like grassroots campaigning—as though he and the dope boys are competing for the same office.

Opa-locka needs Wright's political savvy. Nimbly wielding his political influence, so far he has enlisted eight county and federal agencies to supplement the force, at no expense to the town. He's trying to install cameras and an acoustic gunshot tracking system that's been battle-tested in Iraq. The half-million dollars in various grants he's seeking have yet to come through, but Wright will travel to Tallahassee in May to implore everyone from the governor to the state drug czar for the necessary funds.

He has raised officers' starting salary twice, from $27,000 to more than $34,000, and has waged something of an aesthetic campaign, redesigning the force's patch and badge and purchasing a brand-new fleet of take-home black and white Dodge Chargers.

Wright's aim is to build the department back up to more than fifty officers. Thirteen people have left the department since he became chief; only three have been hired.

One Wednesday morning in March, after thirteen years in Opa-locka, Rojas didn't show up to work. By midafternoon word got around that he had quit.

A week later he handed in a letter to the city manager demanding the water tower be razed. A fire erupted there early this month. The city installed a new chainlink fence, but it was hack-sawed down hours later.

Bidding has begun to consider proposals for the tower's rehabilitation or demolition. "We just voted to revitalize it," said Vice Mayor Dottie Johnson. "I hope we don't tear it down."

With Rojas gone the number of police officers in the city has dropped to twenty six, including the chief and his deputy: fewer than half the number policing the city when Rojas started in 1994.

Rojas now patrols South Miami, where the murder rate is one every ten years, and the pay is better. But he still hasn't gotten used to it. "*It's weird,*" he said by phone, "*patrolling a place without so much violence.*"

Shortly after Rojas left, Pee Wee was arrested and released, twice. According to one arresting officer, the boy admitted to being in the Grand Prix during the murder of Major Johnson, but denied pulling the trigger. Today he can be found wandering the Triangle.

Johnson's murder is still under investigation, one of more than a dozen open murder cases in Opa-locka. Dre remains in police custody, charged with lewd and lascivious assault on a minor.

In the week following Rojas's departure, three people were shot in Opa-locka; one incident took place in an apartment building less than two blocks west of the police station. Late on the evening of 5 April, Guy Shapiro, a prominent North Miami Beach chiropractor, was found in the Triangle, shot to death in his Escalade. This past Sunday night, two men were shot to death outside an apartment in the 1300 block of Ali Baba Avenue. No arrests have been made.

Calvin Godfrey, "Baghdad West: In Opa-locka, gang warfare, drug dealing, and decay are a way of life", originally published in *Miami New Times*, Thursday 26 April 2007.

The following conversation with Antolin Garcia Carbonell was held at the Miami Springs Historical Society where, previously, MaryAnn Goodlett-Taylor had guided us around.

Kenneth Andrew Mroczek & Anne Daems: What is your relationship to Opa-locka?

Antolin Garcia Carbonell: I worked at Miami International Airport for thirty years, and in my last five years there I got involved with documenting the old buildings at Opa-locka Airport. These buildings had been built with federal funds and once you use federal funding for any building and it has to be demolished, you have to document its history. There was a consultant working on this. He wasn't doing a very good job and I just got sucked into it. I realized there was a lot more history surrounding the airport than I first thought.

Glenn Curtiss had a small airfield there—the fifth airport he had in Miami. He had an outfit that was known as the Florida Aviation Camp, which served as the public relation side of his aviation company; they would do aerial photography and stunt flying. He built a film studio in Hialeah and the airport was previously located next to the film studio, but when Hialeah became popular he moved it to Opa-locka. His idea was that if you lived in Opa-locka you could have your own little airplane, you could keep it there and, you know, live there and fly in and out.

The very first building that was built in Opa-locka was the observation tower, which is no longer standing. I found the footprint of the ruins of the tower in Opa-locka Airport. The footprint is the last thing left of the first building that gave the whole look to the town. It was a very functional building because it housed a well and a water tower, and they just covered it up on the outside, with a Moorish design facade. It had an exterior staircase and there was a viewing platform to promote the initial land sales. They would take you up there and point and say, "Well, your lot is gonna be over there and, you know, these streets are coming this way and that way."

Then there was a golf course, just as there was a golf course in Miami Springs, which went all around the airfield. I assume MaryAnn told you about the archery club?

KAM & AD: No.

AGC: Oh! Ah! Glenn Curtiss realized people liked golf. But he wasn't really into golf. He liked archery, so he created an archery club, which was one of the buildings that was within the airport footprint. That building survived until the 1980s, when it was demolished. Curtiss brought an archer in and they developed this game they called "archery-golf" where they set up tripods with coconuts and you would go from one hole to the other shooting arrows—he had this game set up in Miami Springs too. There was also a swimming pool that was just past the archery club—there was this kid who was a swimmer and would do shows there.

KAM & AD: That was Jacky Ott, no?

AGC: Jacky Ott, you got it. I assume you have read *Dream of Araby*, the book by Frank FitzGerald-Bush?

KAM & AD: Yes.

AGC: I'm on the board of the Curtiss Mansion, trying to document more of Curtiss' life here, and at one point I was trying to find out where Frank FitzGerald-Bush's papers had gone, to see if we could source more research material. I mostly wanted to see his father's account books, because his father was the original electrical contractor on Opa-locka. So there is probably a lot more documentation on some of these buildings there than we have currently. Frank FitzGerald-Bush was also a poet and he was a colleague of Vivian Laramore Rader who was the Poet Laureate of Florida. I couldn't find his papers so I looked for her papers and I discovered that we had been neighbors! When I first came to Miami fifty years ago, she lived near me and I had seen her house. We never met but I did this whole study on her that was published in the Florida Book Review about three years ago.

KAM & AD: Were you ever able to track down Frank FitzGerald-Bush's collection?

AGC: Well, he has a nephew who inherited his stuff and I'm not sure where he is or what he did with it. I think Frank FitzGerald-Bush was also a musician and apparently he had a lot of material that was valuable. I think the nephew at some point had a shop and was selling many things.

I started seeing Opa-locka from many different angles. There is the whole story of World War II, for example, and what was built on Opa-locka during this period was incredible—all the buildings went up in a very short period of time. There is a natural hammock, which is actually now set aside as a reserve, you can't touch it anymore. I tried very hard to save a group of buildings from the 1930s, they're all demolished now, that made up the Naval Reserve Airbase, Curtiss' last legacy to Miami before his death. He wanted to develop aviation in Miami but he needed pilots and pilots need to train and in those days most pilots were part of the U.S. Navy and had to go in for regular flight training. Curtiss lobbied Congress to get a Naval Reserve Airbase set up in Miami and he gave them land in Opa-locka, just north of the golf course. So, there was a whole group of buildings that were built in the 1930s using money from the WPA (Works Progress Administration), including a hangar, a whole complex of shops and warehouses, and a particularly nice lounge, a really beautiful building. Unfortunately, it was all knocked down. I did manage to get the doors of the building saved, they're now in the Historical Museum collection. I am working with the Historical Museum right now. Next year there is going to be an exhibition I am guest curating here in Miami to mark 100 years since our first flight.

The Navy set up a dirigible mooring mast in Opa-locka, it took up the entire west half of the airport. The dirigible Graf Zeppelin came here in 1933. It was a huge story at the time and when I was doing research in the National Archives, I found out that the Hindenburg had been approved to come to Miami—they gave them the permit a week before it crashed (in 1936). The reason that the Hindenburg crashed—among other things—was because they were trying to turn its construction around very fast. After the death of King George V, the new king, King George VI, was going to be crowned and there were a lot of very wealthy people who wanted to get to England in time, so they were going to use the Hindenburg to get there. Because they could not wait it crashed, but the original plan was that after it dropped these people off in Europe, it was going to stop here in Miami and dock at Opa-locka.

I am Cuban, and I found a whole dimension of the history of Cuba mostly related to the Opa-locka Airport. Also, during the Cold War, Opa-locka was the site of covert CIA operations: In 1954 the CIA overthrew the government of Guatemala from the base here.

KAM & AD: Oh, we did not know that.

AGC: Yes! Yes. And Opa-locka was also used during the Bay of Pigs Invasion [an unsuccessful military invasion of Cuba in April 1961]. Are you also aware that there was a whole group of houses that were built during WWII in support of the Naval air station?

KAM & AD: Yes the barracks and the other houses that...

AGC: Well, there are about 200 houses on the southern part. And, actually, I found in the National Archive actual plans of all the houses. I found the plans about seven or eight years ago and at that time 190 of the original houses were still there and fairly unchanged.

I think part of the reason why Opa-locka ended up with some of the problems it did was because the Navy controlled those properties up until the 1960s. When the Naval air station was finally de-activated it was declared surplus property and the houses were sold to individuals. Actually, that was part of the reason why all these government operations were held in Opa-locka: because the Navy could put people in these houses without attracting attention.

KAM & AD: That's interesting.

AGC: So, why don't you tell me what you are most interested in?

KAM & AD: We are looking at the timeline of Opa-locka, focusing on the architecture and the creation of the original 'dream', and how it has developed over the years; it's trajectory. We've been taking photographs, making video recordings, and talking with people since our first visit in 2006. We have also done some research in the archives.

AGC: I am sure Mary Ann told you about the Arabian Nights.

KAM & AD: She did not say so much about it, but we know Opa-locka had this festival every year.

AGC: The festival started because of the first train. Because the deal, and this is one of the other important things about Curtiss and, really, this is why Opa-locka happened in the first place. He had made a deal with Davies Warfield to bring the second railroad into Miami. There was Flagler's railroad, the FEC (Florida East Coast Railway), along the coast, but because of its monopoly rates were very high and people in Miami wanted a second railroad to come through.

Davies Warfield had brought his railroad through central Florida as far down as Palm Beach and he wanted to extend it to Miami but 1925 was the height of the land boom, and prices of real estate were so inflated it was outrageous. The Securities and Exchange Commission would not allow you to sell bonds to buy land at these inflated prices so the only way the railroad could come here was through right of way donations [voluntary gifts of land for transportation improvements]. Curtiss and his partner Bright had the 120,000-acre Curtiss-Bright ranch, which went from 36th Street to Miami Gardens Drive. They donated six miles of right of way land that was critical to the railway. Where their property was you have a curve in the railroad, and that is where Opa-locka was created. Opa-locka was going to be the first stop on the railroad out of Miami—the curve on the railroad is what established the design parameter for the street grid of Opa-locka.

Miami Springs, 21 June 2010

ARCHIVAL MATERIAL DESCRIPTIONS

COVER
Cover and dustjacket adapted from Opa-locka newspaper advertisements c.1926. (full citations p.176)

DUST JACKET
Opa-Locka, the City Substancial: Opa-Locka Company Inc., Owners and Developers. 1"=200'–0". Received date of 01/27/26 appear. Actual-scale (not a reduced) plat of the city with area west of Douglas Road (now NW 37th Avenue) platted, containing a golf course and homes. Administration building, pool, school, railroad station, garage and golf clubhouse plotted. Blue-line original print on paper, 97 × 150 cm.

PHOTOGRAPHS
Arrival of the first Seaboard Air Line Rail Road train at Opa-locka, Florida, 8 January 1927. Photographs of celebration:
Page 3: Grand Vizier of the city of Opa-locka, Florida, dressed in Arabian garb and saddled upon a horse, takes a scrolled proclamation of S. Davies Warfield; Governor Martin seated at right. Black and white glossy photographic print, 5" × 7" (13 × 18 cm).
Page 4: Costumed townspeople posing with dignitaries, including governor John W. Martin, State of Florida; E.E. Dammers, Mayor of Coral Gables; and S. Davies Warfield, president of the Seaboard Air Line Rail Road. Arabian costumes were reputedly chosen by B.E. Muller, the city's architect, and supplied by a New York company. Black and white glossy photographic print, 5" × 7" (13 × 18 cm).
Page 5: Arabian Nights fantasy. A scene from the celebration honoring the arrival of the first Orange Blossom Special train of the Seaboard Line in Opa-locka, 7 January 1926. (Photograph by F.N. Irving.)**

Page 6: Photograph Hurt Building, 3.5" × 5.25".*
Page 7: Photograph Administration Building, 3.5" × 5.25".*
Page 8: Suggested treatment in Batchelder Tiles: gate panels, 10 July 1926. By A.J.E. for The Batchelder Tiles, Batchelder-Wilson Co., New York. 3/4"=1'–0". Note stamp imprint at bottom and statement in upper left corner. Partially-rendered drawing of the gatehouse panels with notes at right identifying types of tile used. Blueprint on paper, 45 × 25 cm.
Page 9: Photograph Administration Building, 3.5" × 5.25".*
Page 10: Photograph Administration Building, 3.5" × 5.25".*
Page 11: Photograph of women in costume standing on balcony in front of the Administration Building, Scenario undated. Photo taken from gateway tower. Black and white print, 8" × 10", modern photographic print, 25 × 20 cm.
Page 12: A group posing and talking on stairs and balcony in courtyard, Scenario c. 1927. Photograph of activity around Administration Building, possibly taken at the Arabian Nights Festival. Black and white photographic print, 5" × 7", or 12 × 17 cm.
Page 13: Photograph of about a dozen people in costume standing behind the parapet and in front of the third story dome next to the observation tower. Scenario undated. Black and white print, 5" × 7", modern photographic print, 12 × 17 cm.
Page 14: H. Sayre Wheeler Residence, Opa-locka, Florida, 3.5" × 5.25".*

Photographs of persons at Wheeler house, likely taken during the Arabian Nights Festival on January 8, 1927:
Page 15: Pioneer resident Frank S. Bush, in Arabian costume and standing beyond a vase at the corner of the garage. Black and white photographic print, 13 × 18 cm.
Page 16: Group of fifteen posing outside the gateway to house, all dressed in oriental garb. Black and white photographic print, 13 × 18 cm.
Page 17: Woman in harem outfit sitting on a window ledge. Black and white photographic print, 13 × 18 cm.
Page 18: Photograph of H. Sayre Wheeler Residence, Opa-locka, Florida, 3.5" × 5.25".*
Page 19: Photograph of residence for W.H. Kendrik, Opa-locka, Florida. Lot 2, Block 37 (1006 Sharar Avenue) and residence for (Bostik House) 1010 Sharar Avenue, 3.5" × 5.25".*
Page 20: Photograph of 1111 Sesame Street, 3.5" × 5.25".*
Page 21: Photograph of Duplex Residency's for New England Construction Company

Opa-locka, Florida. Lots 3 and 4, Block 13 (1210/1212 and 1214/1216 Sesame Street), 3.5" × 5.25".

Page 22: Front view, c. 1927. Bernardt E. Muller, architect, N.Y.C. Photograph of Bush apartments. Black and white photographic print, 20 × 26 cm.

Page 23: Photograph of Haislip House 3.5" × 5.25".*

Page 24: Photograph of unknown residence, Opa-locka, Florida. 3.5" × 5.25".*

COLOR CODE CHARTS

Page 45–47: City of Opa-locka Building Structure Color Code, provided by the city of Opa-locka, Florida. http://www.opalockafl.gov/DocumentCenter/Home/View/444.

ARCHITECTURAL DRAWINGS OF BUILDINGS AND RESIDENCES

Page 50: Stores and Apartments. Garage and Gas Station for Curtiss-Bright Properties (Hurt Building), Opa-locka, Florida. Drawing 2. Front elevation, 18 February 1926. Bernardt E. Muller, architect, N.Y.C. 1/4" = 1'–0". Muller's stamped title block with note below drawing title: "Repeat other side." Rendered elevation of arcaded, two-story building with three minarets, two small domes at ends, and a large central dome. Floor lines and building heights dimensioned at center. Pencil on tracing paper, 66 × 94 cm.

Page 63: Residence for Mr. R.D. Logan, Opa-locka, Florida. Lot 2, Block 75 (705 Sharar Avenue), Higgings House. Job 45, drawing 3. Front (south) elevation, side (east) elevation, 18 November 1926. By Carl Jensen for Bernardt E. Muller, architect. 1/4" = 1'–0". Dimensioned facades with many details. Pencil on tracing paper, 44 × 55 cm.

Page 64: Residence for Mr. R.D. Logan, Opa-locka, Florida. Lot 2, Block 75 (705 Sharar Avenue), Higgings House. Job 45, drawing 4. Rear (north) elevation, side (west) elevation, 18 November 1926. By Carl Jensen for Bernardt E. Muller, architect. 1/4" = 1'–0". Dimensioned and detailed elevations. Pencil on tracing paper, 44 × 55 cm.

Page 65: Residence for Mr. R.D. Logan, Opa-locka, Florida. Lot 2, Block 75 (705 Sharar Avenue), Higgings House. Job 45, drawing number absent. Elevation and section of kitchen cupboard, undated. B.E. Muller, architect, Opa-locka, Fla. 3/4" = 1'–0". Cabinetry details and frame construction identified. Pencil on yellow tracing paper, 30 × 40 cm.

Page 66: Residence for Mr. R.D. Logan, Opa-locka, Florida. Lot 2, Block 75 (705 Sharar Avenue), Higgings House. Job 45, drawing number absent. Detail of fireplace, undated. B.E. Muller, architect, Opa-locka, Fla. 3/4" = 1'–0". Plan, elevation and section drawn, dimensioned and detailed as to material used. Pencil on yellow tracing paper, 36 × 35 cm.

Page 67: Residence for Mr. R.D. Logan, Opa-locka, Florida. Lot 2, Block 75 (705 Sharar Avenue), Higgings House. Job 45, Front door detail, undated. B.E. Muller, architect, Opa-locka, Fla. (Elevation at 1" = 1'–0". (Window mullion not to scale.) Dimensions and materials for a door. Pencil on yellow tracing paper, 35 × 32 cm.

Page 79: Residence for Mr. George Cravero, Opa-locka, Florida. Lot 19, Block 38 (1011 Sharar). Job 37, drawing 2. Front elevation, side elevation, 14 September 1926. By C.J.J. for B.E. Muller, architect, Opa-locka, Fla. 1/4" = 1'–0". Drawing details elevations with finishes and dimensions given. Pencil on tracing paper, 45 × 55 cm.

Page 96: Residence for Mr. J.W. Crouse, Opa-locka, Florida. Job 28, drawing 2. Street side elevation, front elevation, 27 August 1926. By P.L. for B.E. Muller, architect, Opa-locka, Fla. 1/4" = 1'–0". Drawing give details of finishes and dimensions for elevations. Pencil on tracing paper, 45 × 55 cm.

Page 110: Proposed Residence for Mr. W.P. Tooker, Opa-locka, Florida. Lot 9, Block 61 (811 Dunad Avenue). Spindle detail, west elevation, south elevation, east elevation, undated. Elevations at 1/4" = 1'–0" ; spindles at full size. Notes made for each drawing. Details of spindled archways, gates and copper hoods on elevations. Pencil on tracing paper, 45 × 55 cm.

Page 117: Residence for Mrs. Walter E. Griffith, Opa-locka, Florida. Lots 7 and 8, Block 36 (1036 Dunad Avenue). Job 83, drawing 4. West elevation, 25 May 1927. By C.J.J. for B.E. Muller, architect, New York. 1/4" = 1'–0". Elevation in rear, with details and treatments shown. Pencil on tracing paper, 37 × 50 cm.

Page 125: Trunk Factory and Showroom for Mr. W.B. King, Opa-locka, Florida. Lot 25, Block 126 (951 Superior). Job 8, drawing 2. Rear elevation, front elevation, street side elevation, 31 August 1926. By P.L. for B.E. Muller, architect, Opa-locka, Fla. 1/4" = 1'–0". Section shows footings, columns, and roof composition; elevation is simple with roof drainage shown. Pencil on tracing paper, 43 × 62 cm.

Page 129: Duplex Residency for New England Construction Company Opa-locka, Florida. Lots 3 and 4, Block 13 (1210/1212 and

1214/1216 Sesame Street, respectively). Lot 4 only. Job 52, drawing 2. Front elevation, side elevation, 27 November 1926. By Carl Jensen for Bernardt E. Muller, architect. 1/4" = 1'–0". Note at left center under front elevation concerns details, and note at bottom center: "Two side elevations similar excepting chimney tops." Detailed elevations with heights dimensioned. Pencil on tracing paper, 44 × 52 cm.

Page 136: Duplex Residency for New England Construction Company Opa-locka, Florida. Lots 3 and 4, Block 13 (1210/1212 and 1214/1216 Sesame Street, respectively). Lot 3 only. Job 51, drawing 2. Front elevation, side elevation, 27 November 1926. By Carl Jensen for Bernardt E. Muller, architect. 1/4" = 1'–0". Notes are similar to companion drawing (see above) regarding elevations and details. Dimensioned and detailed elevations. Pencil on tracing paper, 44 × 52 cm.

Page 140: Four-family dwelling for Mr. Frank S. Bush, Opa-locka, Florida. Lots 9 and 10, Block 13 (1240 Sesame Street). Job 48, drawing 4. Front (north) elevation, side (west) elevation, undated. By Carl Jensen for B.E. Muller, architect, Opa-locka, Fla./New York. Notes at right regarding finish and casement dimensions. Elevations detailed and dimensioned with ceiling heights and arch measurements. Pencil on tracing paper, 58 × 74 cm.

Page 141: Four-family dwelling for Mr. Frank S. Bush, Opa-locka, Florida. Lots 9 and 10, Block 13 (1240 Sesame Street). Stair detail, 18 January 1927. B.E. Muller architect. Three elevations, facing north, east, and west, drawn of the stairs leading to the second floor. Details and a few dimensions given on one elevation. Pencil on tracing paper, 37 × 90 cm.

Page 145: Residence for Mr. S.K. Haislip, Opa-locka, Florida. Lots 17, Block 22 (1141 Jann Avenue).Job 22, drawing 1A. (Revisited) front elevation, side (elevation), 13 September 1926. By C.J.J. for B.E. Muller, architect Opa-locka. 1/4" = 1'–0". Detailed and dimensioned front facade; side elevation crossed through. Pencil on tracing paper, 37 × 50 cm.

NEWSPAPERS ADVERTISEMENTS

Page 181: *Miami Life*, 30 January 1926, 9. Full-page advertisement with engraving of Hurt Building and entitled "Building Begins at Opa-locka, the City Substantial." 55 × 41 cm.

Page 182: *Miami Daily News and Metropolis*, 23 June 1926, page number missing. Large advertisement entitled "Opa-locka Will Be Beautiful," with a short text explaining the architectural and natural beauty of Opa-locka, two photographs of landscaped drives, and several engravings of the features in Opa-locka (golf club, archery club, swimming pool, etc.). Seven columns, 60 × 43 cm.

Page 183: *The Miami Herald*, 10 January 1926, 16. Full page advertisement: "Opa-locka, The city Substantial," beginning with "One thousand and one reasons justify our statement." Indicates Opa-locka's theme before the city's development begins; engraving at right entitled "A Dream of the Arabian Nights." 58 × 44 cm.

Page 184: *Miami Daily News and Metropolis*, 14 February 1926, second news section, 12. Full-page advertisement: "The Overture to the Building Program at Opa-locka, the City Substantial." A lengthy quote from Isabel Stone describes the architectural style of Opa-locka. Sketch of the Administration Building in bottom center, which was due to begin construction that week. 60 × 43 cm.

Page 185: *Miami (Labor) News*, 22 July 1926, not numbered. Large advertisement celebrating the six-month anniversary of Opa-locka, with many small drawings followed by details of the features and progress made at Opa-locka. Six columns, 58 × 43 cm.

Page 186: *The Hialeah Press*, 21 May 1926, 7. Advertisement by Opa-locka Company, Inc., entitled "When Miami is forty years old—What?" Engraving at top of the Miami skyline as envisioned in 1936. Advertisement promotes the favorable climate as the reason for Miami's growth, but Opa-locka claims that the cultural development in western Dade County is most important; makes the connection with the Seaboard Railroad's station in Opa-locka. Bottom has an engraving of a railroad station, the seaboard's symbol, and a conclusion: "Opa-locka—the Seaboard's Gateway to the Everglades." Full page, 56 × 41 cm.

Page 187: *Miami Daily News and Metropolis*, 24 February 1926, Section B, 16. Full page ad for Opa-locka, titled "From the Days of the 'Iron Horse'." Text at left suggests a building boom for Opa-locka with the coming of the railroad. "Points of progress in Opa-locka," list of officers of the Opa-locka Company, Inc., and Seaboard Railway symbol superimposed over a sketch of the front of a locomotive. 60 × 44 cm.

Page 188: *Miami Daily News and Metropolis*, 7 March 1926, main news section, 15. Full-page ad entitled "The Seaboard Will Enter Miami

Through the Golden Gate of Opa-locka, the City Progressive." Large engraving of a locomotive speeding past a Moorish building. At upper right of text, list of features of Opa-locka. Note error in sentence above address: "very" instead of "every." 60 × 43 cm.

NOTE

The descriptions of the advertisements, drawings and unmarked photographs are courtesy of the B.E. Muller Collection, Special Collections at the University of Miami Libraries, Coral Gables, Florida. Photographs marked * are from the Archives & Research Center History Miami, and the photograph marked ** is from Miami Springs Historical Society. Scale and size relate to the original materials.

OPA-TISHA-WOCKA-LOCKA

Architecting 2006–2026

Concept and editors
    Anne Daems &
    Kenneth Andrew Mroczek

Authors
    Kenneth Andrew Mroczek, Catherine Lynn,
    Frank S. FitzGerald-Bush and Calvin Godfrey

Text editors
    Marnie Slater, Carl Skoggard

Color photographs
    Anne Daems &
    Kenneth Andrew Mroczek

Photographs of architectural drawings
    Sid Hoeltzell

Graphic design
    Anne Daems &
    Kenneth Andrew Mroczek
    in conversation with
    Studio Luc Derycke
    (Luc Derycke, Werther Vandenborre,
    Ellen Debucquoy)

Lithography
    Hans Roels

Paper
    Lessebo Design Bright, Luxo Art Samt

Typeface
    Rockwell

Printing and binding
    Cassochrome

Publisher
    MER. Paper Kunsthalle

Texts © the authors, 2014
Images © the artists, 2014

Historical material © Special Collections, University of Miami Libraries, Coral Gables, Florida; Archives & Research Center History Miami and Miami Springs Historical Society, 2014

All rights reserved. No part of this book may be reproduced without permission from the publisher, the artists and authors.

Copies
    500

First edition 2014

ISBN 978 94 9177 540 6
D/2014/7852/222

With the support of
    LUCA – *Faculteit Architectuur en Kunsten*

Additional support by
    Flemish Minister of Culture
    Transitgroep Mechelen

Thanks to
    The many kind friends and folks in Miami and further afield who have guided this project forward: Els Roelandt, Petra Herzog, Frédéric Paul, Herman Van Ingelgem, Anna Kleberg, Joe Holtzman, Ryan Donaldson, Helena Durst, Elisa Platteau, Wouter Davidts, Matthew Stadler, Joseph Grima, Timothy Brock, Johan Lagae, Ans Nys, Sarah Kesenne, town residents Jacky, Charlotte Rapisarda, Robert Knapp, Mrs. Owens and her son, city Commissioner Timothy Holmes, city Commissioner Rose Tydus, townplanner Gerald Lee, Eady from DCP (Dade County Plug), Nicolas Lobo, Gean Moreno & Ernesto Oroza (Tabloid), Rene Morales, Miami Art Museum, Chuck Strouse Editor in Chief of Miami New Times, Dawn Hugh Archives Manager at History Miami Archives & Research Center, Steve Hersh & Cristina Favretto at the University of Miami's Special Collection Department at the Otto G. Richter Library, MaryAnn Goodlett-Taylor and Antolin Garcia Carbonell at Miami Springs Historical Society, Cathy Leff at Wolfsonian FIU and Ruba Katrib at Museum of Contemporary Art North Miami

Special thanks to
    Angelique Campens and Boy Vereecken

LUCA

With the support of
the Flemish authorities

Saturday, January 30th, 1926   MIAMI LIFE   Page Nine

-building begins at
OPA-LOCKA
The City Substantial

Above we show the first building to be started in OPA-LOCKA in the business zone; designed by Bernhardt Muller, of New York, to accommodate seven apartments, five stores, a gas-filling station and a large garage.

Just two weeks ago we announced OPA-LOCKA to the public and now we publish, herewith, a perspective sketch from the architect details. OPA-LOCKA has a building plan now—no waiting, no delay, no disappointment, no "Future."

We mention our building plans thus confidently, because we believe that OPA-LOCKA'S rapid growth into a city of importance is a matter of almost assured fact. OPA-LOCKA Company, Inc., KNOWS that their opening prices are very low, and it KNOWS the great commercial need for a city at OPA-LOCKA, and now it has had its opinion confirmed by the fact that

The Seaboard will build its first Main Line station North of Miami--at OPA-LOCKA

The President of the Seaboard, S. Davies Warfield, has been a far-sighted developer of railroad property throughout his entire life. He "saw" South Florida and has spent millions and years of effort to bring to Miami the S. A. L. R. R. He knows that his right-of-way throughout OPA-LOCKA is ready for Mr. Foley's railroad builders TODAY.

We have long known that this great railroad has looked with favor upon the strategic advantages of a great mainline passenger, freight and express station at OPA-LOCKA.

Drive out to OPA-LOCKA, see the Seaboard Air Line's right-of-way through to Miami, note where they will build their station, and remember, OPA-LOCKA will be the first main line station north Miami.

How to Get to Opa-Locka
Motor out the Dixie Highway and turn left on Gratigny Boulevard and then turn right (north) on Le Jeune Road to OPA-LOCKA

OPA-LOCKA COMPANY INC.
Sales Office at OPA-LOCKA is open every day for visitors to property
CITY SALES OFFICE
132 East Flagler Street

OPA-LOCKA COMPANY, Inc.
132 East Flagler Street, Miami, Florida
Gentlemen:
I am interested in receiving, without any obligation, first-hand information about OPA-LOCKA while I can still buy at opening prices.

Name ....

Street and No. ....

OPA-LOCKA Will Be Beautiful

Below, at the left and right are two photographs of drives through one of the beauty spots at OPA-LOCKA. At the bottom of this page are drawings depicting some of the sports and other activities of OPA-LOCKA.

IT IS this combination of surpassing natural beauty with the "planned" loveliness that is being developed under the trained guidance of Mr. Clinton MacKenzie (our City Planner) and Mr. Bernhardt Muller (our Chief Architect) that is so rapidly bringing into being, at OPA-LOCKA, a complete townsite of altogether unusual attractiveness and unique architecture.

A drive out over the Dixie Highway to Grainger Boulevard, there turning west until you come to Le Jeune Road, will put you within sight of OPA-LOCKA. It's a drive worth taking—whether you go as a visitor or as an investor.

Why Not Make the OPA-LOCKA Trip TODAY?

OPA-LOCKA CO., Inc.
132 East Flagler Street

SWIMMING POOL — ADMINISTRATION BUILDING — COMMUNITY GARDENS — GOLF — ARCHERY CLUB — BRIDLE PATH

one thousand *and* one reasons

Justify our statement that, in The City Substantial, the investor of a moderate sum of money will be getting in on the ground floor in a townsite that will, by its rapid growth, rival the towering cities of the Arabian Tales.

But, at this time, we can tell you but a few of the 1001 reasons why OPA-LOCKA presents a never-to-be-repeated opportunity for the investor who wants fully developed business and residential property from $1,000 to $10,000 per lot.

Behind OPA-LOCKA is a comprehensive plan for development that has been finally accepted, after it has received nearly a year of expert study by Clinton Mackenzie and Bernhardt Muller of New York.

The former has laid out a city of surpassing beauty — winding, eye-appealing boulevards, residential, business, wholesale and industrial sections of great convenience and up-to-dateness, while the latter has designed gorgeous buildings after the manner of the storied buildings described at the Court of Haroun al Raschid.

To the skill of the City Planner and the technique of the Architect, the developers of OPA-LOCKA have added such modern adjuncts for comfort as electricity, city water system, parks and plenty of parking spaces, and a building program which includes both public and private buildings, stores, apartments and homes, and — a suitable home for a well organized and financed bank.

A few lots as low as $1,000 and others up to $10,000. Pre-Development Discount of 10% is now offered for an indefinite period.

A Dream of the Arabian Nights

OPA-LOCKA
The City Substantial

OPA-LOCKA COMPANY INC.

Sales Office at OPA-LOCKA is now open every day!

City Sales Office
132 East Flagler Street

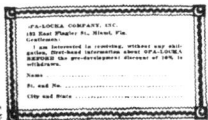

The Overture
to the Building Program at
OPA-LOCKA
The City Substantial

Below, we show a drawing of the OPA-LOCKA Administration Building, which will be erected at the head of BANU Street.

Construction will be started this week

This huge building will serve as the keynote structure of a series designed by Bernhardt Muller which includes a bank, an apartment building, a hotel, several residences, The Club House, and the drawings of the Seaboard Air Line Railway's main line Station soon to be erected at OPA-LOCKA.

A detailed announcement about the Seaboard Air Line Railway's station at OPA-LOCKA may be expected almost any day!

Note: Until the school at OPA-LOCKA is constructed, a school bus will leave OPA-LOCKA daily.

"Weaving a spell of imagery about the substantial back-ground of OPA-LOCKA will be the architecture familiar in the fancy of all those who thrilled over the colorful tales of the Arabian Nights. The lofty domes, the sky-aspiring minarets, the lacy designs of wrought iron gates that have inspired the imagination of generations who have lived by proxy the adventures of The Thousand and One Nights, have been reduced to a fascinating reality by Bernhardt Muller, famous New York architect.

Mr. Muller has developed a series of buildings, including the Administration, Bank, railroad station, hotel and some business and residential structures, that transport one into the very atmosphere of the Far East. From his extensive experience with the technique of the ancient architects of Persia, Arabia and South Central Europe, Mr. Muller has recaptured the charm of the settings of the Tales of Schuherazade." (From Isabel Stone's recent descriptive article in The Miami Herald.)

Co-operating Brokers:

Bertha E. Swank
267 East Flagler Street
Telephone 6311

Lee Horner Corp.
Main Office, 267 New Halcyon Arcade, Phone 22710
Branch Office, 1191 Douglas Rd.

J. L. Criswell
311-312 Exchange Building, Corner N. E. Third Ave. and Second St.
Telephone 7452

Miami Beach
Rice Realty Company
Telephone M. B. 3304

Boston Office
D. H. Thurber, Room 840, Park Square Building, 31 St. James Street, Boston, Mass.

OPA-LOCKA COMPANY INC.

132 East Flagler St.

How to Get to Opa-Locka
Motor out the Dixie Highway and turn left on Gratigny Boulevard and then turn right (north) on Le Jeune Road to OPA-LOCKA.

BRANCH OFFICE
151 East Flagler St
Sales Office at OPA-LOCKA is Open Every Day to Visitors to Property.

OPA-LOCKA COMPANY, Inc.
132 East Flagler Street, Miami, Florida.
Gentlemen:
I am interested in receiving, without any obligation, free land information about OPA-LOCKA, while I still buy at opening prices.

Name ....
Street and No. ....
City and State ....

MIAMI NEWS, JULY 22, 1926.

HE MISAPPREHENDS US

Miami, Fla., July 17, 1926.
Editor of Miami Labor News,
1442 N. W. 1st Court,
Miami, Fla.

7 Dear Sir: Your article in your July 13th issue, "The Necessity for Trades Unions," ably presents the need of trade unions, their functions and their justification. I agree with you that Mr. Abraham Epstein's viewpoint shows not only a lack of understanding of the American workingman but also fails to realize the conditions and the forces which have brought into existence this "rake bees" he speaks about.

But when you say, "Mr. Epstein may be forgiven for not understanding the real purpose of organized labor seeing that his name implies that he is not a native American," meaning by that, I suppose, that he is not of the Anglo Saxon race; may I remind you that neither was Samuel Gompers, the greatest American champion of organized labor of all times.

The fact that Mr. Epstein and the late Mr. Gompers have such widely divergent views proves conclusively that the cause of their race can be found on both sides of all the great questions of today; just like all other Americans. And any argument such as the above is absurd.

Trusting that you will appreciate the spirit of the writer who, at one time, held a union card in a clerks' union, I am,

Respectfully,
JULIUS PEARLMAN,
24 South Miami Ave.

Cigar Makers Local 289

Mr. Grauman, formerly of the Fulford-by-the-Sea Company, has accepted a position from the Old Time Cigar Company as salesman and hereafter will call on his many friends to supply them with Miami Maid's 10 cents, 80s, and Cigar Makers' Smokers, 5 cents, the three leading brands made in Miami.

The Dillon Cigar Company has been taken over by a stock company and the factory has been moved to First street, N. W. The new concern will continue to manufacture the old brands with a new brand known as the Grand Royal, 10 cents. The new concern will operate under the name of Grand Royal Cigar Company.

Fine Watch Repairing

Dealer in high grade watches exclusively.

Here since 1913.

Karl Neuenschwander
123 Central Arcade

A Name That's a Guarantee.
Jule's

A Timely
SHIRT SALE
for these
Shirt Sleeve Days

ENTIRE STOCK OF HIGH GRADE

SHIRTS

at Sacrifice Prices

See Window!

Jule's
4 E. FLAGLER ST.

SERVICE TRANSFER COMPANY
R. E. WARR, Manager
LIGHT and HEAVY HAULING
55 N. W. 3rd St. Tel. 4445

PRESTO RESTAURANT
ALWAYS OPEN
22 N. E. FIRST AVE.

MEN, GET THIS!
Tailor Made Suits—$32.50
MAX THE TAILOR
244 N. E. First Ave.
We do alterating and remodeling

King Undertaking Co.
Lady Undertaker Private Ambulance
Phone 3536 29 N. W. 3rd Av.

For Best Shoe Repairing
Molnar's Shoe Hospital
431 N. MIAMI AVE.
Ladies' Half Sole $1.00
Men's Half Sole $1.25
Rubber Heels 50c
Work Done While You Wait

LIGHT MEANS PROGRESS

The applied force of civilization

Modern Cities cannot come into being without commerce, industry and the advantages for expansion and development.

The prime necessity for these is adequate and dependable utility service.

FLORIDA POWER & LIGHT COMPANY

ONLY 6 MONTHS OLD IS
OPA-LOCKA

SINCERE, SUSTAINED DEVELOPMENT IS MAKING IT MIAMI'S FASTEST GROWING SUBURB

Proof

SIX MONTHS OLD— and already OPA-LOCKA is an incorporated Town, with its own commission form of self government.
(ADMINISTRATION BUILDING)

SIX MONTHS OLD— and with homes being started now, in OPA-LOCKA, at the rate of about two every three days.
(NEW HOMES)

SIX MONTHS OLD— and already OPA-LOCKA is the choice of local authorities for the AIRPORT OF GREATER MIAMI.

The ARCHERY CLUB HOUSE is now in use. If you haven't yet played archery-golf, better come out and "see how it is done" some afternoon, soon.
(ARCHERY)

SIX MONTHS OLD— and with every promised OPA-LOCKA improvement installed, the entire civic development kept steadily and always a little ahead of its schedule.
(IMPROVEMENTS INSTALLED)

Six YEARS is but a moment in the life of almost any town or city—six MONTHS is only a single tick of the clock; but give us another TWELVE months, and you won't "know" OPA-LOCKA.

The great SWIMMING POOL is almost ready for use. Watch for definite announcement of the opening date, very soon!
(SWIMMING POOL)

SIX MONTHS OLD— and already OPA-LOCKA is the site of Miami's SECOND MUNICIPAL 18-HOLE GOLF LINKS. Play on at least nine holes of this course is promised for this Winter. Mr. William S. Flynn, one of the foremost golf architects in the United States has designed this course.
(18 HOLE GOLF LINKS UNDER CONSTRUCTION)

SIX MONTHS OLD— and OPA-LOCKA is destined to be the FIRST main-line-stop on the Seaboard Railway, north of Miami.

SIX MONTHS OLD— and within the year OPA-LOCKA is to be linked with West Flagler Street for those who will commute via the Seaboard Air Line.
(SEABOARD TRANSPORTATION FOR COMMUTERS)

When this course is open for play, this Winter, the great Golf Club House—completely equipped in every last detail—will also be ready for your comfort. Architect-In-Chief Mueller has designed a most commodious building—a beautiful building, of course—and work upon this large structure will be started at once.

Anticipate this sure-to-come growth by selecting, NOW, a home site at OPA-LOCKA. Fifty odd months to pay the balance (is so desire), and but a small down payment required. All this enables you to BUY this excellent investment out of INCOME.

In the entire history of Florida, within the annals of Miami's MAGIC expansion, NOTHING HAS EVER EQUALED the amazing GROWTH of OPA-LOCKA!

OPA-LOCKA COMPANY INC.
132 EAST FLAGLER STREET

When Miami
Miami, Founded 1896 — Is Forty Years Old—What? (1936)

Miami's population in 1920 was less than 30,000. Now it is unquestionably a city of more than 125,000.

This being so, a vitally important question is: WHAT DO THE NEXT TEN YEARS HOLD FOR US WHO LIVE IN "THE MAGIC CITY?"

Before we deal with this question, let us consider Maj. Gen. Ames and John D. Rockefeller, who live in Florida—the former being over 91 and the latter nearing four-score years and ten.

These men live in Florida because of its balmy, healthful climate; and, during the next ten years MILLIONS of other men and women will become residents of our state and our city, for that very same reason.

But Miami's growth during the next ten years, in the opinion of the OPA-LOCKA COMPANY will come with the active farming and industrial development of the vast area comprised in the western part of Dade County.

The Seaboard Railway, with an eye to this impending development work, will build a main-line station at OPA-LOCKA. The lands of this corporation can see growth, profit—yes, richness—for their stockholders in the fertile lands of Dade County. They are building now, so that Dade County may have a direct route for its agricultural products to the Northern markets.

Miami, a city of a million people, will be an assured fact when its rich back country is upon a producing basis!

OPA-LOCKA COMPANY, Inc.
132 East Flagler St.

OPA-LOCKA
The Seaboard's Gateway to the Everglades

From the Days of the "Iron Horse"

The coming of a railroad has, since the days of the Iron Horse, been the signal for prosperity and growth of population.

It is just as true a sign of prosperity and profit today as it was a generation or two ago.

The elements (forces) which operated in the seventies and eighties to upbuild great areas of the United States are now, in a large measure, focussed in the single State of Florida.

Population growth of Florida for the five years prior to 1925 was at the rate of about 30 per cent; while the rate of population increase for the year 1925 was a 10 per cent growth—or a gain over the rate for the previous five years.

Land values are determined, in large measure, by the concentration of population. Population growth in the Miami zone was at a faster rate than 10 per cent, many times the rate for the State.

Hence, property values in the Miami zone mounted apace.

OPA-LOCKA is just a mile and a half north of the city limits of Miami and well within the Miami zone. It is the center of a great area which will be served by the Seaboard Air Line Railway's station which will be built at OPA-LOCKA.

OPA-LOCKA will be a completely planned and developed town. Construction is now going on—buildings are being built, roads are being finished. Hence present prices are much lower than they will be when all improvements are complete.

Points of Progress at OPA-LOCKA

Opa-Locka Company, Inc.

OFFICERS

G. CARL ADAMS, President
C. L. WATERS, Vice-President
J. ALDEN MICHAEL, Secretary
F. S. ARNOLD, Assistant Secretary
H. C. GENUNG, Treasurer
GLENN H. CURTISS
Chairman of the Board

OPA-LOCKA
The City Substantial

OPA-LOCKA COMPANY INC.

Sales Office at OPA-LOCKA is open every day for visitors to property.

City Sales Office: 132 East Flagler Street   Branch Office: 181 East Flagler Street

SUNDAY, MARCH 7, 1926 — MIAMI DAILY NEWS — MAIN NEWS SECTION—FIFTEEN

The Seaboard will enter Miami through the Golden Gate of OPA-LOCKA

The City Progressive

Features in the Development of Opa-Locka

The SEABOARD AIR LINE Passenger Depot is an assured factor in the upbuilding, not only of OPA-LOCKA, but the entire northern area of Greater Miami. Freight terminals of the SEABOARD AIR LINE RAILWAY will be especially provided for at another point in OPA-LOCKA.

A Clubhouse is being erected at the Archery Course. This course has nine targets.

There is an 18-hole golf course projected at OPA-LOCKA, nine holes of which will be built this summer under the direction of W. P. Flynn, one of the foremost Golf Architects in the country. The new links at OPA-LOCKA will afford the sportiest course it is possible for Mr. Flynn, backed by adequate capital, to design.

Pure Water—an almost unlimited supply that will be used, for the present at least, as strategy to supply the domestic, commercial and industrial requirements of OPA-LOCKA.

One of the finest administration buildings ever to be erected in South Florida is under construction at OPA-LOCKA. This building will give the architectural tone to the Arabian Nights Zone.

A Swimming Pool will soon be ready for use for all residents of OPA-LOCKA and to all who desire to visit this growing center.

Numerous Bridle Paths will be maintained throughout OPA-LOCKA, and ample facilities will be provided for those who desire to hire saddle horses.

OPA-LOCKA is the gateway to the entire Miami Zone and South Florida. It will be the Seaboard Railway's first stop upon entering Miami from the north.

Here the traveler will be greeted by the great buildings designed by Bernhardt Muller, here the domes and minarets of the Arabian Nights Zone buildings will be clearly viewed, here at OPA-LOCKA will be gained the first impression of Miami, an impression that will be heightened by the remaining eight-mile ride to the Seaboard's station on Flagler Street.

OPA-LOCKA property—residential, commercial or industrial—is all within a very few blocks of the Seaboard Air Line Railway's OPA-LOCKA Station. Property price increases should be rapid—phenomenal, as OPA-LOCKA grows.

Great main line railway stations are sure builders of property values. Just fancy buying desirable property near the Miami railway station for $1,000 and up per lot. It can't be done today, nor has it been done within the last twenty years, at least.

Follow the Seaboard Air Line Railway to OPA-LOCKA, the gateway and center of northern Dade County, and back your vision with your dollars!

How To Get to Opa-Locka:
Motor out the Dixie Highway and turn left on Gratigny Boulevard and then turn right (north) on Le Jeune Road to OPA-LOCKA.

OPA-LOCKA
The City Progressive

OPA-LOCKA COMPANY INC.
Sales office at OPA-LOCKA is open every day for visitors to property

132 East Flagler Street   **181 East Flagler Street**

Co-operating Brokers